The

Friars Club

BIBLE

OF JOKES, POKES,

ROASTS, AND TOASTS

The Friars Club

BIBLE

OF JOKES,

POKES, ROASTS,

AND TOASTS

Edited by Nina Colman

Edited for the Friars Club by Barry Dougherty

BLACK DOG
& LEVENTHAL
PUBLISHERS
NEW YORK

Published by

Black Dog & Leventhal Publishers, Inc.

151 West 19th Street

New York, NY 10011

Distributed by

Workman Publishing Company

708 Broadway

New York, NY 10003

Manufactured in the U.S.A.

Library of Congress Cataloging-in-Publication Data

The Friars Club Bible of Jokes, Pokes, Roasts, and Toasts: more than 2,000 quips, snips, insults, tumults, jibes, japes, jingles, and rhymes for every speaker and every occasion/ edited by Nina Colman.

       p.   cm.

ISBN 1-57912-166-7 (hardcover)

1. American wit and humor.   I. Colman, Nina.

PN6162.F74 2001

818.02DC21

Designed by Martin Lubin Graphic Design

j i h g f e d c b a

A special thanks to Jean Pierre Trebot,
Barry Dougherty, and Howard Cohl,
without whom this book
could not have come into being.

CONTENTS

A Message from Friars Club Proctor Buddy Hackett   15

A Few Opinions from Friar Jeffrey Ross   17

INTRODUCTION

Barry Dougherty Explains "Who the Hell Are the Friars?"   19

A Brief History of Toasts   22

Why You Need This Book (Besides the fact that you don't want to make a fool of yourself)   22

Why We Toast, Joke, and Occasionally Roast   24

How to Speak in Public and Not Make a Fool of Yourself (Toasting, joking, and roasting attire included)   24

The Art of Joke-Telling, or How to Be a Good Toastmaster   25

Toasting Etiquette (Why stupid or politically incorrect jokes can work)   27

To Toast or to Joke?   27

CHAPTER ONE

Life and Those Not-So-Little Moments   31

Being Single (This is living?!)   32

Dating (It's hunting time)   35

Engagement (Is this the one?)   45

Marriage (The long haul)   46

In-laws (Hold on, it's going to be a bumpy ride)   77

We're Pregnant (Now you've done it!)   78

Childbirth (Is there pain involved?)   86

Children (You better believe it!)   87

Family (But wait, there's more!)   95

Parents (A lifetime commitment)   98

Grandparents (Yes, your parents had parents)   105

■ PROFILE

Milton Berle "The Biggest Friar of Them All"   96

CHAPTER TWO

It's Party Time   107

It's Your Birthday (...and you can cry if you want to)   108

Sweet Sixteen (...and never been...)   114

21 (A lucky number?)   115

30 (...something)   116

Fat and Forty (Lordy, Lordy)   117

When I'm 64   122

So What, You're 80   125

Anniversary (You've been together how long?!)   133

First Anniversary (Gotta start somewhere)   137

Silver Anniversary (When a platter won't do)   137

Nozze D'Oro (Golden Night)   139

Party Till the Cows Come Home (When should you
wear a lampshade?)   140

Confirmation (Are you sure?)   142

Bar/Bat Mitzvah (Now you are a fountain pen)   143

Bris (Watch the guy with the knife)   147

■ PROFILE

Henny Youngman King of the One-liners   130

CHAPTER THREE

You're Growing Up   149

School Days (Or daze...)   150
Grade School (Prison life begins)   150
High School (No, you can't have the keys)   155
College (Let the games begin)   158

■ PROFILE
Who Is Steven Wright?   178

CHAPTER FOUR

Rough Times   187

Get Well Soon (Pass the chicken soup)   188
Death (No more soup for you)   192
Funeral (If you have nothing nice to say...)   197
Memorial Service (...don't say these)   200
You're Caught (Get your hand out of the cookie jar)   200
Divorce (Free at last!)   202

■ PROFILE
Mae West The Original "Scandalous Broad"   198

CHAPTER FIVE

Off to Work   205

The Dreaded Job Interview   208
First Job (Who is this FICA, and why does he get
more money than me?)   209
The Work (Hi-ho, hi-ho...oh, forget it)   212
Accountants (Count those beans)   222
Actors (Is this any way for a grown person to
make a living?)   223

Advertising (New and improved)   224

Agents (Fifteen percent of your ass is mine)   224

Construction (If you build it...)   225

Dentists (Open wide...your wallet, that is)   226

Doctors (This won't hurt a bit...except your wallet, that is)   228

Lawyers (Dewey, Cheatham, and Howe)   240

Models (Can you spell gorgeous? I guess not. So what.)   245

Nurses (Hey, that thing is cold!)   251

Salesperson (Come out, come out, wherever you are)   252

Productivity (More work for me)   253

Announcing Great Results (Like I care)   258

Motivational Speech (Did you say something?)   258

Getting a Promotion (That brown-nosing paid off)   262

Getting Fired (Not enough brown-nosing)   263

Retirement/Going Away Party (I gave you my life,
and all I got was this watch)   264

■ PROFILE

Rodney Dangerfield Lovable Loser   260

CHAPTER SIX

Happy Holidays   267

New Year's (A license to kiss)   268

Valentine's Day (Blissfully happy, or lonely loser?)   271

St. Patrick's Day (Start drinking at 9:00 A.M...)   275

Fourth of July (I saw fireworks)   276

Halloween (Yes, you can wear ladies' clothes)   277

Thanksgiving (Start by being grateful for St. Patrick's Day)   280

Christmas (Deck those halls)   282

■ PROFILE

Phyllis Diller What a Face   272

CHAPTER SEVEN

The Media Circus 285

Books (Like movies, but you have to work) 288

The Book Signing (I didn't know you could *read* one,
let alone write one) 294

Movies (Like TV shows, but you have to pay) 294

The Big Premiere (I want to thank all the little people...) 299

Television (A thousand channels and nothing to watch) 300

■ PROFILE
Groucho Marx "You Bet Your Life" 290

CHAPTER EIGHT

Battle of the Sexes 303

Men (Lord of the remote control) 305

High Holy Days (Poker night, Super Bowl Sunday,
and The Final Four) 313

Bachelor Party (Does anyone have change for a $20?) 322

The Confirmed Bachelor (Just say it...he's gay) 325

Women (Forget the "B" word, and don't even
think about the "C" word) 326

Blondes (How many does it take...?) 335

Baby Showers (Better you than me) 343

Bridal Showers (Better me than you) 343

Bachelorette Party (What are we supposed to do
at these things again?) 344

The Confirmed Bachelorette (You can tell by the shoes) 346

■ PROFILE
Billy Crystal "Face" 310

CHAPTER NINE

Politics—How to Be the Life of the Party 349

Meet the Pundits (The lunatics have taken over the asylum)   352
Working for the People (Elevating lying to a fine art)   361

■ PROFILE
Rita Rudner High Anxiety   362

CHAPTER TEN

It's Just a Game—Isn't It?   375

Baseball (A stick and a couple of balls)   376
Basketball (More ball jokes)   378
Bowling (Please, no more ball jokes)   379
Boxing (This is a sport?)   380
Fishing (THIS is a sport?)   381
Football (What fun, I can't feel my toes...)   383
Golf (Who came up with the outfits?)   385
Skiing (I'm in complete controlllllllllllllll)   395
Skydiving (When "oops" matters)   396
Tennis (More balls)   397
Gambling (Don't bet the ranch)   398

■ PROFILE
Drew Carey "Regular Guy"   390

CHAPTER ELEVEN

All the World Is a Joke   401

Ethnic/Regional (No, nothing is sacred)   402

Texans (Guns, oil, and a pick-up)   408

Americans (You bet!)   411

New Yorkers (You talkin' to me?)   412

Canadian (Sorry, my mind wandered...)   413

Irish (Enough said)   415

Italian (Points for the food)   418

Polish (*No* points for the food)   419

Russians (...are coming)   419

WASPs (Cocktail time)   420

Religion (Hallelujah!)   421

Amish (Is nothing sacred?)   422

Catholics (Bless me, Father...)   423

Christians (Fire and brimstone)   432

Jews (See, also, the rest of this book)   435

Mormons (Take my wives...)   447

Miscellany (Wit, wisdom...whatever)   450

■ PROFILE

Jerry Seinfeld "Did you ever notice...?"   448

INDEX OF CONTRIBUTORS   469

ACKNOWLEDGMENTS   473

A MESSAGE FROM
FRIARS CLUB PROCTOR
BUDDY HACKETT

Jokes last forever, and if they don't, they never were a joke to start with. Things that make us laugh will always make someone laugh. However, there is a new generation of people who learned what is funny from television, where they tell the jokes and put the laffs in later on. Ergo—some of the T.V. audience has never heard a joke, unless they have been lucky enough to have been to one of the great casinos in New Jersey or Nevada.

Of course, the best place is usually a "Friars Function" of some sort—which had real jokes and real comedians. Sometimes a joke depends on what is going on in the world and if the world changes the joke may become obsolete unless the listener has a great memory.

In 1951, I wrote a joke that has been used by many comics. They are not thieves using my joke but are brilliantly selective. The joke was, "If you are going to Las Vegas you will lose your money. If you don't want to lose your money—when you get off the plane walk into the propeller—this way you get an even split." Followed by, "If you don't like that joke—you and your whole family can fall down a well—especially your brother who was here last night."

Naturally, "dear reader," the propeller plane to Las Vegas doesn't fly anymore, and getting sucked into a jet pod sounds somewhat painful. However, there are still guys around using the propeller joke. Naturally, these guys also have an icebox in the kitchen of their rented garage.

War jokes, Army routines, moon landings, may still be funny but usually need a reformed base to make them play. We can go back to colonial times and recall jokes about splinters on Martha Washington's ass from George Washington's wooden teeth, which also proves that back then we had more carpenters than dentists.

However, I hope the jokes that follow in this book are selected properly for you—but I take no credit nor blame for whatever is to follow.

BUDDY HACKETT

A FEW OPINIONS FROM
FRIAR JEFFREY ROSS

Why are you reading this book? Are you trying to be funny? Well, either you're funny or you're not. And if you need this book, then chances are you are not funny. So stop bothering people.

However, if you're already at least a little bit funny (and most people are), then maybe we can help you along—because we at the Friars Club know what's funny.

Fat guys are always funny. If you have to make a speech or a toast or a dedication, bring along a fat guy.

The first thing Buddy Hackett ever said to me was, "Y'know who hates farts the most? Midgets." Midgets are hilarious and always will be. That is a definitive rule of comedy. Our ancestors laughed at midgets the same way we laugh at midgets today. Same goes for farts, or noises that sound like farts. Or seeing someone stumble.

They say that hard "K" sounding words are funny—except of course for the words "kike," "Ku Klux Klan," and "cunt." However, when Milton Berle uses that last one at the infamous Friars roasts—it's always hilarious.

I love tradition. Getting to know the pioneers of television comedy like Milton Berle and Sid Caesar is a big part of why I love the Friars Club. Legend has it that our elegant townhouse on east 55th Street was originally purchased by Milton Berle to be his home—but his wife thought it was too big for the two of them, so he gave it to the Friars.

Since then, almost every superstar in the world (except maybe Marilyn Manson) has passed through the New York Friars Club dining room at least once. And the health club on the fifth floor is probably the last gym in the world with a medicine ball.

It was in the Beverly Hills branch of the Friars Club where Uncle Miltie gave me my first cigar. He cut it, stuck it in my mouth, and lit it. I'm still gagging. He also taught me (and then demonstrated) that if you stick a cigar all the way up your nostril and it smells like you're inhaling horseshit—you can be sure it's a genuine Cubano.

Comedy is an art, and the Friars Club is its greatest gallery. Within our walls is an ever-evolving exhibition of one-liners, stories, put-downs, parodies, and all types of verbal ammunition. So go ahead—steal! Take! Borrow! It's only our jokes—our lifeblood. Just give us Friars credit once in a while. You seem like a nice person. Try the veal. Thanks, I'll be here all week.

JEFFREY ROSS

Jeffrey Ross is a producer and regular performer at the Friars Club Celebrity Roasts, broadcast on Comedy Central. He's written for a number of television shows, including The Man Show *and the* 2000 Academy Awards™, *which afforded him the opportunity to write with one of his idols, Billy Crystal. He's acted in independent films, and in* The Adventures of Rocky and Bullwinkle, *a film that he notes "made so little money I have to send them residuals."*

He performs in clubs around the country, and, regarding his television appearances, he states, "I have appeared on all the late-night TV shows, including The Late Show, Late-Late Show, Late Friday, Later, Go to Sleep Already, Are You Still Up? Call a Hooker! *and* Cock-a-Doodle-Doo!"

INTRODUCTION

BARRY DOUGHERTY EXPLAINS
"WHO THE HELL ARE THE FRIARS?"

How many Friars does it take to change a light bulb? None. They don't need to see anybody, they just need to hear the laughs! For a Friar, laughter is what showbiz is all about and it doesn't take a brain surgeon to figure out that if there were no jokes there would be no laughs. The Friars' whole existence today is based on a joke played out almost a hundred years ago, only at that time nobody was laughing.

Depending upon which comedian you ask how the Friars Club started, chances are pretty good you'll get a detailed, hysterically funny account—of a place more enticing than Brigadoon. But just as farfetched. If you prefer to remain in the blissful yet funny darkness of a jokester's punch line, then by all means, run along to another page. This tale, however, tells about the Friars' century-long reign of comedy.

Back in 1904...okay stop with the yawning already, this is good stuff...there was a group of theater press agents who gave out free Broadway show tickets to newspaper reporters. This way the journalists would see the shows, write really nice things about them, and make the agents very happy. That is, until the agents got wind of the fact that many of these reporters were frauds. Can you imagine people being dishonest just to get something for nothing? The agents wised up when one of the scoundrels (that's how they talked back then), Colonel Marshall E. Lee, was busted. A couple of the press agents discovered he didn't really work for the *Washington Post* the way he said he did.

To clear out the dead wood, eleven of these press agents

got together at a place called Browne's Chophouse, in New York City. Their solution to the problem was to just blacklist the lot of them. After this council of Sherlock Holmeses resolved their ticket woes, they decided to keep on meeting, once a week, because they just plain liked each other. It gave them an opportunity to split from the wives and kids for a bit, hang out together, smoke cigars, drink, and yes, tell some jokes.

They even came up with a name for themselves—The Press Agents Association. They must have spent weeks of discussion over vodka gimlets to come up with that one. Eventually, however, the big guns started to join them. Actors like George M. Cohan; music makers Victor Herbert, Oscar Hammerstein, and Irving Berlin; and wits such as Will Rogers would stop by adding so much more excitement than these press agents could muster. They became so diverse, they formed a new organization and called themselves the Friars Club. "Friars" stemming from the Latin "Frater," meaning brother. Oh, in case you haven't picked up on this—it was just the guys—no women allowed! Well, not until 1988 that is, when the Supreme Court played another joke on the Friars and said all men's clubs had to let the ladies in. Alright, so maybe a lot of the guys didn't think that was very funny, but in spite of them Liza Minnelli became the very first official female New York Friar.

From the very beginning the Friars held a reputation of being naughtier than your average social club. They held lavish Testimonial Dinners where they elevated the joke to an art form and they definitely had a monopoly on the "dirty joke." They developed their ribald skills so intently that they eventually created a forum specifically designed for the less-than-pure at heart—the "Roast." This new badge of honor was proudly handed over to those tough enough to endure hours of verbal tongue-lashings at the hands of the funniest people in entertainment.

The Friars even came up with their own motto to help the victim—I mean, guest of honor—through the hilarious tirade that left their ego obliterated and their self-esteem in shreds. "We only Roast the ones we love" is the mantra of bullshit that enables the Roastee to walk away with at least a little dignity intact—that and a crystal statue. The statue serves as a very special memento of their Roast— and if they choose to smash it they will be reminded of their own pride left on the Friars floor that fateful day. All because of jokes, no less!

There are so many legends of comedy that have laughed their way through the portals of the New York Friars Club: Milton Berle, who single-handedly saved the club in the 1940s and '50s so he could have a fresh supply of jokes to steal; George Burns, who hung around for a hundred years just so he could hear every joke ever told; Jack Benny, who complained about paying his dues but would rather part with that money than lose access to all the laughter—needless to say, the list of immortal Friars is endless.

Alan King is the leader of this band of merry men and women, holding court as Abbot of the New York Friars from their elegant Victorian Townhouse located in mid-town Manhattan.

The Friars don't mind if you can't *tell* a joke, because hopefully this book can help you with that. But if you can't *take* a joke, well then that's a problem. You see, the members of this legendary Club may not have invented banana peels or seltzer or toilet paper on your shoe or even dirty words—but you can be damn sure they know how to put them all together to make them funny! And that's no joke.

Barry Dougherty is the author of New York Friars Club Book of Roasts *and is editor of the Friars' own magazine, the* Epistle. *He has been writing jokes for Friars Roasts and Dinners for ten years.*

A Brief History of Toasts

Toasting, roasting, and joking have been around since prehistoric times.

Brief enough.

Why You Need This Book

(BESIDES THE FACT THAT YOU DON'T WANT TO MAKE A FOOL OF YOURSELF)

Not all of us are born with the wit and wisdom of the ages on the tips of our tongue-tied tongues. Very few of us are fortunate enough to know exactly what to say and exactly when to say it. Thank God the Friars do! They can help us when it comes to breaking the ice, telling a joke, giving a toast, and making others feel at home (or really uncomfortable)—even if we are scared witless standing front-and-center in a lecture hall, board room, Bar Mitzvah reception, bachelorette party, wedding, family reunion, or holiday party.

This book contains the perfect toast, joke, or roast for every occasion. What you are holding here is a guide to speaking in public, making people laugh, and most important, not making a fool of yourself when asked to get up in front of a group of people. They are now all here at your disposal. And by the way, a toast can be a joke, a joke can be a toast, and a roast is often both.

There are lots of toasts and quotes in here, too, because sometimes "sweet" wins out over "saucy," and a little rhyme or pearl of wisdom succeeds where a mother-in-law joke might fall flat. Neither Shakespeare nor Ben Franklin were Friars, but sometimes quoting them is just the ticket.

This book will make you as funny as the Friars (and occasionally, as vulgar and inappropriate, too!). You will be able to say the right thing at the right time (and occasionally, the wrong thing at the right time or the right thing at the wrong time—but hey, that's the Friars Club for you). After consulting its various sections, you'll be the best you can be when making a toast, telling a joke, or making a speech. You will seem smart, funny (and occasionally crude and inappropriate), but you'll make people laugh and you'll make people cry and you'll make them think—and that's what a good speaker does.

Whether you want to be raunchy, funny, sentimental, or serious, this book serves as the perfect guide. For every key moment there is a quote, for every occasion there is a joke. This book will free you from the throngs of mediocrity and propel you into a life of success and wealth filled with witty banter and clever conversation. Then again, none of this may happen for you. You may stay the same old schmuck you've always been—but you'll know deep down that you have the potential to be a Friar. So use this book and enjoy. Or make kindling out of it if you need to, just remember that all the answers to the age-old question, "What the hell am I going to say at Jerry's wedding?" are somewhere in these pages.

The answer to, "Oh, no, Sheryl's Bat Mitzvah is next weekend and she asked me to speak—what am I gonna say?" is between these covers. The solution for "I totally spaced on Karen's bachelorette dinner—I gotta give a toast—does anybody know any man-bashing jokes?" is right here. It's got what to say at Cousin Manny's funeral, Uncle Ted's 50th, the guy from shipping's 25th, the woman in 3R's anniversary...you get the picture. Read the book. It doesn't make such great kindling anyway, and you'll get a helluva lot of use out of it. I promise. It's great stuff. And besides, you know you need it.

Why We Toast, Joke, and Occasionally Roast

Tradition!! Tradition!! Oh, sorry, that's a little ditty from *Fiddler on the Roof*. But anyway, it's true: Tradition. It's all about Tradition. Tevye knew what he was singing about. Life offers us many occasions filled with friends, family, coworkers, people we detest, former lovers, and people who smell, and it's always nice to have something to say to them.

We toast at those occasions in life that are filled with tradition, whether they be sentimental (a first wedding) or pathetic (a fourth wedding), happy (a baby shower) or sad (baby all grown up and going to prison). Whatever the case, at these times it is important to have something to say.

It's up to you how you use this book. A toast, a joke, a poem, a quotation, a roast—something to remember, something to record. A memento of a special time, a great day, an awesome occasion. A way of commemorating an event, a feeling, an experience. Or, just to be funny, to get a laugh and make people feel comfortable.

How to Speak in Public and Not Make a Fool of Yourself
(TOASTING, JOKING, AND ROASTING ATTIRE ARE INCLUDED)

First of all, do not, under any circumstances, wear a bow tie if you are over eleven years old. I don't care how cute your Republican friends think it is, people will stare at you. That's number one. Usually, the event dictates the wardrobe. Nudity is always a big hit (unless you are Abe Vigoda), but, often, arrests are made and no one gets to laugh at all. Best to look nice, clean, and pulled together. Sort of like you did when you took a family vacation in the 1970s and wore nice cords and a turtleneck. Look nice. Or look cool. But not if you're not cool. Lou Reed is cool. Don't try to look like Lou if you know in your heart that the vintage leather jacket couldn't possibly be dry-cleaned enough times to satisfy your anal-retentive soul. You know what? Stick to what you know best. (Nice cords and a turtleneck will do the trick nicely.)

It's also important, while speaking in public, not to sweat profusely (think Albert Brooks in *Broadcast News*). Mop your brow often and wear an undershirt. Your mother will be proud.

Not making a fool of yourself is really about making a fool of others (just ask the Friars). That's really all you need to know. And if there is a piece of spinach between your teeth or a scrap of toilet paper trailing from your shoe, pretend you know it's there and you did it for effect. Works every time.

The Art of Joke Telling, or How to Be a Good Toastmaster

When we are asked to speak in public, whether it be before four people or four hundred, it's important to have a sense of humor (unless you're Amish, and then it's only important to look good in a garment with no buttons). If you are not Amish, the most important characteristic of a good joke-teller or toastmaster is to make others feel comfortable.

The only real way to do this, is to be comfortable yourself and to have a sense of humor—even at the most serious of occasions.

Little Johnny got hit by a bus. Do you say, "Did you hear the one about the drunk driver?" Obviously, this is not what is meant by "a sense of humor," but it is important that lightheartedness be an ingredient in any toast or joke. It makes people more at ease, makes them more receptive, and therefore, you'll look better and everyone will like you. And that's really what you are concerned with, isn't it?

It's also good to know a few names of the people in the room—or, even better, to know a few of the people. Refer to them, bring them into the joke, make them a part of your story. The Friars are masters at this and it works every time. Even if you are making fun of someone, at least he's a part of it. You are laughing with him, not, as they say, at him. Okay, a little bit at him, no harm done. Tell a story about him or change the name in a joke to incorporate his name. Change the situation to one that perhaps you and he have been in together. Make it more personal. Do you perhaps know something really gross and private about his sexual practices? Go ahead! Let the crowd at Aunt Rita's 85th hear the twisted details. They'll all laugh.

It's always been the mark of a good joke-teller or toast-master to start off with a laugh. Not just you laughing, that would be creepy, but a joke. Get your audience to smile, warm 'em up. Pretend you're Sammy in Vegas and Dean is backstage getting sauced and no one knows where the hell Frank is. Dance around if you have to. Just don't sing "The Girl from Ipanema." That might not go over so well.

Most important, the mark of a good joke-teller, toastmaster, or speech-maker is this: Be yourself. Unless you're an awful bore. Then be someone else. But relax, have fun, and try not to drool.

Toasting Etiquette

(WHY STUPID OR POLITICALLY INCORRECT
JOKES CAN WORK)

In regard to etiquette, there is none. At least not where
the Friars are concerned. For instance, I am sure that
Drew Carey's mother was watching the Friars Club Roast
in honor of Drew when "giving it to her son up the ass"
was a topic of conversation. Everyone likes to laugh,
even Drew's mother. If they can't take the humor, you
don't really want them around, now do you? People like
to be shocked, they like to laugh hard, and they usually
get the joke. Everyone's grandmother was young once
and got felt up. They've been there, too. They get the
joke.

For every event in life, there are reasons to be serious
and reasons to joke. The fact of the matter is, we can be
funny, we can be serious, but chances are, the funnier we
are, the more we get laid. And that my friends, is the
most important thing of all—getting laid.

To Toast or To Joke?

To toast or to joke, that is the question, and it's a stupid
one. Do not tell a raunchy joke at Fiona's wake. Tell an
Irish joke, but not a raunchy one. Unless Fiona was a
fun-loving slut, and then by all means, tell the raunchy
joke. She would have loved it.

Often, we speak in public because we have been asked or
even begged to do so (unless we're a spotlight-grabbing
moron). Or there is some legitimate reason we "have the
floor," like it's part of our job or something. So…to toast
or to joke? One often compliments the other. For
instance, "I toast to your health—you're 95—I toast to
you having a pulse! Here's to you!" See how well that
worked? You, too, can be funny and mean…just toast

and joke at the same time. No, really, seriously, it doesn't matter which you do—it's all about the spirit in which you do it. Be funny, be sentimental, be sweet, be vulgar, just SAY SOMETHING, DAMN IT! You'll do great.

So use these jokes, toasts, quips, and oddly satisfying little stories to entertain a room, break the ice, stand out in a crowd, make your grandmother proud. Isn't that what life is about? Enjoy the humor of the Friars.

NINA COLMAN

The concept of the roast is that you honor someone by dishonoring them.

ED MCMAHON

SUSIE ESSMAN TO PAUL SHAFFER—ROAST OF RICHARD BELZER:

I had no idea you were so funny. Such a sharp tongue! That must really hurt David Letterman's ass.

KEVIN JAMES—ROAST OF JERRY STILLER:

Do you think the guy who invented the tuxedo would have pressed on if he knew a head like that would be popping out of it?

JEFFREY ROSS—ROAST OF DREW CAREY:

Dr. Ruth is here, 90 and horny. She went down on me standing up.

MICHAEL MCKEON—ROAST OF ROB REINER:

Tonight we honor a man big enough to come here and let his peers piss all over him.

BILLY CRYSTAL—ROAST OF ROB REINER:

Vincent Pastore is here, Dr. Ruth is here...So Big Pussy and Little Pussy are here.

BILLY CRYSTAL—ROAST OF ROB REINER:

Rob, you're so fucking fat, you're like Orson Welles without all that genius baggage.

KEVIN POLLAK—ROAST OF ROB REINER:

Seriously, when did you start looking older than your father? Rob, they say every man looks great in a tuxedo. You look like someone crammed you up a firehose and shoved it up a penguin's ass.

ADAM FERRARA—ROAST OF ROB REINER:

You know, I rented *The Story of Us* and you owe me $3.50. Seriously, that movie was so bad my VCR spit it out.

I'm delighted to be here again, especially with Milton Berle. Milton has been suffering from a disease called Berlesheimer Disease. That's where he forgets everything except everybody else's jokes.

DICK CAPRI

I'm not talking about your penis today because my mother told me I should always respect the dead.

DICK CAPRI TO MILTON BERLE

CHAPTER ONE:
LIFE AND THOSE NOT-SO-LITTLE MOMENTS

Life is made up of a plethora of events—most of which we'd rather not attend. Excuses can be made, lies can be told, but in the long run we're better off putting on our happy face and going. This means, of course, getting off the couch and turning off *Who Wants to Marry a Dentist and Be a Zillionaire*—even if we'd rather be locked in a steam room with the Village People. We're guests at the festival of life and it is always good to have something to say, should you be called upon to do so.

For instance: Your best friend gets engaged, and even if you have slept with the groom (and so has everybody else you know, including the guy from the Texaco station), try not to bring it up at the engagement party. Make a joke, but do not give yourself away. Feel free to make innuendoes about the ambiguity of his sexual persuasion, hell, everyone is gay nowadays. (Unless he is a member of the Church of Scientology, then he is not gay. No way. Been married for years. Just look at the beautiful beard and kids. I mean wife and kids.)

Now, where were we? Ah yes, life's big moments and all that they entail. From an engagement party to the birth of a child, to the friends and relatives and enemies we are forced to spend time with, life gives us the opportunity to say "Thanks," "I love you," "Did you hear the one about the pregnant nun?" and "My son the moron is your new CEO!" This has everything you've always wanted in a chapter about life and its events and what to say along the way. If not, try the next chapter, there's some great stuff in there, too.

JEFFREY ROSS:

I was dating this girl for awhile, and the first time she saw me naked, she said, "Is everything a joke with you?"

JEFFREY ROSS—ROAST OF ROB REINER:

I was really nervous. How do you insult a guy who married Penny Marshall?

MARGARET CHO—ROAST OF DREW CAREY:

Drew, your dick is so big, no one knows where it ends and the sky begins.

Being Single (This is living?!)

I'm single because I was born that way.

MAE WEST

RESPONSES TO "WHY AREN'T YOU MARRIED YET?"

You haven't asked yet.

I was hoping to do something meaningful with my life.

What? And spoil my great life?

Nobody would believe me in white.

Because I just love hearing this question.

Just lucky, I guess.

It gives my mother something to live for.

My fiancé is awaiting parole.

I'm still hoping for my shot at Miss America.

Do you know how hard it is to get two tickets to *The Producers*?

I'm waiting until I get to be your age.

It didn't seem worth the blood test.

I THINK, THEREFORE I'M SINGLE

Q: How does a woman in New York get rid of cockroaches?

A: She asks them for a commitment.

Q: What do you call a woman with no asshole?

A: Single.

WHAT I WANT IN A MAN (AGE 22):

1. Handsome
2. Charming
3. Financially successful
4. A caring listener
5. Witty
6. In good shape
7. Dresses with style
8. Appreciates finer things
9. Full of thoughtful surprises
10. An imaginative, romantic lover.

WHAT I WANT IN A MAN (AGE 32):

1. Nice looking (prefer hair on his head)
2. Opens car doors, holds chairs
3. Has enough money for a nice dinner
4. Listens more than talks
5. Laughs at my jokes
6. Carries bags of groceries with ease
7. Owns at least one tie
8. Appreciates a good home-cooked meal
9. Remembers birthdays and anniversaries
10. Seeks romance at least once a week.

WHAT I WANT IN A MAN (AGE 42):

1. Not too ugly (bald head OK)
2. Doesn't drive off until I'm in the car
3. Works steady—splurges on dinner out occasionally
4. Nods head when I'm talking
5. Usually remembers punch lines of jokes
6. Is in good enough shape to rearrange the furniture
7. Wears a shirt that covers his stomach
8. Knows not to buy champagne with screw-top lids
9. Remembers to put the toilet seat down
10. Shaves most weekends.

WHAT I WANT IN A MAN (AGE 52):

1. Keeps hair in nose and ears trimmed
2. Doesn't belch or scratch in public
3. Doesn't borrow money too often
4. Doesn't nod off to sleep when I'm venting
5. Doesn't re-tell the same joke too many times

6. Is in good enough shape to get off couch on weekends
7. Usually wears matching socks and fresh underwear
8. Appreciates a good TV dinner
9. Remembers my name on occasion
10. Shaves some weekends.

WHAT I WANT IN A MAN (AGE 62):

1. Doesn't scare small children
2. Remembers where bathroom is
3. Doesn't require much money for upkeep
4. Only snores lightly when asleep
5. Remembers why he's laughing
6. Is in good enough shape to stand up by himself
7. Usually wears clothes
8. Likes soft foods
9. Remembers where he left his teeth
10. Remembers that it's the weekend.

WHAT I WANT IN A MAN (AGE 72):

1. Breathing
2. Doesn't miss the toilet

Dating (It's hunting time)

Zabiski saved up his money for an excursion to Reno, where he soon found himself at the bar next to a very attractive brunette.

"Say, could I buy you a drink?" he asked boldly.

"Forget it, Buddy," she replied, not unkindly. "I'm gay."

Zabiski looked blank.

"I'm a lesbian," she elaborated.

Zabiski shook his head. "What's a lesbian?"

"See that woman over there?" She pointed at a lovely blond waitress serving drinks on the far side of the bar.

Zabiski nodded, perking up.

"Well, I'd like to take her to my room," the brunette said, "take off all her clothes, and nibble her tits and lick every curve and suck every inch of that sweet young thing, all night long."

At this Zabiski burst into tears and buried his head in his arms.

"Why the hell are you crying?" asked the woman.

"I think I'm a lesbian too," he sobbed.

DATING VS. MARRIAGE

When you're dating...he takes you out to have a good time.

When you're married...he brings home a six pack and says, "What are you going to drink?"

When you're dating...you picture the two of you growing old together.

When you're married...you wonder who will die first.

When you're dating...he knows what the "hamper" is.

When you're married...the floor will suffice.

My girlfriend always laughs during sex—no matter what she's reading.

STEVE JOBS

TEN PICK-UP LINES FOR MEN:

1. "I'm going to give you a quarter so you can phone your mom and tell her you won't be coming home."

2. "Why not sit on my lap, and we'll see if anything comes up."

3. "Can I check the label on your bra? Why? To see if those tits really are made in heaven."

4. "I like your dress, but it would look better around your ankles."

5. "I want to melt in your mouth, not your hand."

6. "Do you fuck?"

7. "My name's [fill in]. That's so you know what to scream later on."

8. "Do you want to see something really swell?"

9. "Want to play carnival? That's where you sit on my face and I guess your weight."

10. First you beckon a girl over, then you say: "I made you cum with one finger. Imagine what I could do with my whole hand..."

Stage 1: Kissing/Light Petting

What he hopes you're thinking: "Oh, I can't resist: I'm powerless before your seductive ways!"

What he's afraid you're thinking: "Garlic breath—ewwww!"

Stage 2: Undressing

What he hopes you're thinking: "My God, look at the size of that!"

What he's afraid you're thinking: "My God, look at the size of that!"

Stage 3: Foreplay/Oral Sex

What he hopes you're thinking: "I could worship at the altar of your impressive manhood for hours."

What he's afraid you're thinking: "If he doesn't warn me before he comes, I'm going to kill him."

Stage 4: Penetration

What he hopes you're thinking: "You stallion, you're splitting me in half!"

What he's afraid you're thinking: "Is it in yet?"

Stage 5: Your Orgasm

What he hopes you're thinking: "Yes, [his name here], yes!"

What he's afraid you're thinking: "I deserve an Academy Award for this performance."

What he's even more afraid you're thinking: "Yes, [other guy's name here], yes!"

Stage 6: Postcoital Bliss

What he hopes you're thinking: "Now I know what an earthquake feels like."

What he's afraid you're thinking: "Maybe I should let my lesbian friend, Sue, take me to that females-only dance club after all."

TOP 10 REJECTION LINES USED BY MEN
(AND WHAT THEY ACTUALLY MEAN):

1. I think of you as a sister. (You're ugly.)

2. There's a slight difference in our ages. (You're ugly.)

3. I'm not attracted to you in "that" way. (You're ugly.)

4. My life is too complicated right now. (You're ugly.)

5. I've got a girlfriend. (You're ugly.)

6. I don't date women where I work. (You're ugly.)

7. It's not you, it's me. (You're ugly.)

8. I'm concentrating on my career. (You're ugly.)

9. I'm celibate. (You're ugly.)

10. Let's be friends. (You're ugly.)

MAN: Where have you been all my life?

WOMAN: Hiding from you.

MAN: Haven't I seen you someplace before?

WOMAN: Yes, that's why I don't go there anymore.

MAN: Is that seat empty?

WOMAN: Yes, and *this* one will be if you sit down.

MAN: Your place or mine?

WOMAN: Both. You go to yours, I'll go to mine.

MAN: So, what do you do for a living?

WOMAN: I'm a female impersonator.

MAN: Hey baby, what's your sign?

WOMAN: Do not enter.

MAN: How do you like your eggs in the morning?

WOMAN: Unfertilized.

MAN: Your body is like a temple.

WOMAN: Sorry, there are no services today.

MAN: I would go to the end of the world for you.

WOMAN: But would you stay there?

MAN: If I could see you naked, I'd die happy.

WOMAN: If I saw you naked, I'd probably die laughing.

I date this girl for two years—and then the nagging starts: "I wanna know your name!"

Women try on several outfits to make sure they look good, stylish, are the right color....

Men smell their clothes, then put them on.

TOP TEN PRINCE CHARLES PICK-UP LINES

1. "Wanna hold the royal scepter?"

2. "Put a flag over my head and do it for England."

3. "Ever done it with an outdated historical anachronism?"

4. "If you think my ears are big..."

5. "Come upstairs with me and I'll make you the Princess of Wails."

6. "Care to join a family of inbred freaks?"

7. "Would you like to sit in a giant bowl of eggnog with me?"

8. "Why don't you lose that hayseed you're with, Hillary?"

9. "Let's put the bucking in Buckingham Palace."

10. "I've got Big Ben in my pants."

Q: Do you mind if I smoke?

A: I don't care if you burst into flames and die.

On their first date, Joe took Rose to the carnival. When he asked her what she wanted to do first, Rose replied, "Get weighed."

So Joe took her to the man with the scale who guesses your weight. He looked at Rose and said, "One hundred and twenty pounds." Since Rose weighed in at one seventeen, she collected a prize.

Next they went on the roller coaster. When the ride was finished, Joe asked Rose what she wanted to do next. "Get weighed," she said. So they went back to the man with the scale, who of course guessed Rose's weight correctly. Leaving without a prize, they went for a ride on the merry-go-round. After they got off, Joe asked Rose what she wanted to do next. "I want to get weighed!" she said again.

Now Joe began to think this girl was quite strange, and decided to end the evening quickly. He left her at the door with a quick handshake.

Rose's roommate was waiting up for her return and asked how the evening went.

"Wousy!" Rose replied.

A drunk is leaning against a lightpost on the corner of a busy street.

While gazing blearily around, he notices a smartly dressed young man standing a few feet away, watching the people pass by. As the drunk is watching, a lovely lady comes walking along, and the young man says something to her. She immediately smiles, shakes her head, and takes his hand. The two of them together go up the stairs of a nearby row house, and inside.

A short while later, the two come back down, grinning from ear to ear. They embrace affectionately, and the lady departs.

This happens several times in the next few hours with different ladies. Once the lady frowned, and after some further words from the young man, merely nodded her head and walked on. The drunk strained his ears to hear what was being said, but just couldn't make it out. Finally, his curiosity overcame his need for vertical support, and he stumbled over to the young man.

DRUNK: Shay, bud. Wha's goin' on?

YOUNG MAN: Yes, I saw you watching. I wondered when you would come over. Well, it's like this. I watch the people. When I see a lady that takes my fancy, I walk up to her and say, softly, "Tickle your ass with a feather?" If she is agreeable to the idea, we go upstairs to my room and have a good time. If she becomes upset, I merely say, "Typical nasty weather." She assumes that she misheard me the first time, and just keeps going. I can't lose!

DRUNK: (now swaying): Thas a great idea! I'll have to run home and try it mysel'.

So the drunk wobbles to his own home and stands leaning against the fence. Soon a very lovely lady comes walking briskly along, and the drunk decides that this is his big chance. So he stumbles over to the lady and grabs her arm.

VERY LOVELY LADY: Yes?

DRUNK (shouting): HEY BABE, C'N I STICK A FEATHER UP YOUR ASS?

VERY LOVELY LADY: WHAT?!

DRUNK (looking at the sky): Fuckin' rain!

May I have the pleasure of the next sadly outdated courting ritual?

MICHAEL LEUNIG

I'm glad you don't recognize me. I'd rather have you like me for myself.

This guy pulls into his driveway after a long day at work to find all his belongings out in the front yard. He enters his house and asks his girlfriend, "What's going on?"

She says, "I found out you're a pedophile, and I want you to leave."

He looks at her and says, "Pedophile, huh? That's a pretty big word for a ten year old."

After finishing dinner with a new girlfriend, a French fighter pilot retires to a couch where he immediately starts kissing her on the neck. After a few minutes of this the girlfriend says, "Kiss my lips." The French fighter pilot dips two fingers in some red wine, rubs it on her lips, and in a thick French accent says, "When I have red meat, I have red wine."

After kissing his girlfriend on her lips for a while she says, "Kiss me lower." The French fighter pilot then dips two fingers in some white wine, rubs them on her breasts, and says, "When I have white meat, I have white wine." Then he begins to kiss her breasts.

After a few minutes of this the girlfriend says, in complete passion, "Kiss me lower!" The French fighter pilot then takes a bottle of cognac, pours it between her legs, and with a match he sets the cognac on fire. In disbelief the girlfriend jumps up and says, "What the hell are you doing?"

To which the French fighter pilot replies, "When I go down, I go down in flames."

Infatuation is when you think that he's as sexy as Robert Redford, as smart as Henry Kissinger, as noble as Ralph

Nader, as funny as Woody Allen, and as athletic as Andre Agassi. Love is when you realize that he's as sexy as Woody Allen, as smart as Andre Agassi, as funny as Ralph Nader, as athletic as Henry Kissinger, and nothing like Robert Redford—but you'll take him anyway.

JUDITH VIORST

I don't date women my own age. There *are* no women my own age.

GEORGE BURNS

"I went out with a pair of twins last night."

"Did you have a good time?"

"Yes and no."

Engagement (Is this the one?)

Here's to health and prosperity,
To you and all your posterity.
And them that doesn't drink with sincerity,
That they may be damned for all eternity!

Drink, my buddies, drink with discerning,
Wedlock's a lane where there is no turning;
Never was owl more blind than lover;
Drink and be merry, lads, and think it over.

Four blessings upon you:
Older whiskey,
Younger women,
Faster horses,
More money.

Here's to the perfect girl,
I couldn't ask for more.
She's deaf 'n dumb 'n oversexed,
and owns a liquor store.

I love the girls that say they won't.
I love the girls that say they do,
And then they say they don't.
But the girls that I do love the most,
And I know you'll think I'm right,
Are the girls that say they normally don't,
"But for you I think I might."

"I hear you're engaged. So who's the lucky woman?"

"Her mother!"

Marriage (The long haul)

Like life isn't stressful enough. People have to get married! Planning a wedding is the most stressful thing a person can ever do (except have a conversation with someone who works in a post office). Trying to figure out how to pay for it, who is paying for it, who is coming, why they are coming (do you really like them that much anyway?) and how the hell you are going to get through the next fifty years sleeping with just one person. Do you really know that much about him? Is anyone interesting enough to spend fifty years with? Should you consider a Labrador instead?

What about the pre-nup? What about taxes, will you have to consult someone else every time you want to do something? Guess what?

Her family, your family, oy. First there is the engagement. We are so happy for you! (Looks like you guys
found each other just in time—we were getting worried.)
Presents, endless gifts for every occasion leading up to
the big day when you will probably spend two grand on
plane tickets and hotels, five hundred on clothes, and two
hundred on a gift, all adding up to the same price as that
vacation in Tahiti you wanted to take and all for someone
whom you find slightly annoying. Someone you can't
even remember where you met. And someone who, by the
way, you will NEVER see again.

There's the endless showers—could you spend more
money on this chick you don't even like? Bachelor parties, and now, bachelorette parties. Naked men and
women performing live! And it's socially acceptable and
we even get dressed up for it. Call it entertainment. Call
it fun. It calls for a toast—and that's where you come in.

ABOUT THAT PRE-NUP!

Say it with flowers
Say it with eats,
Say it with kisses,
Say it with sweets,
Say it with jewelry,
Say it with drink,
But always be careful
Not to say it with ink.

If it weren't for marriage, men and women would have to
fight with total strangers.

Man is incomplete until he is married. Then he is really
finished.

I'm so miserable without my husband, it's almost like having him here.

Love is one long dream and marriage is the alarm clock.

May your wedding night be like a kitchen table...all legs and no drawers.

May your neighbors respect you,
Trouble neglect you,
The angels protect you,
And heaven accept you.
May the Irish hills caress you.
May her lakes and rivers bless you.
May the luck of the Irish enfold you.
May the blessings of Saint Patrick behold you.

May all your ups and downs be between the sheets.

I love them, all the ladies,
With their frilly little things.
I love them with their diamonds,
Their perfumes and their rings.
I love them, all the ladies,
I love them big and small,
But when a lady isn't quite a lady,
That's when I love them most of all.

Here's to them that sail to sea
And the ladies that stay on land.
May the former be well-rigged
And the latter be well-manned!

May the winds of fortune sail you,
May you sail a gentle sea.
May it always be the other guy
Who says, "This drink's on me."

I married a German. Every night I dress up as Poland
and he invades me.

BETTE MIDLER

On the first day of their honeymoon, the very naive
blonde virgin bride slipped into a sexy but sweet nightie
and, with great anticipation, crawled into bed, only to
find that her new Christian husband had settled down on
the couch.

When she asked him why he was apparently not going to
make love to her, he replied, "Because it's Lent."

Almost in tears, she remarked, "That's terrible! Who on
earth did you lend it to?"

One night a father overheard his son saying his prayers.

"God bless Mommy and Daddy and Grammy. Good-bye,
Grampa."

Well, the father thought it was strange, but he soon forgot about it. The next day, the grandfather died.

About a month or two later the father heard his son saying his prayers again.

"God bless Mommy. God bless Daddy. Good-bye,
Grammy."

The next day the grandmother died. Well, the father was
getting more than a little worried about the whole situa-

tion. Two weeks later, the father once again overheard his son's prayers.

"God bless Mommy. Good-bye, Daddy."

This alone nearly gave the father a heart attack. He didn't say anything, but he got up early to go to work so that he would miss the traffic. He stayed all through lunch and dinner. Finally, after midnight, he went home. He was still alive!

When he got home he apologized to his wife. "I am sorry, honey. I had a very bad day at work today."

"YOU THINK YOU HAD A BAD DAY?!" his wife yelled, "The mailman dropped dead on my doorstep this morning!"

HE SAID... SHE SAID

He said...I don't know why you wear a bra; you've got nothing to put in it.

She said...You wear briefs, don't you?

He said...Do you love me just because my father left me a fortune?

She said...Not at all honey, I would love you no matter who left you the money.

She said...What do you mean by coming home half-drunk?

He said...It's not my fault...I ran out of money.

He said...Since I first laid eyes on you, I've wanted to make love to you in the worst way.

She said...Well, you succeeded.

He said...Two inches more, and I would be king.

She said...Two inches less, and you'd be queen.

Priest said...I don't think you will ever find another man like your late husband.

She said...Who's gonna look?

He said...What have you been doing with all the grocery money I gave you?

She said...Turn sideways and look in the mirror.

He said...Let's go out and have some fun tonight.

She said...Okay, but if you get home before I do, leave the hallway light on.

He said...Why don't you tell me when you have an orgasm?

She said...I would, but you're never there.

He said...Shall we try a different position tonight?

She said...That's a good idea...you stand by the ironing board while I sit on the sofa and fart.

Q: What's the difference between a Catholic wife and a Jewish wife?

A: A Catholic wife has real orgasms and fake jewelry.

YOU BET YOUR LIFE BANTER:

GROUCHO: So, Mrs. Smith, do you have any children?

MRS. SMITH: Yes, thirteen.

GROUCHO: Thirteen! Good lord, isn't that a burden?

MRS. SMITH: Well, I love my husband.

GROUCHO: Lady, I love my cigar, but I take it out of my mouth every once in a while.

Two guys are talking about their boss's upcoming wedding. One says, "It's ridiculous. He's rich, but he's 93 years old, and she's just 26! What kind of a wedding is that?"

"Well, we have a name for it in my family."

"What do you call it?"

"We call it a football wedding."

"What's a football wedding?"

"She's waiting for him to kick off."

When I can no longer bear to think of the victims of broken homes, I begin to think of the victims of intact ones.

PETER DEVRIES

SOME THOUGHTS ON WIVES BY
THE LATE FRIAR HENNY YOUNGMAN:

A woman says to a man, "I haven't seen you around here."

"Yes, I just got out of jail for killing my wife."

"So...you're single...."

Take my wife, please!

I've been in love with the same woman for 49 years. If my wife ever finds out, she'll kill me!

My wife and I have the secret to making a marriage last. Two times a week, we go to a nice restaurant, a little wine, good food.... She goes Tuesdays, I go Fridays.

Someone stole all my credit cards, but I won't be reporting it. The thief spends less than my wife did.

I asked my wife, "Where do you want to go for our anniversary?" She said, "Somewhere I have never been!" I told her, "How about the kitchen?"

We always hold hands. If I let go, she shops.

My wife will buy anything marked down. Last year she bought an escalator.

All my wife does is shop. Once she was sick for a week and three stores went under.

She was at the beauty shop for two hours. That was only for the estimate.

She got a mudpack and looked great for two days. Then the mud fell off.

Q: What did the wife do when she found out her husband was gay?

A: She turned around and took it like a man.

A little boy asked his father, "Daddy how much does it cost to get married?"

"I don't know," his father replied, "I'm still paying."

After a quarrel, a woman said to her husband, "I was a fool when I married you."

"I know," the husband replied. "But I was in love and I didn't notice."

Every mother generally hopes that her daughter will snag a better husband than she managed to do...but she's certain that her boy will never get as great a wife as his father did.

Long engagements give people the opportunity of finding out each other's character before marriage, which is never advisable.

OSCAR WILDE

Will you marry me? Do you have any money? Answer the second question first.

GROUCHO MARX

To keep your marriage brimming,
With love in the wedding cup,
Whenever you're wrong, admit it;
Whenever you're right, shut up.

OGDEN NASH

An archaeologist is the best husband a woman can have; the older she gets the more interested he is in her.

AGATHA CHRISTIE

One cardinal rule of marriage should never be forgotten: "Give little, give seldom, and above all, give grudgingly." Otherwise, what could have been a proper marriage could become an orgy of sexual lust.

RUTH SMYTHERS, *MARRIAGE ADVICE FOR WOMEN*, 1894

Marriage isn't a word...it's a sentence.

KING VIDOR, IN THE 1928 FILM *THE CRAWL*

Here's a toast to your new bride who has everything a girl could want in her life, except for good taste in men!

Marriage is the only war where one sleeps with the enemy.

Never go to bed angry. Stay up and fight.

PHYLLIS DILLER

Marriage is a great institution, but I'm not ready for an institution.

MAE WEST

I think men who have a pierced ear are better prepared for marriage. They've experienced pain and bought jewelry.

RITA RUDNER

Many a man owes his success to his first wife, and his second wife to his success.

Be tolerant of the human race. Your whole family belongs to it—and some of your spouse's family does too.

YOUNG SON: Is it true Dad, I heard in some parts of Africa a man doesn't know his wife until he marries her?

DAD: That happens in every country, son.

A man inserted an ad in the classifieds: "Wife Wanted."

The next day he received a hundred letters.

They all said the same thing: "You can have mine."

I haven't spoken to my wife for 18 months.

I don't like to interrupt her.

Marriage is a three-ring circus:

Engagement ring, wedding ring, and suffering.

The last fight was my fault. My wife asked, "What's on the TV?" I said, "Dust!"

In the beginning, God created earth and rested. Then God created man and rested. Then God created woman and rested. Since then, neither God nor man has rested.

Why do men die before their wives?

They want to.

What is the difference between a dog and a fox?

About five drinks.

A man and a woman who have never met before find themselves assigned to the same sleeping room on a transcontinental train. After the initial embarrassment and uneasiness, they both go to sleep, the man in the upper berth and the woman in the lower berth.

In the middle of the night the man leans over, wakes the woman and says, "I'm sorry to bother you, but I'm awfully cold and I was wondering if you could possibly reach over and get me another blanket?"

The woman leans out and, with a glint in her eye says, "I have a better idea. Just for tonight let's pretend that we are married."

The man happily says, "OK. Great!"

The woman says "Good…get your own blanket."

The most effective way to remember your wife's birthday is to forget it once.

You never know what true happiness is until you are married, and then it is too late.

Q: How do you turn a fox into an elephant?

A: Marry it.

Q: Where does a husband hide money from his wife?

A: Under the vacuum cleaner.

Q: How do you keep your husband from reading your e-mail?

A: Rename the mail folder, "Instruction Manuals."

For Sale By Owner: Complete set of *Encyclopedia Britannica.* 45 volumes. Excellent condition. No longer needed. Got married last weekend. Wife knows everything.

A popular airline recently introduced a special half-rate fare for wives who accompany their husbands on business trips. Expecting great feedback, the company sent out letters to all the wives of businessmen who had used the special rates, asking how they enjoyed their trip.

Letters are still pouring in asking, "What trip?"

FIRST GUY (proudly): "My wife's an angel!"

SECOND GUY: "You're lucky, mine's still alive."

An elderly women decided to have her portrait painted. She told the artist, "Paint me with diamond earrings, a diamond necklace, emerald bracelets, a ruby brooch and a gold Rolex."

"But you are not wearing any of those things."

"I know. It's in case I should die before my husband. I'm sure he will remarry right away, and I want his new wife to go crazy looking for the jewelry."

In olden times, sacrifices were made at the altar. Obviously this is still very much practiced.

HELEN ROLAND

Before marriage, a man will lie awake all night thinking about something you said; after marriage, he'll fall asleep before you finish saying it.

HELEN ROLAND

Compromise: An amiable arrangement between husband and wife whereby they agree to let her have her way.

When a girl marries, she exchanges the attentions of many men for the inattention of one.

HELEN ROLAND

When you are dating…you are turned on at the sight of him naked.

When you are married…you think to yourself "Was he ALWAYS this hairy?"

Some of us are becoming the men we wanted to marry.

GLORIA STEINEM

When a man steals your wife, there is no better revenge than to let him keep her.

Your marriage is in trouble if your wife says, "You're only interested in one thing," and you can't remember what it is.

MILTON BERLE

I told my wife the truth. I told her I was seeing a psychiatrist. Then she told me the truth: that she was seeing a psychiatrist, two plumbers, and a bartender.

RODNEY DANGERFIELD

Eighty percent of married men cheat in America. The rest cheat in Europe.

JACKIE MASON

I wouldn't mind my wife having the last word—if only she'd get to it.

HENNY YOUNGMAN

A man was in court for a double murder, and the judge said, "You are charged with beating your wife to death with a hammer."

A man at the back of the courtroom yelled out, "You bastard!"

The judge continued, "You are also charged with beating your mother-in-law to death with a hammer."

Again, the man at the back of the courtroom yelled out, "You damn bastard!"

The judge stopped, looked at the man and said, "Sir, I can understand your anger and frustration at this crime, but I will not have any more of these outbursts from you, or I shall charge you with contempt! Now is that a problem?"

The man at the back of the court stood and responded, "For fifteen years, I have lived next door to that bastard, and every time I asked to borrow a hammer, he said he never had one!"

A Code of Honor: Never approach a friend's girlfriend or wife with mischief as your goal. There are just too many women in the world to justify that sort of dishonorable behavior. Unless she's really attractive.

BRUCE FRIEDMAN

A mother had three virgin daughters who were all getting married within a short period of time. Because Mom was a bit worried about how their sex life would get started, she made them all promise to send a postcard from the honeymoon with a few words on how marital sex felt.

The first daughter sent a card from Hawaii two days after the wedding. The card said nothing but "Nescafe."

Mom was puzzled at first, but then went to the kitchen and got out the Nescafe jar. It said: "Good till the last drop." Mom blushed, but was pleased for her daughter.

The second girl sent the card from Vermont a week after the wedding, and the card read, "Benson & Hedges." Mom now knew to go straight to her husband's cigarettes, and she read from the Benson and Hedges pack: "Extra Long. King Size." She was again slightly embarrassed but still happy for her daughter.

The third girl left for her honeymoon in the Caribbean. Mom waited for a week. Nothing. Another week went by and still nothing. Then after a whole month, a card finally arrived. Written on it with shaky handwriting were the words: "British Airways." Mom took out her latest *Harper's Bazaar* magazine, flipped through the pages fearing the worst, and finally found the ad for British Airways. The ad said, "Three times a day, seven days a week, both ways."

Mom fainted.

Men have a much better time of it than women: for one thing, they marry later; for another thing, they die earlier.

H.L. MENCKEN

Bigamy is having one wife too many. Monogamy is the same.

OSCAR WILDE

A young couple hadn't been married for long when, one morning, the man came up behind his wife as she got out of the shower and grabbed her ass.

"You know, Babe," he said smugly, "if you firmed your ass up a bit you wouldn't have to keep tying a sweater around your waist."

Her feelings were so hurt she didn't talk to him for the rest of the day.

A week later, he stepped into the bathroom again just as she was getting into the shower.

He grabbed her tits and said, "You know Babe, if you firmed up your tits a bit you wouldn't have to wear a bra."

The young wife was infuriated but she had to wait until the next morning to exact her revenge. When her husband stepped out of the shower, she grabbed him by the penis and hissed, "You know, Babe, if you firmed this up a bit, I wouldn't have to keep using your brother."

A man comes home to find his wife packing her bags. "Where are you going?" he asked.

"To Las Vegas! I found out that there are men that will pay me four hundred dollars to do what I do for you for free!"

The man pondered that thought for a moment and then began packing *his* bags. "What do you think you are doing?" his wife screamed.

"Going to Las Vegas with you...I want to see how you live on eight hundred dollars a year!"

All marriages are happy. It's living together afterwards that is difficult.

Marriage is like a hot bath. Once you get used to it, it's not so hot.

I'd marry again if I found a man who had fifteen million dollars and would sign over half of it to me before the marriage and guarantee he'd be dead within a year.

BETTE DAVIS

Keep your eyes wide open before marriage and half shut afterwards.

BENJAMIN FRANKLIN

I was married by a judge. I should have asked for a jury.

GROUCHO MARX

During sex my wife always wants to talk to me. Just the other night she called me from a hotel.

RODNEY DANGERFIELD

My marriage is on the rocks again. Yeah...my wife just broke up with her boyfriend.

RODNEY DANGERFIELD

WEDDING NIGHT

At 85 years, Morris marries a lovely 25-year-old woman. Because her new husband is so old, the woman decides that on their wedding night they should have separate bedrooms.

She is concerned that the old fellow might overexert himself. After the wedding festivities she prepares herself for bed and for the knock on the door she is expecting.

Sure enough the knock comes and there is her groom ready for action. They unite in conjugal union and all goes well whereupon he takes his leave of her and she prepares to go to sleep for the night.

After a few minutes there's a knock on the door and there is old Morris again ready for more action. Somewhat surprised, she consents to further coupling which is again successful, after which the octogenarian bids her a fond good night and leaves.

She is certainly ready for slumber at this point, and is close to sleep for the second time when there is another knock at the door and there he is again, fresh as a 25-year-old and ready for more.

Once again they go at it. As they're lying in afterglow, the young bride says to him, "I am really impressed that a man your age has enough juice to go at it three times. I've been with guys less than half your age who were only good for one time. You're a great lover, Morris."

Morris looks confused, turns to her, and says, "I was here already?"

I feel like Zsa Zsa Gabor's sixth husband. I know what I'm supposed to do, but I don't know how to make it interesting.

MILTON BERLE

My mother-in-law broke up my marriage. My wife came home from work one day and found me in bed with her.

LENNY BRUCE

If variety is the spice of life, marriage is the big can of leftover Spam.

JOHNNY CARSON

Marriage is an adventure, like going to war.

G. K. CHESTERTON

It is with true love as it is with ghosts; everyone talks about it, but few have seen it.

FRANÇOIS DE LA ROCHEFOUCALD

A man's wife has more power over him than the state has.

RALPH WALDO EMERSON

Where there is marriage without love, there will be love without marriage.

BENJAMIN FRANKLIN

Immature love says, "I love you because I need you." Mature love says, "I need you because I love you."

ERICH FROMM

It is wrong to think that love comes from long companionship and persevering courtship. Love is the offspring of spiritual affinity and unless that affinity is created in a moment, it will not be created for years or even generations.

KAHLIL GIBRAN

Love is an ideal thing, marriage a real thing; a confusion of the real with the ideal never goes unpunished.

JOHANN WOLFGANG VON GOETHE

Thank heaven. A bachelor's life is no life for a single man.

SAMUEL GOLDWYN

If I were a girl, I'd despair. The supply of good women far exceeds that of the men who deserve them.

ROBERT GRAVES

I don't think I'll get married again. I'll just find a woman I don't like and give her a house.

LEWIS GRIZZARD

An ideal wife is one who remains faithful to you but tries to be just as charming as if she weren't.

SACHA GUITRY

People need loving the most when they deserve it the least.

JOHN HARRIGAN

Beware of men on airplanes. The minute a man reaches thirty thousand feet, he immediately becomes consumed by distasteful sexual fantasies which involve doing uncomfortable things in those tiny toilets. These men should not be encouraged, their fantasies are sadly low-rent and unimaginative. Affect an aloof, cool demeanor as soon as any man tries to draw you out. Unless, of course, he's the pilot.

CYNTHIA HEIMEL

If you want to sacrifice the admiration of many men for the criticism of one, go ahead, get married.

KATHARINE HEPBURN

Last time I tried to make love to my wife, nothing was happening, so I said to her, "You can't think of anybody either?"

I take my wife everywhere I go. She always finds her way back.

HENNY YOUNGMAN

Marriage: the only sport in which the trapped animal has to buy the license.

WIFE: Okay, today's Friday. Where's your pay envelope?

MAN: I already spent all my pay. I bought something for the house.

WIFE: What? What could you buy for the house that cost $480?

MAN: Eight rounds of drinks.

FIRST MAN: My wife suggested that I take up a new sport this summer.

SECOND MAN: Well, that's nice. It shows that she has your interests at heart. Did she make any suggestions?

FIRST MAN: As a matter of fact, she did. By the way, how do you play this Russian Roulette?

Here's to the man who loves his wife,
And loves his wife alone.
For many a man loves another man's wife,
When he ought to be loving his own.

BURNING QUESTIONS ABOUT MARRIAGE
(AS ANSWERED BY ELEMENTARY SCHOOL STUDENTS)

How do you decide who to marry?

You got to find somebody who likes the same stuff. Like, if you like sports, she should like it that you like sports, and she should keep the chips and dip coming.

ALAN, AGE 10

No person really decides before they grow up who they're going to marry.

God decides it all way before, and you get to find out later who you're stuck with.

KIRSTEN, AGE 10

What is the right age to get married?

Twenty-three is the best age because you know the person FOREVER by then.

CAMILLE, AGE 10

No age is good to get married at. You got to be a fool to get married.

FREDDIE, AGE 6

How can a stranger tell if two people are married?

You might have to guess, based on whether they seem to be yelling at the same kids.

DERRICK, AGE 8

What do you think your mom and dad have in common?

Both don't want any more kids.

LORI, AGE 8

What do most people do on a date?

Dates are for having fun, and people should use them to get to know each other. Even boys have something to say if you listen long enough.

LYNETTE, AGE 8

On the first date, they just tell each other lies, and that usually gets them interested enough to go for a second date.

MARTIN, AGE 10

What would you do on a first date that was turning sour?

I'd run home and play dead. The next day I would call all the newspapers and make sure they wrote about me in all the dead columns.

CRAIG, AGE 9

When is it okay to kiss someone?

When they're rich.

PAM, AGE 7

The law says you have to be eighteen, so I wouldn't want to mess with that.

CURT, AGE 7

The rule goes like this: If you kiss someone, then you should marry them and have kids with them. It's the right thing to do.

HOWARD, AGE 8

Is it better to be single or married?

It's better for girls to be single but not for boys. Boys need someone to clean up after them.

ANITA, AGE 9

How would the world be different if people didn't get married?

There sure would be a lot of kids to explain, wouldn't there?

KELVIN, AGE 8

How would you make a marriage work?

Tell your wife that she looks pretty even if she looks like a truck.

RICKY, AGE 10

Give me a kisse, and to that kisse a score;
Then to that twenty, adde a hundred more;
A thousand to that hundred; so kiss on,
To make that thousand up a million;
Treble that million, and when that is done,
Let's kisse afresh, as when we first begun.

ROBERT HERRICK, "HESPERIDES"

Here's to the bride that is to be,
Here's to the groom she'll wed,
May all their troubles be light as bubbles
Or the feathers that make up their bed!

Let us toast the health of the bride;
Let us toast the health of the groom,
Let us toast the person that tied;
Let us toast every guest in the room.

Love, be true to her; Life, be dear to her;
Health, stay close to her; Joy, draw near to her;
Fortune, find what you can do for her,
Search your treasure-house through and through for
her,
Follow her footsteps the wide world over,
And keep her husband always her lover.

ANNA LEWIS

May you have enough happiness to keep you sweet;
Enough trials to keep you strong;
Enough sorrow to keep you human;
Enough hope to keep you happy;
Enough failure to keep you humble;
Enough success to keep you eager;
Enough friends to give you comfort;
Enough faith and courage in yourself, your business,
and your country to banish depression;
Enough wealth to meet your needs;
Enough determination to make each day a better day
than yesterday.

Here's to the man who takes a wife,
Let him make no mistake:
For it makes a lot of difference
Whose wife it is you take.

Since 50 percent of marriages now end in divorce, good
luck.

What's mine is yours, and what is yours is mine.

SHAKESPEARE

Here's to the husband and here's to the wife,
May they be lovers for the rest of their life.

Here's to the bride and the mother-in-law,
Here's to the groom and the father-in-law,
Here's to the sister and the brother-in-law,
Here's to the friends and the friends-in-law,
May none of them need an attorney-at-law.

Here's to the bride and here's to the groom,
And to the bride's father who paid for this room.

Nothing is worth more than this day.

JOHANN WOLFGANG VAN GOETHE

A time to celebrate and think
Last chance to size up life.
'Cause soon the pants in the family shrink
Yet will oddly fit the wife.

Marriage is for a lifetime... with no opportunity for
parole.

Diplomacy, n. The art of letting somebody else have your
way.

DAVID FROST

Best wishes for a happy and successful first marriage.

MARC ROSEN

A couple have been married forty years and are revisiting the same places they went to on their honeymoon. As they are driving through the secluded countryside, they pass a ranch with a tall deer fence running along the road.

The woman says, "Sweetheart, let's do the same thing we did here forty years ago."

The guy stops the car. His wife backs against the fence, and he immediately jumps her like a bass on a June bug. They make love like never before.

Back in the car, the guy says, "Darlin', you sure never moved like that forty years ago—or any time since that I can remember."

The woman says, "Forty years ago that goddamn fence wasn't electrified!"

Husbands are like fires. They go out if unattended.

ZSA ZSA GABOR

LOUD SEX:

A wife went in to see a therapist and said, "I've got a big problem, doctor. Every time we're in bed and my husband climaxes, he lets out this ear-splitting yell."

"My dear," the shrink said, "that's completely natural. I don't see what the problem is."

"The problem is," she complained, "it wakes me up!"

QUIET SEX:

Tired of a listless sex life, the man came right out and asked his wife during a recent love-making session, "How come you never tell me when you have an orgasm?"

She glanced at him casually and replied, "You're never home!"

CONFOUNDED SEX:

A man was in a terrible accident, and his "manhood" was mangled and torn from his body.

His doctor assured him that modern medicine could give him back his manhood, but that his insurance wouldn't cover the surgery, since it was considered cosmetic. The doctor said that the cost would be $3500 for "small," $6500 for "medium," and $14,000 for "large."

The man was sure he would want a medium or large, but the doctor urged him to talk it over with his wife before he made any decision.

The man called his wife on the phone and explained their options.

The doctor came back into the room, and found the man looking quite dejected. "Well, what have the two of you decided?" asked the doctor.

The man answered, "She'd rather remodel the kitchen"

A man phones home from the office and tells his wife, "Something has just come up. I have the chance to go fishing for a week. It's the opportunity of a lifetime. We leave right away, so pack my clothes, my fishing equipment, and especially my blue silk pajamas. I'll be home in an hour to pick them up."

He hurries home, grabs everything and rushes off. A week later he returns. His wife asks, "Did you have a good trip?"

He says, "Oh yes, great! But you forgot to pack my blue silk pajamas."

The wife responds in an angry tone, "Oh no, I didn't. I put them in your tackle box."

An old man of ninety got married,
The bride was so young and so bold,
In his car they both went honeymooning—
She married the old man for gold.
A year later he was a daddy,
At ninety he still had the knack;
He took one look at the baby—
And then gave the chauffeur the sack.
MAX MILLER

A good marriage lasts forever and a bad one seems to.

I'm so miserable without her, it's almost like having her here.

My wife and I have finally come to terms. Hers!

My wife and I started arguing on our wedding day. When I said, "I do," she said, "Oh no, you don't!"

I know I'm old-fashioned but I believe my wife shouldn't work. She should just stay at home and do the cooking, the washing, the ironing, the cleaning....

Real happiness is when you marry a girl for love and find out later she has money.

I was cleaning out the attic last night with my husband—filthy, dusty, covered in cobwebs. Still, he's good to the kids!

GROOM: Darling, was I the first?

BRIDE: Why does everyone have to ask me that question?

In-laws (Hold on, it's going to be a bumpy ride)

Ah, the mother-in-law...the much laughed at, criticized member of the family—but the question remains: Is there anyone really more annoying than your *own* mother? Think about that.

Mother-in-law: A woman who destroys her son-in-law's peace of mind by giving him a piece of hers.

Q: What's the definition of mixed emotions?

A: When you see your mother-in-law backing off a cliff in your brand-new car.

Do you know the punishment for bigamy? Two mothers-in-law.

HENNY YOUNGMAN

I just got back from a pleasure trip. I took my mother-in-law to the airport.

HENNY YOUNGMAN

I keep telling my wife that I like her mother-in-law better than I like mine!

It's strange. One day I wasn't good enough to marry her daughter. The next, I've fathered the brightest grand-child on earth.

My mother-in-law may live with us for ever. I can't really complain—it *is* her house!

We're Pregnant (Now you've done it!)

The problem with the gene pool is that there is no life-guard.

STEVEN WRIGHT

Women should not have children after 35.
Really...35 children are enough.

FATAL THINGS TO SAY TO YOUR PREGNANT WIFE

"Not to imply anything, but I don't think the kid weighs forty pounds."

"Y'know, looking at her, you'd never guess that Pamela Lee had a baby!"

"I sure hope your thighs aren't gonna stay flabby forever!"

"Well, couldn't they induce labor? The 25th is the Super Bowl."

"Damn if you ain't about five pounds away from a surprise visit from that Richard Simmons fella."

"Fred at the office passed a stone the size of a pea. Boy, that's gotta hurt."

"Whoa! For a minute there, I thought I woke up next to Willard Scott!"

"Are your ankles supposed to look like that?"

"Get your own ice cream, Buddha!"

"Got milk?"

"Maybe we should name the baby after my secretary, Tawney."

"Man! That rose tattoo on your hip is the size of Madagascar!"

"Retaining water? Yeah, like the Hoover Dam retains water."

"You don't have the guts to pull the trigger, Lard Ass."

"Sure you'll get your figure back—we'll just search 1985 where you left it."

"Keys are by the fridge, honey. I'll see you at the hospital at half-time."

"Sure, the doctor said you're eating for two—but he didn't mean two Orcas."

"Honey—come show the guys your Brando impression!"

"Roseanne, what have you done with my wife?!"

"How come you're so much fatter than the other chicks in Lamaze?"

"Sweetheart, where'd you put that Victoria's Secret catalog?"

"What's the big deal? If you can handle me going in, surely you can handle a baby coming out."

"Hey, when you're finished pukin' in there, get me a beer, will ya?"

"Why in the world would I want to rub your feet?"

"That's not a bun in the oven—it's the whole friggin' bakery!"

"You know, now that you mention it, you are getting fat and unattractive."

"Oh, this is great! Now, on top of everything else, child support."

"Yo, Fat Ass! You're blocking the TV!"

"No, I don't know where the remote is! Have you looked under your breasts?"

"I know today's your due date, but Larry just got a 10-point buck and that's a reason to celebrate, too."

We meet today to celebrate,
Your baby's pending birth,
You'll be so happy when she is born,
And you can lose that girth.

PREGNANCY QUESTIONS AND ANSWERS

Q: Am I more likely to get pregnant if my husband wears boxers rather than briefs?

A: Yes, but you'll have an even better chance if he doesn't wear anything at all.

Q: What is the easiest way to figure out exactly when I got pregnant?

A: Have sex once a year.

Q: What is the most common pregnancy craving?

A: For men to be the one to get pregnant.

Q: My blood type is O-positive and my husband's is A-negative. What if my baby is born, say, type AB-positive?

A: Then the jig is up.

Q: My husband and I are very attractive. I'm sure our baby will be beautiful enough for commercials. Who should I contact about this?

A: Your therapist.

Q: I'm two months pregnant now. When will my baby move?

A: With any luck, right after he finishes college.

Q: How will I know if my vomiting is morning sickness or the flu?

A: If it's the flu, you'll get better.

Q: My brother tells me that since my husband has a big nose, and genes for big noses are dominant, my baby will have a big nose as well. Is this true?

A: The odds are greater that your brother will have a fat lip.

Q: Since I became pregnant, my breasts, rear end, and even my feet have grown. Is there anything that gets smaller during pregnancy?

A: Yes, your bladder.

Q: Ever since I've been pregnant, I haven't been able to go to bed at night without onion rings. Is this a normal craving?

A: Depends on what you're doing with them.

Q: The more pregnant I get, the more often strangers smile at me. Why?

A: Cause you're fatter then they are.

Q: My wife is five months pregnant and so moody that sometimes she's borderline irrational.

A: So what's your question, dipshit?

Q: Will I love my dog less when the baby is born?

A: No, but your husband might get on your nerves.

Q: Under what circumstances can sex at the end of pregnancy bring on labor?

A: When the sex is between your husband and another woman.

Q: What's the difference between a nine-months-pregnant woman and a *Playboy* centerfold?

A: Nothing, if the pregnant woman's husband knows what's good for him.

Q: My childbirth instructor says it's not pain I'll feel during the labor, but pressure. Is she right?

A: Yes, in the same way that a tornado might be called an air current.

Q: When is the best time to get an epidural?

A: Right after you find out you're pregnant.

Q: Is there any reason I have to be in the delivery room while my wife is in labor?

A: Not unless the word "alimony" means anything to you.

Q: I'm modest. Once I'm in the hospital to deliver, who will see me in that delicate position?

A: Authorized personnel only—doctors, nurses, orderlies, photographers, florists, cleaning crews, journalists, etc.

Q: Does labor cause hemorrhoids?

A: Labor causes anything you want to blame it for.

Q: Where is the best place to store breast milk?

A: In your breasts.

Q: Is there a safe alternative to breast pumps?

A: Yes, baby lips.

Q: What does it mean when a baby is born with teeth?

A: It means that the baby's mother may want to rethink her plans to nurse.

Q: How does one sanitize nipples?

A: Bathe daily and wear a clean bra. It beats boiling them in a saucepan.

Q: What are the terrible twos?

A: Your breasts after baby stops nursing cold turkey.

Q: What is the best time to wean the baby from nursing?

A: When you see teeth marks.

Q: What is the grasp reflex?

A: The reaction of new fathers when they see a new mother's breasts.

Q: Can a mother get pregnant while nursing?

A: Yes, but it's much easier if she remove the baby from her breast and puts him to sleep first.

Q: What happens to disposable diapers after they are thrown away?

A: They are stored in a silo in the Midwest, in the event of global chemical warfare.

Q: Do I have to have a baby shower?

A: Not if you change the baby's diaper very quickly.

Q: What causes baby blues?

A: Tanned, hard-bodied bimbos.

Q: What is colic?

A: A reminder for new parents to use birth control.

Q: What are night terrors?

A: Frightening episodes in which the new mother dreams she's pregnant again.

Q: Our baby was born last week. When will my wife begin to feel and act normal again?

A: When the kid is in college.

PREGNANCY CLASS

The room was full of pregnant women and their partners, and the class was in full swing. The instructor was teaching the women how to breathe properly, along with informing the men how to give the necessary assurances at this stage of the plan.

The teacher then announced, "Ladies, exercise is good for you. Walking is especially beneficial. And, gentlemen, it wouldn't hurt you to take the time to go walking with your partner!"

The room really got quiet.

Finally, a man in the middle of the group raised his hand.

"Yes?" asked the teacher.

"Is it all right if she carries a golf bag while we walk?"

Afterbirth: When the hard part begins.

Cravings: An excuse to gluttonize your way through pregnancy.

Dilation: One of those things a pregnant woman has to take her doctor's word for.

Elastiphobia: Fear of making it into the *Guinness Book of World Records* for "Most Stretch Marks."

First Trimester: The first three months of pregnancy when you wonder, "Is it too late to hire a surrogate mother?"

Maternity clothes: What a pregnant woman wears to show people there's a reason she's fat.

Miracle: 1. The birth of a baby. 2. The fact that you lived to tell about it.

Obstetrician: The doctor who tells you you're doing fine when you think you're caught in the jaws of death.

Pregnant pause: The time it takes for a nine-month-pregnant woman to get out of a chair.

Prenatal: When your life was still your own.

Pushing: The final effort to get a ten-pound baby through an opening the size of a dime.

Second Trimester: The time when you ask the question, "Will my husband notice if I eat this gallon of ice cream and side of beef before he gets home?"

Third Trimester: The final months of pregnancy when you wonder, "How much longer can I keep from waddling?"

Here is the toast of the moon and the stars,
To the child...who will soon be ours.

Childbirth (Is there pain involved?)

A woman goes to her doctor who verifies that she is pregnant. This is her first pregnancy. The doctor asks her if she has any questions.

She replies, "Well, I'm a little worried about the pain. How much will childbirth hurt?"

The doctor answers, "Well, that varies from woman to woman and from pregnancy to pregnancy, and besides, it's difficult to describe pain."

"I know, but can't you give me some idea?" she asks.

"Grab your upper lip and pull it out a little..."

"Like this?"

"A little more..."

"Like this?"

"No. A little more..."

"Like this?"

"Yes. Does that hurt?"

"A little bit."

"Now stretch it over your head!"

Here's to the stork, a most valuable bird,
That inhabits the residence districts.
He doesn't sing tunes, nor yield any plumes,
But he helps with the vital statistics.

When he was born, his father came into the room and gave him a funny look. And as you can see, he's still got it!

Children (You better believe it!)

The first half of our life is ruined by our parents and the second half by our children.

CLARENCE DARROW

A man was taking his wife, who was pregnant with twins, to the hospital when his car went out of control and crashed. Upon regaining consciousness, he saw his brother, a relentless practical joker, sitting at his bedside.

He asked his brother how his wife was and his brother replied, "Don't worry, everybody is fine and you have a son and a daughter. But the hospital was in a real hurry to get the birth certificates filed and since both you and your wife were unconscious, I named them."

The husband asked with trepidation, "Well what did you name them?"

The brother replied, "I named the little girl Denise."

Relieved, the husband said, "That's a very pretty name! What did you come up with for my son?"

"Denephew."

Children are like a poor man's riches.

ENGLISH PROVERB

There was a boy whose father was a pastor in a small church. One day, the father told the boy that a very important bishop was coming and that he would be staying with them. The boy became very excited and asked his father if he would get to meet the guest. The father thought about this and decided that he would let the boy bring the bishop tea in the morning and wake him up. The boy agreed to do this and was very excited. His father gave him instructions: First, knock on the door of the bishop's room and then say to him, "It's the boy, my Lord, it's time to get up."

The young boy rehearsed his lines, repeating them over and over. Finally, the day came. He went to the door and knocked. He was so excited and nervous, though, that he got his lines mixed up and said, "It's the Lord, my boy, and your time is up!"

Children should be like waffles—you should be able to throw the first one away.

MARY ALICE MESSENGER

My Dad says that kids today are sure different, much more biased than when he was a kid. For example, when he takes them to the store, they say, "Bias this" and "Bias that."

Never raise your hand to your children; it leaves your midsection unprotected.

ROBERT ORBAN

TOP 10 SIGNS YOUR CHILD HAS GROWN TOO OLD FOR BREAST-FEEDING

1. He can open your blouse by himself.

2. While sucking at one breast, he caresses the other.

3. He has developed a bad habit of flicking his tongue.

4. He keeps slipping dollar bills into your belt.

5. He uses your milk as a creamer for his coffee.

6. Your birth control pills interfere with his acne medicine.

7. After each feeding, he has a smoke.

8. He frequently invites his friends over for dinner.

9. You feel an uncontrollable urge to listen to "Dueling Banjos."

10. Beard abrasions on areola.

TOP 20 CHILDREN'S BOOKS NOT RECOMMENDED BY THE NATIONAL LIBRARY ASSOCIATION

1. *Clifford the Big Red Dog Is Put to Sleep*

2. *Charles Manson's Bedtime Stories*

3. *Daddy Loses His Job and Finds the Bottle*

4. *Babar Becomes a Piano*

5. *Controlling the Playground: Respect Through Fear*

6. *Curious George and the High-Voltage Fence*

7. *The Boy Who Died from Eating All His Vegetables*

8. *Harry the Perverted Dentist*

9. *Let's Draw Betty and Veronica Without Their Clothes On*

10. *The Care Bears Maul Some Campers and Are Shot Dead*

11. *Strangers Have the Best Candy*

12. *The Little Faggot Who Snitched*

13. *Some Kittens Can Fly!*

14. *Where Would You Like to Be Buried?*

15. *Kathy Was So Bad Her Mom Stopped Loving Her*

16. *Garfield Gets Feline Leukemia*

17. *Daddy Drinks Because You Cry*

18. *You Are Different and That's Bad*

19. *Pop Goes the Hamster and Other Great Microwave Games*

20. *Things Rich Kids Have But You Never Will*

Ask a child what he wants for dinner only if he's buying.

FRAN LIEBOWITZ

The trouble with children is that they are not returnable.

QUENTIN CRISP

When I was born, the doctor came out to the waiting room and said to my father, "I'm very sorry. We did everything we could, but he pulled through."

My father carries around the picture of the kid who came with his wallet.

I remember the time I was kidnapped and they sent back a piece of my finger to my father. He said he wanted more proof.

RODNEY DANGERFIELD

A bright junior executive struggled to achieve company quotas assigned to her. At lunch one day, she asked her senior mentor how she managed the multiple priorities in her job.

"I learned a long time ago," responded the seasoned veteran, "that there are basically three ways to get things done. You can do it yourself, get someone else to do it, or ask your children *not* to do it."

A child is the perfect example of minority rule.

Do your children a favor—don't have any.

I love children, especially when they cry, for then someone takes them away.

NANCY MITFORD

Alligators have the right idea, they eat their young.

EVE ARDEN

"What's the latest dope on Wall Street?" "My son!"

HENNY YOUNGMAN

In some cultures they don't name their babies right away.
They wait and see how the child develops, like in *Dances
With Wolves*.

Unfortunately, our kids names would be less romantic
and poetic.

"This is my oldest boy, Falls Off His Tricycle, and his
friend Dribbles His Juice, and my beautiful daughter,
Allergic to Nuts."

PAUL REISER

If your parents never had children, chances are, neither
will you.

DICK CAVETT

A father comes home and asks where his son is. His wife
replies that the boy is downstairs playing with his new
chemistry set. The father is curious so he wanders down
stairs to see what his son is doing. As he's walking down
the steps he hears a banging sound. When he gets to the

bottom he sees his son pounding a nail into the wall. He asks, "What are you doing? I thought you were playing with your chemistry set. Why are you hammering a nail into the wall?"

His son replies, "This isn't a nail, dad, it's a worm. I put these chemicals on it and it became as hard as a rock."

His dad thinks about it for a minute and says, "I'll tell you what son, give me those chemicals and I'll give you a new Volkswagen." His son quite naturally says, "Sure, why not."

The next day his son goes into the garage to see his new car. Parked in the garage is a brand new Mercedes. Just then, his dad walks in. He asks his father where his Volkswagen is. His dad replies, "It's right there behind the Mercedes. By the way, the Mercedes is from your mother."

A police recruit was asked during the exam, "What would you do if you had to arrest your own mother?" He said, "Call for backup."

I could tell that my parents hated me. My bath toys were a toaster and a radio.

RODNEY DANGERFIELD

Ah, children. A woman knows all about her children. She knows about dentist appointments and soccer games and romances and best friend and favorite foods and secret fears and hopes and dreams.

A man is vaguely aware of some short people living in the house.

"Mommy, one of the kids at school called me a fairy."

"So what did you do, Johnny?"

"I hit him with my purse."

I was definitely a gay kid. My tree house had a breakfast nook.

BOB SMITH

Little Johnny is visiting the zoo with his mother. They get to the elephant exhibit, where a big old bull elephant is taking a leak. Johnny points to the pachyderm's privates and says, "Mommy, what's that?"

Mommy, seeing the huge member, turns bright red and says, "Oh, that's nothing. Never mind. Come along now."

A few weeks later, Johnny is at the zoo with his father. Johnny grabs his dad by the hand and pulls him over to the elephants, saying he has a question. Johnny points to the elephant's member and says, "Daddy, what's that?"

Dad replies, "Didn't your mother tell you?"

"Yes, she told me it was nothing."

"Well, your mom is spoiled, son."

We haven't all the good fortune to be ladies; we have not all been generals, or poets or statesmen; but when the toast works down to the babies we stand on common ground. We've all been babies.

MARK TWAIN

Ah, the patter of little feet around the house. There's nothing like having a midget for a butler.

W.C. FIELDS

When I was kidnapped, my parents snapped into action. They rented out my room.

WOODY ALLEN

Childhood is a time of rapid changes. Between the ages of twelve and seventeen, a parent can age 30 years.

SAM LEVENSON

Family (But wait, there's more!)

The old believe everything, the middle-aged suspect everything, the young know everything.

OSCAR WILDE

We've toasted the mother and daughter
We've toasted the sweetheart and wife;
But somehow we missed her,
Our dear little sister,
The joy of another man's life.

Happiness is having a large, loving, caring, close-knit family in another city.

GEORGE BURNS

Last year on Father's Day, my son gave me something I've always wanted: the keys to my car.

Friar Milton Berle
"The Biggest Friar of Them All"

"Mr. Television," "Uncle Miltie," "Big Daddy," he's been called 'em all. What did Lucille Ball and Marilyn Monroe, among others, see in him that they found so "irresistible?"

Gee, I wonder... Was it his unmatched wit? The way he delivered lines like, "...cocksucker"? Maybe not. Perhaps it was his experience and savoir-faire?

I don't know about that, but the rumor that's been circulating almost as long (no pun intended) as Uncle Miltie himself, is that he's hung like a horse. No wonder he's so revered in Hollywood.

Born Mendel Berlinger, July 12, 1908, in New York City, this Friar got his start in vaudeville and eventually moved into silent movies as a child actor. Some of his early credits include *The Perils of Pauline*, *Tillie's Punctured Romance*, and *The Mask of Zorro* (not the one with Catherine Zeta-Jones), as well as working with Charlie Chaplin.

Mr. Berle made his Broadway debut in 1920 in *Floradora* and eventually appeared in numerous Broadway shows including: *Ziegfeld Follies*, *Vanities*, *Sandals*, and *See My Lawyer*.

With the advent of television, Milton became a household name (and face) when he starred on *Texaco's Star Theater*, also known as *The Milton Berle Show*, and eventually the *Buick-Berle Show*. NBC had meant to use a rotation of hosts when it launched the program in 1948, but Uncle Miltie was so instantly popular that he became the only host of the show, ever. Milton's popularity is also believed to have aided the sale of TV sets to working-class families. He truly was "Mr. Television."

In the '60s, Berle refocused his career to concentrate only on acting. He appeared in dramatic roles on TV programs and series as well as in feature films. Some of his film credits include *Always Leave Them Laughing*, *Tall, Dark and Handsome*, *The Oscar*, *It's a Mad, Mad, Mad, Mad World*, and Woody Allen's *Broadway Danny Rose*.

Milton Berle was one of the first comedians to earn a star on NBC's Walk of Fame, and in 1984 he was inducted into the Television Hall of Fame.

The only remaining question about Miltie's greatness is whether he is indeed profoundly endowed. Well if talent is any indication...

Parents (A lifetime commitment)

WHAT MY MOTHER TAUGHT ME

My mother taught me to appreciate a job well done: "If you are going to kill each other, do it outside, I just finished cleaning."

My mother taught me religion: "You better pray that will come out of the carpet!"

My mother taught me time travel: "If you don't straighten up, I'm going to knock you into the middle of next week."

My mother taught me logic: "Because I say so, that's why."

My mother taught me foresight: "Make sure you wear clean underwear in case you're in an accident."

My mother taught me irony: "Keep crying and I'll give you something to cry about."

My mother taught me about contortionism: "Will you look at the dirt on the back of your neck!"

My mother taught me about stamina: "You'll sit there 'til all that spinach is finished."

My mother taught me about the weather: "It looks as if a tornado swept through your room."

My mother taught me how to solve physics problems: "If I yelled because I saw a meteor coming towards you, would you listen, then?"

My mother taught me about hypocrisy: "If I told you once, I told you a million times, don't exaggerate!"

My mother taught me about the circle of life: "I brought you into this world and I can take you out."

My mother taught me about envy: "There are millions of less fortunate children in this world who don't have wonderful parents like you do!"

My mother never saw the irony in calling me a son-of-a-bitch.

JACK NICHOLSON

My mother never breast fed me. She told me that she only liked me as a friend.

RODNEY DANGERFIELD

MOTHERHOOD

If it was going to be easy, it never would have started with something called labor!

Shouting to make your children obey is like using the horn to steer your car, and you get about the same results.

Life's golden age is when the kids are too old to need baby-sitters and too young to borrow the family car.

Any child can tell you that the sole purpose of a middle name is so he can tell when he's really in trouble.

God gave you two ears and one mouth...so you should listen twice as much as you talk.

You know the only people in this world who are always sure about the proper way to raise children? Those who've never had any.

Oh, to be only half as wonderful as my child thought I was when he was small, and half as stupid as my teenager now thinks I am.

There are only two things a child will share willingly: communicable diseases and his mother's age.

Adolescence is the age at which children stop asking questions because they know all the answers.

An alarm clock is a device for awakening people who don't have small children.

No wonder kids are confused today. Half the adults tell them to find themselves; the other half tell them to get lost.

Avenge yourself: Live long enough to be a problem to your children.

ANATOMY OF A MOTHER

Ears: Ears should be well-placed, incredibly attuned to a child's utterings—i.e. "you suck!" even when spoken under the breath and in another room. Yet strong enough to tune out Limp Bizkit played full blast when preparing dinner.

Eyes: Eyes can be of any color, should be able to see (although there have been many very successful mothers who were blind—they simply used the all-powerful "eyes at the back of the head" tool). Expression should be soft and gentle, yet capable of "shooting bullets" at appropriate times. The "I will turn your little butt to salt right here" look may be used in times of extreme stress.

Nose: Ah, the nose, able to smell a soiled diaper at 50 yards! I have not found the "bigger is better" theory at work here. I have known mothers with tiny little turned-up noses that look completely ineffectual, actually "scent" the time (10 minutes) when her little offspring smoked his/her first cigarette. A fantastic feat, it was a treat to watch her. She made one small error once—completely understandable—she mistook the Scotch he tried for a single-malt, rather than a blend. I could forgive her this—she was a Gin-drinker.

Mouth: Not quite so large as Rush Limbaugh's (God forbid), nor so small as Betty Boop (I do not think she would make an effective mother). It should be able to sing a soft, albeit out-of-key nursery rhyme, or raise the rafters when "mother" is displeased. It should never, never be used to insult, demean or humiliate the child. Anger is all right, but verbal abuse is forbidden. Also, the mouth is needed for eating—quite often, and in small doses usually—because mothers do not have enough time to actually sit down to eat a full meal at one time. "Mom, I need this done now," "Mom can you take me here now," "Mom where is my...," "Mom, come here and look at this!" and the dreaded, "Oops...Oh God...MOM!!!!!!"

Shoulders: The actual size is not so important, as long as they can bear the weight of the world, especially during High School.

Breasts: These particular accoutrements to the human body are there for one reason and one reason only: Milk Machines! They were put there to nourish a baby and when the time comes, boy are they handy! Now, there are some women out there who look like they could feed Nicaragua single-handedly and some who look as if they were drier than the Sahara Desert. But the good Lord has provided just such a large range of sizes to make men look like idiots in their admiration of something that every other mammal in the world has.

Stomach: This includes the waist, which many of us have not had since 1971. It is truly amazing that one can lose it so suddenly and not even hear it drop. This particular part of the body can change dramatically after having a child. There are stretch marks that have inspired gynecologists to spend an enormous amount of time trying to decipher hidden pictures. Sort of like a Rorschach Test. Some have had five babies and have a stomach that you could bounce a dime off of, and not only that, there's not a mark on them. (Others have lost several coins in the folds of their big bellies. Look at it as a kind of retirement fund.)

You may have a friend,
You may have a lover,
But don't forget,
Your best friend is your mother.

We have toasted our futures,
Our friends and our wives,
We have toasted each other
Wishing all happy lives:
But I tell you my friends,
This toast beats all others,
So raise your glasses once more
In a toast to our mothers.

MONA LISA'S MOTHER:
"After all that money your father and I spent on braces, Mona, that's the biggest smile you can give us?"

HUMPTY DUMPTY'S MOTHER:
"Humpty, If I've told you once, I've told you a hundred times not to sit on that wall. But would you listen to me? Noooo!"

COLUMBUS' MOTHER:
"I don't care what you've discovered, Christopher. You still could have written!"

BABE RUTH'S MOTHER:

"Babe, how many times have I told you—quit playing ball in the house! That's the third broken window this week!"

MICHELANGELO'S MOTHER:

"Mike, can't you paint on walls like other children? Do you have any idea how hard it is to get that stuff off the ceiling?"

NAPOLEON'S MOTHER:

"All right, Napoleon. If you aren't hiding your report card inside your jacket, then take your hand out of there and prove it!"

ABRAHAM LINCOLN'S MOTHER:

"Again with the stovepipe hat, Abe? Can't you just wear a baseball cap like the other kids?"

BARNEY'S MOTHER:

"I realize strained plums are your favorite, Barney, but you're starting to look a little purple."

MARY'S MOTHER:

"I'm not upset that your lamb followed you to school, Mary, but I would like to know how he got a better grade than you."

BATMAN'S MOTHER:

"It's a nice car, Bruce, but do you realize how much the insurance is going to be?"

GOLDILOCKS' MOTHER:

"I've got a bill here for a busted chair from the Bear family. You know anything about this, Goldie?"

LITTLE MISS MUFFET'S MOTHER:

"Well, all I've got to say is if you don't get off your tuffet and start cleaning your room, there'll be a lot more spiders around here!"

PAUL REVERE'S MOTHER:

"I don't care where you think you have to go, young man. Midnight is past your curfew!"

MARY, MARY, QUITE CONTRARY'S MOTHER:

"I don't mind you having a garden, Mary, but does it have to be growing under your bed?"

ALBERT EINSTEIN'S MOTHER:

"But, Albert, it's your senior picture. Can't you do something about your hair? Styling gel, mousse, something...?"

GEORGE WASHINGTON'S MOTHER:

"The next time I catch you throwing money across the Potomac, you can kiss your allowance good-bye!"

JONAH'S MOTHER:

"That's a nice story, but now tell me where you've really been for the last three days."

SUPERMAN'S MOTHER:

"Clark, your father and I have discussed it, and we've decided you can have your own telephone line. Now will you quit spending so much time in all those phone booths?"

EDISON'S MOTHER:

"Of course I'm proud that you invented the electric light bulb, Thomas. Now turn off that light and get to bed!"

John invited his mother over for dinner. During the meal, his mother couldn't help noticing how beautiful John's roommate, Julie, was. Over the course of the evening, while watching the two interact, she started to wonder if there was more between John and Julie than met the eye. Reading his mom's thoughts, John volunteered, "I know what you must be thinking, but I assure you, Julie and I are just roommates."

About a week later, Julie came to John and said, "Ever since your mother came to dinner, I've been unable to find the beautiful silver gravy ladle. You don't suppose she took it, do you?" John said, "Well, I doubt it, but I'll write her a letter just to be sure."

So he sat down and wrote:

Dear Mother,

I'm not saying you "did" take a gravy ladle from my house, and I'm not saying you "did not" take a gravy ladle. But the fact remains that one has been missing ever since you were here for dinner. Love, John

Several days later, John received a letter from his mother which read:

Dear Son,

I'm not saying that you "do" sleep with Julie, and I'm not saying that you "do not" sleep with Julie. But the fact remains that if she was sleeping in her own bed, she would have found the gravy ladle by now. Love, Mom

---

It isn't easy being a mother. If it were, fathers would do it.

If a mother's place is in the home, how come I spend so much time in the car?

Grandparents
(Yes, your parents had parents)

You have to stay in shape. My grandmother, she started walking five miles a day at 60. She's 97 today and we don't know where the hell she is.

ELLEN DEGENERES

Grandma and Grandpa are sitting, watching TV when Grandpa decides he's hungry for some ice cream.

"Hey, Grandma, I'm gonna head to the kitchen and get myself a dish of ice cream. You want I should get you some, too?"

"Sure, Grandpa, sounds good. But you better write down what you're going out there for or else you'll forget."

"I will not! In fact, tell me what you want on it and I'll show you I can remember that, too."

"OK," says Grandma, "I'll have some chocolate sauce. But you're gonna' forget..."

Grandpa heads out to the kitchen and disappears for about 20 or 30 minutes, accompanied by a cacophonous banging of pots and pans. Finally he emerges, carrying a plate of scrambled eggs.

"See there, Grandpa. I told you you'd forget!" chides Grandma.

"Whaddya' mean, 'forget,' Grandma? What did I forget?" demands Grandpa.

"You fool," says Grandma. "You forgot my bacon!"

My grandmother is over 80 and still doesn't need glasses. Drinks right out of the bottle.

HENNY YOUNGMAN

CHAPTER TWO:
IT'S PARTY TIME

Whether we were playing Pin-the-Tail-on-the-Donkey or crying because we didn't get a flower from the cake, we have been guests at the party of life since we were little tots. People love throwing parties for themselves and for others, and it's always good to be prepared no matter what the occasion. It's also important not to get shit-faced and make out with the caterer, but that's for another chapter. No, it's actually in this one. It's all here: the vulgar, the petty, the funny, the not-so-funny, the really dumb, the sentimental, and the sincere. Take your pick.

Whether the Bar Mitzvah is a 30-thousand-dollar spectacle of bad taste at Tavern on the Green or a tasteful affair at the home of a rich uncle, you need to know what to say and who to say it to. If your friend is turning 40, your aunt and uncle are celebrating their fiftieth, or your niece is being confirmed, you'll need a joke, a story, a toast. And if you (or more likely your spouse) doesn't like what you come up with on your own, you've got a whole chapter here of witty, dirty, or even sort of sweet remarks to choose from. So here you go, have a ball, be the hit of the party—but never let 'em see you schvitz.

I'm glad to be part of this resurgence of youth at the Friars Club. We need it. When I joined the club a few years ago, there were no children, yet there was a diaper machine in the Men's room.

JEFFREY ROSS

Bill Maher's a great guy. The only time he has a funny bone in his body is when I fuck him in the ass.

RICHARD BELZER AT HIS OWN ROAST

KEVIN POLLAK—ROAST OF ROB REINER

You came into this world a sweet little baby, tears rolling down your rosy cheeks after the doc slapped your ass. You're now an enormous fucking cry baby and we'd all like to slap the shit out of you.

JON LOVITZ—DANNY AIELLO LUNCH

First time I met Danny Aiello was twelve years ago. I was 28 and he was 55. Now I'm 40 and Danny is 57.

It's Your Birthday
(... and you can cry if you want to)

INTERNATIONAL TOASTS AND THEIR TRANSLATIONS:

Cheers (British): To your health.

Chu nin chien kang (Chinese): Wishing you good health.

Skal (Danish): Cheers.

Prost (Dutch): Your health.

Kippis (Finnish): Cheers.

A votre santé (French): To your health.

Cead Mile Failte! (Gaelic): One hundred thousand welcomes.

Prost, or *prosit* (German): Your health.

L'Chaim (Hebrew): To life.

Slainte (Irish): To your health.

Salute (Italian): Your health.

Kan pai (Japanese): Empty your glass.

Sto lat (Polish): Live to a hundred.

A sua saude (Portuguese): To your health.

Kamjab raho (Punjabi): Be successful.

Na zdorovie (Russian): Be healthy.

Salud (Spanish): Your health.

Furah (Swahili): Be happy.

Lechyd Da (Welsh): Your good health.

Don't worry about the future,
The present is all thou hast,
The future will soon be present,
And the present will soon be past.

ZODIAC TOASTS

Aquarius (January 20 to February 18)

An Aquarian is a water-bearer
A friend through thick and thin.
Perhaps the most famous of all,
Was that guy named Gunga Din.

Pisces (February 19 to March 20)

On this birthday of Pisces the Fish
We all get together to grant you this wish.
Here's to long life and always good health,
And just for good measure, a large dose of wealth.

Aries (March 21 to April 20)

To Aries, it's a mighty sign,
Symbolized by the Ram.
We wish you happy birthday,
And hope you're happy as a clam.

Taurus (April 21 to May 20)

As we make this toast,
Let us join like a chorus,
And wish happy birthday,
To our friend the Taurus.

Gemini (May 21 to June 21)

Here's to Gemini,
Represented by the twins.
With you as our friend,
We can't help but win.

Cancer (June 22 to July 22)

Hey, Crabby, here's a toast to you,
'Cause you're a Cancer through and through.
You are sensitive and very loyal,
But when you get mad it's a big crab boil.

Leo (July 23 to August 22)

Leo the Lion has the characteristics of generosity, courage and strength. Here's a toast to our friend who becomes more lion-like every day.

Virgo (August 23 to September 22)

This toast does not rhyme, ergo;
It's perfect for our friend, Virgo.

Libra (September 23 to October 22)

Born under the sign of Libra the Scales, our friend was given a great gift for spotting beauty, so it must please him greatly to be able to look out at the rest of us this evening.

Scorpio (October 23 to November 21)

While Scorpions are considered creatures of the desert, our friendship with our Scorpio friend will always prosper and bloom.

Sagittarius (November 22 to December 21)

A toast to our friend the Sagittarius; we know that the arrows you fire have all gone straight to our hearts. We love you, man.

Capricorn (December 22 to January 19)

As I propose this birthday toast I mean it in the best possible way. Happy birthday to a Capricorn...you old goat.

The family wheeled Grandma out on the lawn in her wheelchair, to where the activities for her 100th birthday were taking place. Grandma couldn't talk very well but she could write notes when she needed to communicate.

After a short time out on the lawn, Grandma started leaning off to the right. Some family members grabbed her and straightened her up and stuffed pillows on her right.

A short time later, she started leaning off to her left and again the family grabbed her and stuffed pillows on her left.

Soon she started leaning forward and the family members again grabbed her and tied a pillow around her waist to hold her up.

A nephew who arrived late came running up to Grandma and said, "Hi, Grandma you're looking good, how are they treating you?"

Grandma took out her little notepad and slowly wrote a note to the nephew: "They won't let me fart."

On the very first day, God created the cow. He said to the cow, "Today I have created you! As a cow, you must go to the field with the farmer all day long. You will work all day under the sun! I will give you a life span of 50 years."

The cow objected, "What? This kind of tough life you want me to live for 50 years? Let me have 20 years, and the 30 years I'll give back to you." God agreed.

On the second day, God created the dog. God said to the dog, "What you are supposed to do is to sit all day by the door of your house. Any people that come in, you will have to bark at them! I'll give you a life span of 20 years."

The dog objected, "What? All day long to sit by the door? No way! I give you back 10 years of my life!" God agreed.

On the third day, God created the monkey. He said to the monkey, "Monkeys have to entertain people. You've got to make them laugh and do monkey tricks. I'll give you a 20-year life span."

The monkey objected. "What? Make them laugh? Make monkey faces and do tricks all day? Ten years will do, and the other 10 years I'll give you back." God agreed.

On the fourth day, God created man and said to him, "Your job is to sleep, eat, and play. You will enjoy your life very much, and you don't really need to exert yourself. This kind of life, I'll give you a 20-year life span."

The man objected. "What? Such a good life! Eat, play, sleep, do nothing? Enjoy the best and you expect me to live for only 20 years? No way! Why don't we make a deal? Since the cow gave you back 30 years and the dog gave you back 10 years and the monkey gave you back 10 years, I will take them from you! That makes my life span 70 years, right?" So God agreed.

AND THAT'S WHY....

In our first 20 years, we eat, sleep, play, enjoy the best and do nothing much.

For the next 30 years, we work all day long, suffer and get to support the family.

For the next 10 years, we entertain our grandchildren by making monkey faces and doing monkey tricks.

And for the last 10 years, we stay at home, sit by the front door and bark at people!

Sweet Sixteen (and never been...)

May your troubles be less
And your blessings be more.
And nothing but happiness
Come through your door.

I wish thee health,
I wish thee wealth,
I wish thee gold in store,
I wish thee heaven upon earth
What could I wish thee more?

May you be merry and lack nothing.

WILLIAM SHAKESPEARE

Forget about the past, you can't change it.
Forget about the future, you can't predict it.
Forget about the present, I didn't get you one.

What did George Washington, Abraham Lincoln, and Christopher Columbus all have in common?

They were all born on holidays.

21 (A lucky number?)

Here's to living single and drinking double.

But the greatest love—the love above all loves,
Even greater than that of a mother,
Is the tender, passionate, undying love,
Of one beer-drunken slob for another.

Here's to a long life and a merry one.
A quick death and an easy one.
A pretty girl and an honest one.
A cold beer and another one!

If you are rich you are an alcoholic, if you are poor, you are just a drunk.

His problem is he doesn't just drink to excess, he drinks to anything.

I drive way too fast to worry about the cholesterol.

We grow neither better nor worse as we get old, but more like ourselves.

MAY L. BECKER

I hope I never get so old I get religious.

INGMAR BERGMAN

You don't look like twenty-one
I think that's plain to see.
But now at least you will not need
That counterfeit I.D.

Today you have turned twenty-one,
You'll watch your dreams unfurl,
I just suggest you watch your drinks,
So that you do not hurl.

30 (... something)

A health to you,
A wealth to you,
And the best that life can give to you.
May fortune still be kind to you.
And happiness be true to you,
And life be long and good to you,
Is the toast of all your friends to you.

Here's to the four hinges of Friendship:
Swearing, Lying, Stealing, and Drinking.
When you swear, swear by your country;
When you lie, lie for a pretty woman;
When you steal, steal away from bad company;
And when you drink, drink with me.

He that drinks fast, pays slow.

BENJAMIN FRANKLIN

The only time you really live fully is from thirty to sixty. The young are slaves to dreams; the old servants of regrets. Only the middle-aged have all their five senses in the keeping of their wits.

HERVEY ALLEN

Old age is like everything else. To make a success of it, you've got to start young.

FRED ASTAIRE

Fat and Forty (Lordy, Lordy)

I wish you healthy, I wish you well, and happiness galore.
I wish you luck for you and friends; what could I wish you more?
May your joys be as deep as the oceans, your troubles as light as its foam.
And may you find, sweet peace of mind, wherever you may roam.

May you live as long as you want,
And never want as long as you live.

May the road rise to meet you.
May the wind be always at your back.
May the sun shine warm upon your face.
And rains fall soft upon your fields.
And until we meet again,
May God hold you in the hollow of His hand.

A man decides to give himself a facelift as a birthday present. He's thrilled with the results and on his way home he stops for a newspaper. "How old do you think I am?" he asks the sales clerk.

"About 35," is the reply.

"Actually, I'm 47," the man says, feeling really happy.

He goes to McDonalds for lunch and asks the order-taker, "How old do you think I am?"

"Around 29?"

"I'm 47!" the man answers, feeling on top of the world.

While standing, waiting for the bus, he asks an old woman the same question.

She says, "I'm 85 years old, and I can't see all that well, but if you let me put my hand down your pants for about ten minutes I'll tell you exactly how old you are."

As there is no one around the man agrees.

Ten minutes later, the old lady says, "You're 47!"

"That was brilliant!" the man says, "How did you do it?"

"Easy," the old woman says. "I was on line behind you at McDonalds."

YOU KNOW YOU'RE OVER 25 IF...

You learned to swim about the same time *Jaws* came out, and you carry the emotional scars to this day.

You can sing "99 Red Balloons" in English and German.

You're starting to believe that maybe having kids go to school year-round wouldn't be such a bad idea after all.

You did the LeFreak with Chic.

"All-skate, change directions" means something to you.

In high school, you and all your friends made elaborate plans to get together again at the end of the century and play "1999" by Prince over and over again.

You wore anything Izod, especially collar-up, or the windbreakers that folded up into a pouch you could wear around your waist.

You owned a Jordache anything, or you remember when Jordache jeans were really cool.

Wrinkles: Something other people have. You have character lines.

Another candle on your cake?
Well, that's no cause to pout,
Be glad that you have strength enough
To blow the damn thing out.

Many happy returns of the day of your birth:
Many blessings to brighten your pathway on earth;
Many friendships to cheer and provoke you to mirth;
Many feastings and frolics to add to your girth.

Now I, friend, drink to you, friend,
As my friend drank to me,
And I, friend, charge you, friend,
As my friend charged me,
That you, friend, drink to your friend,
As my friend drank to me;
And the more we drink together, friend,
The merrier we'll be!

To your birthday, glasses held high,
Glad it's you who's older—not I.

I guess I don't so much mind being old as I mind being
fat and old.

PETER GABRIEL

To know how to grow old is the master work of wisdom,
and one of the most difficult chapters in the great art of
living.

HENRI FRÉDÉRIC AMIEL

In youth we run into difficulties. In old age difficulties
run into us.

JOSH BILLINGS

There are only three ages for women in Hollywood—
Babe, District Attorney, and Driving Miss Daisy.

GOLDIE HAWN

She was a handsome woman of forty-five and would
remain so for many years.

ANITA BROOKNER

Probably the happiest period in life is in middle age,
when the eager passions of youth are cooled and the
infirmities of age have not yet begun; as we see that the
shadows, which are at morning and evening so large,
almost entirely disappear at midday.

THOMAS ARNOLD

One time we were the same age,
But now I am behind.
'Cause though you're turning forty,
I'm remaining thirty-nine.

May thy life be long and happy,
Thy cares and sorrows few;
And the many friends around thee
Prove faithful, fond, and true.
Happy are we met, happy have we been,
Happy may we part, and happy meet again.

He says he's looking forward to his twenty-ninth birthday. But I'm afraid he's looking in the wrong direction.

Middle age is when women stop worrying about becoming pregnant and men start worrying about looking like they are.

She recently had bad luck: she ran into someone she knew when they were the same age.

When I went to my class reunion, all the guys were so fat and bald they hardly recognized me.

When I'm 64

What is but Age? Something to count?
Some people fight it as if climbing the mount.
I choose to live with dignity and grace
And offer a drink to all in this place!

To Age! To Age! Why does one care?
As the wrinkles grow longer and gray graces your hair.
Life should be simple because when push comes to shove,
The only one counting is the good Lord above!

A toast to your coffin.
May it be made of 100-year-old oak.
And may we plant the tree together tomorrow.

May your glass be ever full.
May the roof over your head be always strong.
And may you be in heaven half an hour before the devil
knows you're dead.

May the most you wish for
Be the least you get.

To keep the heart unwrinkled, to be hopeful, kindly,
cheerful, reverent, that is to triumph over old age.

THOMAS B. ALDRICH

Age is something that doesn't matter, unless you are a cheese.

BILLIE BURKE

I'm at the age where food has taken the place of sex in my life. In fact, I've just had a mirror put over my kitchen table.

RODNEY DANGERFIELD

I refuse to admit that I am more than 52, even if that makes my children illegitimate.

LADY NANCY ASTOR

I will never be an old man. To me, old age is always 15 years older than I am.

BERNARD M. BARUCH

NOW THAT I'M OLDER, HERE'S WHAT I'VE DISCOVERED:

1. I started out with nothing, and I still have most of it.

2. My wild oats have turned into prunes and All-Bran.

3. I finally got my head together; now my body is falling apart.

4. Funny, I don't remember being absent-minded....

5. All reports are in: Life is now officially unfair.

6. If all is not lost, where is it?

7. It is easier to get older than it is to get wiser.

8. Some days you're the dog; some days you're the hydrant.

9. I wish the buck stopped here; I sure could use a few.

10. Kids on the back seat cause accidents.

11. Accidents on the back seat cause…kids.

12. It's hard to make a comeback when you haven't been anywhere.

13. The only time the world beats a path to your door is when you're in the bathroom.

14. If God wanted me to touch my toes, he would have put them on my knees.

15. When I'm finally holding all the cards, why does everyone decide to play chess?

16. It's not hard to meet expenses…they're everywhere.

17. The only difference between a rut and a grave is the depth.

18. These days, I spend a lot of time thinking about the hereafter…I go somewhere to get something, and then wonder what I'm here after.

You're never to old to become younger.

MAE WEST

A retired gentleman went to the Social Security office to apply. After waiting in line a long time he got to the counter.

The woman behind the counter asked him for his driver's license to verify his age.

He looked through his pockets and told the woman that he was very sorry but he seemed to have left his wallet at home. "I will have to come back later."

The woman said, "Unbutton your shirt."

So he opened his shirt, revealing lots of curly silver hair. She said, "That silver hair on your chest is proof enough for me." She processed his social security application.

When he got home, the man excitedly told his wife about his experience.

She said, "You should have dropped your pants, you might have gotten disability too."

So What, You're 80

Age is strictly a case of mind over matter. If you don't mind, it doesn't matter.

JACK BENNY

By the time you're eighty years old, you've learned everything. You only have to remember it.

GEORGE BURNS

You are never too old to set another goal or to dream a new dream.

LES BROWN

A man of eighty has outlived probably three new schools of painting, two of architecture and poetry, and a hundred in dress.

JOYCE CAREY

Two elderly ladies have been friends for many decades. Over the years they have shared all kinds of activities and adventures. Lately, their activities have been limited to meeting a few times a week to play cards.

One day they are playing cards when one looks at the other and says, "Now don't get mad at me...I know we've been friends for a long time...but I just can't think of your name! I've thought and thought, but I can't remember it. Please tell me what your name is."

Her friend glares at her. For at least three minutes she just stares and glares at her. Finally she says, "How soon do you need to know?"

There are three classes into which all the women past seventy that ever I knew can be divided:

1. That dear old soul;

2. That old woman;

3. That old witch.

SAMUEL TAYLOR COLERIDGE

He is so old that his blood type was discontinued.

BILL DANA

"How was your golf game, dear?" asked Jack's wife, Tracy.

"Well, I was hitting pretty well, but my eyesight's gotten so bad, I couldn't see where the ball went."

"You're seventy-five years old, Jack!" admonished his wife. "Why don't you take my brother Scott along?"

"But he's eighty-five and doesn't even play golf anymore," protested Jack.

"Yes, but he's got perfect eyesight and can watch your ball for you," Tracy pointed out.

The next day Jack teed off with Scott looking on. Jack swung and the ball disappeared down the middle of the fairway. "Did you see where it went?" asked Jack.

"Yup," Scott answered.

"Well, where is it?" yelled Jack, peering off into the distance.

"I forget."

A man goes to visit his grandfather in the hospital.

"How are you, Grandpa?" he asks.

"Feeling fine," says the old man.

"What's the food like?"

"Terrific, wonderful menus."

"And the nursing?"

"Just couldn't be better. These young nurses really take care of you."

"What about sleeping? Do you sleep OK?"

"No problem at all—nine hours solid every night. Before I go to sleep, they bring me a cup of hot chocolate and a Viagra tablet…and that's it. I go out like a light."

The grandson is puzzled and a little alarmed by this, so he rushes off to question the nurse in charge. "What are you people doing," he says, "I'm told you're giving a 95-year-old Viagra on a daily basis. Surely, that can't be true!"

"Oh, yes," replies the head nurse. "Every night at 10 o'clock we give him a cup of chocolate and a Viagra tablet. It works wonderfully well. The chocolate makes him sleep and the Viagra stops him from rolling out of bed."

A senior citizen was driving down the freeway when his car phone rang.

Answering, he heard his wife's voice urgently warning him, "Russ, I just heard on the news that there's a car going the wrong way on Interstate 70. Please be careful!"

Said Russ, "It's not just one car. It's hundreds of them!"

A man is only as old as the woman he feels.

GROUCHO MARX

You're not too old when your hair turns gray
You're not too old when your teeth decay.
But you'll know you're awaiting that final sleep,
When your mind makes promises your body can't keep.

I intend to live forever. So far, so good.

It worries me that I'm getting absent-minded. I mean, sometimes, in the middle of a sentence I....

A senior citizen visits his doctor for a routine checkup and everything seems fine.

The doctor asks him about his sex life.

"Well..." the man drawled, "Not bad at all to be honest. The wife ain't all that interested anymore, so I just cruise around. In the past week I was able to pick up and bed at least three girls, none of whom were over 30 years old."

"My goodness Frank, and at your age too," the doctor said. "I hope you took at least some precautions."

"Yep. I may be old, but I ain't senile yet doc. I gave 'em all a phony name."

On hearing that her elderly grandfather had just passed away, Jenny went straight to visit her grandmother.

When she asked how her grandpa had died, her granny explained, "He had a heart attack during sex on Sunday morning."

Horrified, Jenny suggested that having sex at the age of 94 was surely asking for trouble.

"Oh no," her granny replied, "we had sex every Sunday morning, in time with the church bells—in with the dings and out with the dongs."

She paused, and wiped away a tear.

"If it wasn't for that damn ice cream van going past, he'd still be alive."

Bernie was invited to his friend's home for dinner. Morris, the host, called his wife by many endearing terms, calling her Honey, My Love, Darling, Sweetheart, Pumpkin, etc.

Bernie looked at Morris and remarked, "That is really nice. After all these years, you still call your wife those pet names."

Morris hung his head and whispered, "To tell the truth, I forgot her name years ago."

Henny Youngman
King of the One-Liners

The beloved Friar Henny Youngman was one of America's most durable and enduring comedians. He was called "King of the One-Liners" because he could tell 250 jokes during a 45-minute appearance—but were they funny?

I hope so, because he almost never changed his act. Henny told some of the same jokes for 60 years. Maybe he thought that if you tell a joke over and over, it gets funnier.

How do most men define marriage? An expensive way to get laundry done for free.

Just think, if it weren't for marriage, men would go through life thinking they had no faults at all.

Born Henry Youngman, he grew up in Brooklyn and began his career playing the violin with an orchestra in a New Jersey nightclub. He used to tell jokes backstage, and the legend goes that one night, when the resident comedian didn't show up, the club owner asked Henny to fill in. Well, he was such a hit that the club owner told him to leave the orchestra (they stunk anyway) and become the club's emcee (more jokes per mile).

"I bet on a horse at ten-to-one. It didn't come in until half-past five."

"I miss my wife's cooking—as often as I can."

Henny developed his machine-gun style delivery during the late 1920s in the "Borscht Belt," the cluster of Jewish resorts in the Catskills. Henny was the fastest joker in town. He had to tell the jokes fast, or his audience would go to sleep.

Youngman got his big break in the 1930s on Kate Smith's radio show. He was scheduled to perform for six minutes, but the producers thought he was so funny, and he was speaking so fast, they had no choice but to let him run on for more than ten. He told close to 100 jokes (still a world record). After the appearance, his mother looked at him and said, "Since when are you funny?" He showed her his paycheck and she started laughing hysterically.

If you want your wife to pay undivided attention to every word you say, try talking in your sleep.

Then there was a man who said, "I never knew what real happiness was until I got married; and then it was too late."

Youngman's wife Sadie became the most famous part of his routine when she showed up one night at a radio show demanding free tickets for eight of her friends. Henny stood dumbstruck with embarrassment, he saw his career flash before his eyes. All of a sudden he shouted to the usher, "Take my wife." Then, as an afterthought, he added, "Please." The audience loved it. Henny continued to use the line even after Sadie died in 1987, at age 82.

For many, many years, Youngman, who was known as the "Human Joke Machine," worked about 200 club dates a year across the country. He told thousands of jokes, on a nightly basis.

"A man goes to a psychiatrist who tells him, 'You're crazy.' The man says, 'I want a second opinion.' The psychiatrist says, 'OK, you're ugly, too.'"

Before he died, Henny asked a group of reporters to meet him at a Manhattan restaurant for a reading of his Last Will and Testament.

"To my nephew Irving, who still keeps asking me to mention him in my will, hello, Irving!"

Two 90-year-olds had been dating for a while, when the man told the woman, "Well, tonight's the night we have sex!"

And so they did.

As they were lying in bed afterward, the man thought to himself, "My God, if I had known she was a virgin, I would have been much more gentle with her!"

And the woman thought to herself, "My God, if I had known the old geezer could actually do it, I would have taken off my pantyhose!"

The great thing about turning 75 is you don't get any more calls from insurance salesmen.

SOUPY SALES

At my age, sex is like shooting pool with a rope.

GEORGE BURNS ON HIS 90TH BIRTHDAY

SENILITY PRAYER

God, grant me the senility to forget the people I never liked anyway, the good fortune to run into the ones that I do, and the eyesight to tell the difference.

Here's to health in homely rhyme
To our oldest classmate, Father Time;
May our last survivor live to be
As bold and wise and as thorough as he!

OLIVER WENDELL HOLMES

By the time we'd lit the last candle on his birthday cake, the first one had gone out.

At seventy-five I feel like a twenty-year-old—but unfortunately, there's never one around.

I'm at the age when, if a girl says no, I'm grateful.

Anniversary
(You've been together how long?!)

Here's to you both
A beautiful pair,
On the birthday of
Your love affair.
Here's to the husband and here's to the wife.
May they be lovers
The rest of their life.

MODERN ZEN FOR THE MARRIED MAN

1. Do not walk behind me, for I may not lead. Do not walk ahead of me, for I may not follow. Do not walk beside me, either. Just leave me the hell alone.

2. The journey of a thousand miles begins with a broken fan belt and a leaky tire.

3. It's always darkest before dawn. So if you're going to steal your neighbor's newspaper, that's the time to do it.

4. Sex is like air. It's not important unless you aren't getting any.

5. No one is listening until you make a mistake.

6. Never test the depth of the water with both feet.

7. It may be that your sole purpose in life is simply to serve as a warning to others.

8. If you think nobody cares that you're alive, try missing a couple of car payments.

9. Before you criticize someone, you should walk a mile in their shoes. That way, when you criticize them, you're a mile away and you have their shoes.

10. If at first you don't succeed, skydiving is not for you.

11. Give a man a fish and he will eat for a day. Teach him how to fish and he will sit in a boat and drink beer all day.

12. If you lend someone $20, and never see that person again, it was probably worth it.

13. Don't squat with your spurs on.

14. If you tell the truth, you don't have to remember anything.

15. If you drink, don't park. Accidents cause people.

16. Some days you are the bug, some days you are the windshield.

17. Don't worry, it only seems kinky the first time.

18. The quickest way to double your money is to fold it in half and put it back in your pocket.

19. Timing has an awful lot to do with the outcome of a rain dance.

20. A closed mouth gathers no foot.

21. Duct tape is like the Force. It has a light side and a dark side, and it holds the universe together.

22. There are two theories to arguing with women. Neither one works.

It's Saturday morning and John's just about to set off on a round of golf when he realizes that he forgot to tell his wife that the guy who fixes the washing machine is coming by at noon. So John heads back to the clubhouse and phones home.

"Hello?" says a little girl's voice.

"Hi, honey, it's Daddy," says John. "Is Mommy near the phone?"

"No, Daddy. She's upstairs in the bedroom with Uncle Fred."

After a brief pause, John says, "But you haven't got an Uncle Fred, honey!"

"Yes, I do, and he's upstairs in the bedroom with Mommy!"

"Okay, then. Here's what I want you to do. Put down the phone, run upstairs and knock on the bedroom door and shout in to Mommy and Uncle Fred that my car just pulled up outside the house."

"Okay, Daddy!" A few minutes later, the little girl comes back to the phone. "Well, I did what you said, Daddy."

"And what happened?"

"Well, Mommy jumped out of bed and ran around screaming, then she tripped over the rug and went out the front window and now she's all dead."

"Oh, my God! What about Uncle Fred?"

"He jumped out of bed too, and he was all scared, and he jumped out the back window into the swimming pool. But he must have forgot that last week you took out all the water to clean it, so he hit the bottom of the swimming pool and now he's dead too."

There is a long pause.

"Swimming pool? Is this 555-3097?"

Three buddies decided to take their wives on a week's vacation in Las Vegas. The week flew by and they all had a great time. After they returned home and the men went back to work, they sat around at break and discussed their vacation.

The first guy said, "I don't think I'll ever do that again! Ever since we got back, my old lady flings her arms and hollers 'seven come eleven' all night, and I haven't had a wink of sleep!"

The second guy said, "I know what you mean. My old lady played blackjack the whole time we were there and she slaps the bed all night and hollers 'hit me light or hit me hard' and I haven't had a wink of sleep either!"

The third guy said, "You guys think you have it bad? My old lady played the slots the whole time we were there and I wake up each morning with a sore dick and an ass full of quarters."

A young couple, just married, were in their honeymoon suite on their wedding night. As they were undressing for bed, the husband, who was a big burly man, tossed his pants to his bride and said, "Here, put these on."

She put them on and the waist was twice the size of her body. "I can't wear your pants," she said.

"That's right," said the husband, "and don't you ever forget it. I'm the man and I wear the pants in this family."

With that she flipped him her panties and said, "Try these on." He tried them on and found he could only get them on as far as his kneecaps.

"Heck," he said, "I can't get into your panties!"

She replied, "That's right, and that's the way its going to stay until your attitude changes!"

First Anniversary
(Gotta start somewhere)

Sla'inte: Gaelic for "To your health!"

(It's pronounced as if you quickly slurred "It's a lawn chair!")

Here's to the prettiest, here's to the wittiest,
Here's to the truest of all who are true,
Here's to the neatest one, here's to the sweetest one,
Here's to them all in one—here's to you.

To keep your marriage brimming,
With love in the loving cup,
Whenever you're wrong, admit it;
Whenever you're right, shut up!

OGDEN NASH

To two people who were made for each other.
Think about it, who else would have them?

The biggest surprise you can give your wife on your anniversary is to remember it.

Silver Anniversary
(When a platter won't do)

I've been asked to say a couple of words about my husband. How about "short" and "cheap"?

PHYLLIS DILLER

Grow old with me, the best is yet to come.

ROBERT BROWNING

We've holidays and holy days, and memory days galore;
And when we've toasted every one, I offer just one more.
So let us lift our glasses high, and drink a silent toast,
The day, deep buried in each heart, that each one loves
the most.

To our best friends, who know the worst about us but
refuse to believe it.

A toast to your anniversary and the love
That has held you together these many years.
When the times are good, it's easy, brother.
When the times are tough is when you need one another.

The secret to our success is that on the day we were married I let my wife know who was the boss. I looked her right in the eye and said, "You're the boss."

She had a terrible time trying to pick out an anniversary gift for her husband. It's hard to find something for the man who has everything. But it's even harder to get something for the man who understands nothing.

A silver-wedding party is the occasion on which a married couple celebrate the fact that twenty-five years of their marriage is over.

Nozze d'Oro (Golden Night)

Always remember to forget
The things that made you sad.
But never forget to remember
The things that made you glad.
Always remember to forget
The friends that proved untrue.
But never forget to remember
Those that have stuck by you.
Always remember to forget
The troubles that passed away.
But never forget to remember
The blessings that come each day.

A couple was celebrating their golden wedding anniversary. Their domestic tranquility had long been the talk of the town. A local newspaper reporter was inquiring as to the secret of their long and happy marriage.

"Well, it dates back to our honeymoon," explained the man. "We visited the Grand Canyon and took a trip down to the bottom on mules. We hadn't gotten too far when my wife's mule stumbled. My wife quietly said, 'That's once.'

"We proceeded a little farther and the mule stumbled again. Again, my wife quietly said, 'That's twice.'

"We hadn't gone a half a mile when the mule stumbled a third time. My wife quietly removed a revolver from her pocket and shot the mule, dead.

"I started to protest over her treatment of the mule when she looked at me and quietly said, 'that's once.'"

An elderly couple went to their attorney's office and told him that they wanted a divorce. The lawyer looked shocked and said, "How long have you been married to each other?"

The old man replied, "Fifty-seven years."

"Then why on earth have you decided to get divorced now?" asked the lawyer.

The old man looked at his wife, then turned to the lawyer and said, "We wanted to wait until the kids were all dead."

When we celebrated our 50th wedding anniversary, I said, "Honey, it just doesn't seem like 50 years."

She said, "Speak for yourself."

Party Till the Cows Come Home (When should you wear a lampshade?)

I love to drink martinis.
Two at the very most.
Three, I'm under the table.
Four, I'm under the host!

DOROTHY PARKER

Let us sing our own treasures, Old England's good cheer,
To the profits and pleasures of stout British beer;
Your wine tippling, dram sipping fellows retreat,
But your beer drinking Britons can never be beat.

The French with their vineyards and meager pale ale,
They drink from the squeezing of half-ripe fruit;
But we, who have hop-yards to mellow our ale,
Are rosy and plump and have freedom to boot.

ENGLISH DRINKING SONG, CIRCA 1757

Sam decided to go on a safari. Three days into the jungle, Sam was attacked by a savage lion. He lost an eye, his arm was pulled out, and his genitals were chewed up.

The native guides carried Sam to the nearby village where the old witch doctor performed surgery not known in western medicine. He filled the empty socket with the eye of an eagle. He attached the arm of an ape to Sam's shoulder. For the genitals, the witch doctor searched far and wide and finally attached the trunk of a baby elephant.

Six months later, Sam ran into Harry on Seventh Avenue. "Sam," Harry said, "I heard all about it! How terrible, how awful, are you all right?"

"Am I all right?" Sam said. "Let me tell you, Harry, the whole experience was a mitzvah, a blessing in disguise. Now, when I'm in the shop and some nogoodnik worker is cutting on the bias, I can see him with my eagle eye all the way across the shop and I holler *stop*. And when the union bums come up to bother me, I give them one punch from my gorilla arm, and they're out in the street. But the best of all, *the beauty part* is at cocktail receptions. When they pass around the peanuts—*I'm the life of the party!!!*"

Good company, good wine, good welcome make good people.

WILLIAM SHAKESPEARE

First you take a drink, then the drink takes a drink, then the drink takes you.

F. SCOTT FITZGERALD

Confirmation (Are you sure?)

A new life begun,
Like father like son.
Like one, like the other,
Like daughter, like mother.

Tommy Shaughnessy enters the confessional box and says, "Bless me, Father, for I have sinned. I have been with a loose woman."

The priest asks, "Is that you, little Tommy Shaughnessy?"

"Yes, Father, it is."

"And who was the woman you were with?"

"I can't be tellin' you, Father. I don't want to ruin her reputation."

"Well, Tommy, I'm sure to find out sooner or later, so you may as well tell me now. Was it Brenda O'Malley?"

"I cannot say."

"Was it Patricia Kelly?"

"I'll never tell."

"Was it Liz Shannon?"

"I'm sorry, but I'll not tell her name."

"Was it Cathy Morgan?"

"My lips are sealed."

"Was it Fiona McDonald, then?"

"Please, Father, I cannot tell you."

The priest sighs in frustration. "You're a steadfast lad, Tommy Shaughnessy, and I admire that. But you've sinned, and you must atone. Be off with you now."

Tommy walks back to his pew. His friend Sean slides over and whispers, "What'd you get?"

"Five good leads."

When we drink, we get drunk.
When we get drunk, we fall asleep.
When we fall asleep, we commit no sin.
When we commit no sin, we go to heaven.
So, let's all get drunk, and go to heaven!

Bar/Bat Mitzvah
(Now you are a fountain pen)

An old man had a dog as his only companion for nearly 15 years. Sadly, the dog died. The man had been so attached to the dog that he went to see his Rabbi and asked if he would arrange to say Kaddish for the dog.

The Rabbi said, "Mr. Bernbaum, you know we are an Orthodox congregation. Kaddish is only for humans, not for animals."

"However," added the Rabbi, "there's a new Reform congregation a block or two down the street. Go there and ask if they'll say Kaddish for the dog. You know, they may just be meshugenah enough to do this for you."

The old man thanked him, and said, "Do you suppose they'll also accept my $75,000 donation in memory of my little Moshe?"

"Hold it!" shouted the Rabbi. "You didn't tell me that your dog was Jewish?!"

WELCOME TO "SO YOU WOULDN'T MIND BEING A KOSHER MILLIONAIRE"

You have three lifelines to help you, as follows:

1. You may call your Rabbi for his opinion.

2. You may ask the congregation for their opinion.

3. You may consider your spouse's opinion...or not.

4. Bonus lifeline! Your Mother will give you her opinion, whether you ask for it or not.

Okay, lets play.

For $500:

Q: Who is Israel's favorite Internet provider?

A: Netanyahoo.

For $1,000:

Q: What is the name of a facial lotion made for Jewish women?

A: Oil of Oy Vey.

For $2,000:

Q: What is the title of the new horror film for Jewish women?

A: *Debbie Does Dishes.*

For $4,000:

Q: What is the technical term for a divorced Jewish woman?

A: "The Plaintiff."

For $8,000:

Q: How does a Jewish kid verbally abuse his playmates?

A: "Your Mother pays retail."

For $16,000:

Q: In the Jewish doctrine, when does the fetus become human?

A: When it graduates from medical school.

For $32,000:

Q: What does a Jewish woman do to keep her hands soft and her nails long and beautiful?

A: Nothing. She does nothing at all.

For $64,000:

Q: Define "Genius."

A: A "C" student with a Jewish mother.

For $125,000:

Q: What do you call a bloodthirsty Jew on a rampage?

A: Genghis Cohen.

For $250,000:

Q: Why did the Moyel retire?

A: He just couldn't cut it anymore.

For $500,000:

Q: If Tarzan and Jane where Jewish, what would Cheetah be?

A: A fur coat.

For $1,000,000:

Q: What is the difference between a Jewish grandmother and an Italian grandmother?

A: 10 lbs.

How do we know Jesus was Jewish?

He went into the family business, he lived at home until he was 30, and his mother thought he was God.

A homeless person walked up to a Jewish-American Princess on Fifth Avenue and said, "I haven't eaten anything in four days."

She looked at him and said, "God, I wish I had your will power."

A young Jewish man excitedly tells his mother he's fallen in love and is going to get married. He says, "Just for fun, Ma, I'm going to bring over three women and you try to guess which one I'm going to marry." The mother agrees.

The next day he brings three beautiful women into the house and sits them down on the couch and they chat for a while. He then says, "Okay, Ma. Guess which one I'm going to marry."

She immediately replies, "The redhead in the middle."

"That's amazing, Ma. You're right. How did you know?"

"I don't like her."

Bris (Watch the guy with the knife)

STEWEY STONE—ROAST OF ROB REINER

Your father, the great director, even directed your bris. He kept saying, "Rabbi, one more time." Forty-three takes, it's a wonder you can walk at all.

JEFFREY ROSS—ROAST OF ROB REINER

Everybody knows he's a control freak. At his son's bris he yelled "cut."

ADAM FERRARA—ROAST OF ROB REINER

He's tough. He was circumcised with piano wire.

AN AMAZING TALENT

A man walks into a talent agency, sporting a briefcase under one arm. He approaches the agent sitting behind the desk and opens the briefcase. Inside, there's a miniature piano and bench, and a small dressing room with a star on the door.

"Introducing the amazing Phallini!" the man announces to the agent. Just then, a one-foot-tall man walks out of the tiny dressing room wearing a scaled-down tuxedo with tails. The little man strides silently to the shrunken piano and sits on the tiny bench. He fluffs the small tails behind him and pops his little knuckles.

Suddenly, the foot-tall man begins to play the most fantastic sonatas and concertos, masterfully replicating the complex works of the world's musical geniuses. His tiny fingers expertly play a piece by Beethoven followed by a work of Wolfgang Amadeus Mozart.

When the foot-tall performer is finished, the agent leaps from his seat with tears in his eyes, crying, "This is incredible! We're going to be *rich!*" The agent can barely contain himself. "Where on *earth* did you find such an amazing talent?"

"Well," the man explained. "I was walking along the beach when I found this bottle, and when I dusted it off, a genie came out. And apparently she had lousy hearing, because she thought I asked for a 'twelve-inch pianist'!"

CHAPTER THREE:
YOU'RE GROWING UP

Remember the first time you got caught smoking cigarettes or drinking with your friends? If not, you're spending way too much time hanging around bookstores perusing cheesy joke books. Go out and live a little! If you do remember those times and can smile now about being grounded for three weeks, then you passed through adolescence with a key portion of your brain intact. Growing up is a great time, a scary time, a time filled with odd fashion choices and questionable taste in accessories, but always, a time to remember. So, help those young 'uns out, let them know that you went through it, that you know what it's like, you know what they are feeling and you are so fucking glad you are not there anymore.

Tell them what graduation day feels like (if you weren't tripping your brains out), let them know how it feels to be a student in higher education (not that kind of higher). Let them know how much this time should mean to them because soon, the free ride will be over and the terror of adulthood will begin. Okay, don't scare the little fuckers, just don't tell them everything. Tell them how easy they have it. How they don't know what working for a living is like. Tell them...oh, forget it, just read the chapter.

School Days (Or daze...)

I never let my schooling interfere with my education.

MARK TWAIN

Sixty years ago I knew everything; now I know nothing. Education is a progressive discovery of our own ignorance.

WILL DURANT

Grade School (Prison life begins)

Why does your nose run and your feet smell? Shouldn't it be the other way around?

One day at school, Johnnie's teacher got up in front of the class and announced that they were going to play a guessing game. The teacher said, "I have something behind my back. It's red in color and round. It's soft, but it's hard."

Johnnie raised his hand and said, "Teacher, I know it's a red rubber ball."

The teacher said, "No Johnnie, it's an apple, but I like the way that you think."

Next the teacher grabbed another object and put it behind her back. "I have something behind my back. It's orange in color and round. It's soft, but it's hard."

Johnnie raised his hand again and said, "Teacher, teacher, I know it's an orange rubber ball."

The teacher looked at Johnnie and said, "No Johnnie, it's an orange, but I like the way that you think."

Johnnie was now getting the hang of it so he asked the teacher if he could try one. Johnnie grabbed an object and put it behind his back and said, "I have something behind my back. It's pink in color and it's LONG. It's soft, but it's HARD."

The teacher, first blushing, then getting upset, yelled at Johnnie, "Now Johnnie, I'm going to have to tell the principal about this inappropriate behavior."

Johnnie stopped her and said, "Teacher, all I have is my pink eraser—but I like the way that YOU think!!!"

Little Johnny comes home with a homework paper to do. He asks his dad to help him write about the difference between theory and reality.

His dad says, "Go to your mom and ask her if she would sleep with another man for a million dollars."

Little Johnny does as he is told, and Mom says, "Well, yes, I suppose I would."

His dad then says, "Now go ask your big sister if she would sleep with another man for a million dollars."

Little Johnny does this too, and Sis says, "Yes, I suppose I would."

Little Johnny and his dad then sit down, and Dad says, "Now son, you've learned the difference between theory and reality. In theory, we're sitting on two million dollars. In reality, we're living with a couple of whores."

How many teachers does it take to change a light bulb? Well, teachers don't change light bulbs but they can help make a dim one brighter!

Two 6-year-old boys were attending religious school and giving the teachers problems. The teachers had tried everything to make them behave—time outs, notes home, missed recesses—but could do nothing with them. Finally the boys were sent to see the priest. The first boy went in and sat in a chair across the desk from the priest. The priest asked, "Do you know where God is?" The little boy just sat there. The priest stood up and asked again, "Son, do you know where God is?" The little boy trembled but said nothing. The priest leaned across the desk and again asked, "Do you know where God is?" The little boy bolted out of the chair and ran past his friend in the waiting room, all the way home. He got in bed and pulled the covers up over his head. His friend had followed him home and asked, "What happened in there?" The boy replied, "God is missing and they think we did it!"

MOTHER: Come on, Victor, you have to get out of bed or you'll be late for school.

VICTOR: Aw, Mom do I have to? All the teachers hate me, and all the students hate me too.

MOTHER: Yes you do.

VICTOR: Give me one good reason

MOTHER: You're 34 and you're the Principal!

TEACHER: (Looking over Teddy's homework) I don't see how it's possible for one person to make so many mistakes.

TEDDY: Oh it isn't one person, my dad helped me.

TEACHER: Alice, to what class of the animal kingdom do I belong?

ALICE: I don't know. My dad says you're a horse's ass and my mom says you're a bitch.

"I believe this school is haunted."

"Why?"

"They're always talking about the school spirit."

TEACHER: Jimmy, is "pants" singular or plural?

JIMMY (after much thought): Singular at the top and plural at the bottom.

Louise had just read her composition and her teacher said: "That is good, Louise. Is it original?"

Louise replied, "No, I made it up."

TEACHER: Billy, how much is three and four?

BILLY: I'd like very much to tell you teacher, but I think it'll do you more good if you look it up yourself.

A teacher was telling her class little stories in natural history and she asked if anyone could tell her what a groundhog was. A little hand went up, waving frantically. "Well, Carl, you may tell us what a groundhog is."

The boy replied, "It's a sausage!"

A teacher was quizzing her students. "Little Johnny, who signed the Declaration of Independence?" He was older than some of the others, but he said, "Damned if I know."

She was a little put out by his swearing, so she told him to go home and to bring his father with him when he came back.

Next day, Little Johnny's father came with him, and sat in the back of the room to observe as the teacher requested. She started back in on her quiz and finally got back to the boy. "Now, Little Johnny, I'll ask you again. Who signed the Declaration of Independence?"

"Well, hell, teacher," Little Johnny said, "I told you I didn't know."

His father jumped up in the back, pointed a stern finger at Little Johnny, and said, "Little Johnny, if you signed that thing, you damn well better own up to it!"

Three boys, one black and two white, all third-graders, are playing after school. As boys tend to do, inevitably they start discussing who has the biggest one. To settle the matter, they agree to determine this once and for all by means of comparison. It turns out in favor of the black boy, who self-confidently boasts that he won because he's black.

He runs home to tell his mother: "Mom, mom, guess what! We compared our pee-pees at the playground today, and I had the biggest one! That's because I'm black, right?"

"No, honey…that's because you're nineteen."

High School (No, you can't have the keys)

A teacher was trying to persuade her class to buy the class picture. The teacher said, "Won't it be nice to look at the picture and think, 'Hey, there's Jennifer, she's a congresswoman,' or 'Hey, there's Justin, he's a doctor.'"

A wiseass at the back said, "Hey, there's teacher, she's dead!"

TEACHER: Why the blank stare? Dreaming of your family?

STUDENT: No, sir. Haven't gotten that far yet.

TEACHER: Peter, your lessons aren't done today. Where did you go last night?

PETER: To the movies with a girl.

TEACHER: Get out of this class for a week.

TEACHER: Where did you go last night, Tommy?

TOMMY: Out parking with a girl.

TEACHER: Go home and stay there two weeks.

TEACHER: Where are you going, Oscar?

OSCAR: Teacher, my school days are over!

Bubba needed to further his eduction so he decided to go to night school.

The teacher wrote on the blackboard: "Like I ain't had no fun in months."

She asked the class, "How should I correct this sentence?"

Bubba raised his hand and replied, "Hey, like get a new boyfriend."

CHEERLEADERS

Female cheerleaders are cute, sexy, fresh, and all-American.

Male cheerleaders are scary.

He who laughs last thinks slowest.

To steal ideas from one person is plagiarism; to steal from many is research.

Monday is an awful way to spend one-seventh of your life.

You never really learn to swear until you learn to drive.

Knowledge is power...
But power corrupts...
And corruption is a crime...
And crime doesn't pay...
So if you keep on studying you'll go broke!

Congratulations graduate
I think it's plain to see,
That you've been drinking lots of beer
That you bought with fake ID.

School days, school days,
Let's break all the rule days.
Piercings and brandings and big tattoos,
We'll do to our bodies whatever we choose.

To Mom and Dad
Who have helped me so far,
May I ask one small favor?
Buy me a car.

TEACHER: What do you get if you multiply 13,362 by 476?

STUDENT: Confused.

College
(Let the games begin)

Brown: Hey, kids! Is half of your head shaved? Do you have a nose ring? Are you terribly progressive and do you have a shitload of empathy? Are you sick and tired of silly things like grades or majors? COME TO BROWN!!!

Columbia: Hey, kids! Do you like Harlem? Do you like commuters? Are you planning on transferring to another Ivy school after your freshman year? COME TO COLUMBIA!!!

Harvard: Hey, kids! Do you hate teachers? I mean really hate them? Do you never want to have another teacher again? And what about a social life? Do you hate that, too? COME TO HARVARD!!!

Princeton: Hey, kids! Do you have any idea what the fuck an eating club is? Are you pompous? Can you learn to be? Have you always dreamed of living in the great state of New Jersey? COME TO PRINCETON!!!

Penn: Hey, kids! Did you like high school a lot? How about four more years of the same? Are you dying to visit scenic west Philadelphia? Does the concept of rigorous academics scare you? COME TO PENN!!!

Cornell: Hey, kids! Do you hate intimacy? Are you interested in jumping off high places? Have you ever wanted to converse with future hotel managers? COME TO CORNELL!!!

Yale: Hey, kids! Do you want to get shot? COME TO YALE!!!

Dartmouth: Hey, kids! Do you hate civilization? Looking to get away from stuff like culture and people? Do you like to drink? Do you like to drink some more? Do you like to sexually harass women? Do you like to continue to drink? And what's your feeling on drinking? COME TO DARTMOUTH!!!

EXTRA-SPECIAL BONUS SCHOOLS

MIT: Hey, kids! Are you a freakish nerd? Do you want to be? Do you hate doing anything that doesn't involve math? That's right, math! Math math math math math! COME TO MIT!!! PLEASE!!!!!!!!!!!!!!

Wellesley: Hey, kids! Are you a psycho feminist bitch who likes to hit men? Do you like having short hair? Do you think you're a lesbian? Do you wanna be a lesbian? COME TO WELLESLEY!!!

University of California at Berkeley: Hey, dude! Do you like walking around campus naked? Do you like to march? Are you in Greenpeace? Do you enjoy harassing school officials? Do you enjoy clashing with police? Wow...COME TO BERKELEY!!!

BEFORE I CAME TO COLLEGE I WISH I HAD KNOWN...

That it didn't matter how late I scheduled my first class, I'd sleep right through it.

That I could change so much and barely realize it.

That I can love a lot of people in a lot of different ways.

That college kids throw paper airplanes too.

That if I wore polyester, everyone would ask me why I'm so dressed up.

That every clock on campus shows a different time.

That if someone was smart in high school—so what?

That I would go to a party the night before a final.

That chem labs require more time than all my other classes put together.

That you can know everything and fail a test.

That you can know nothing and ace a test.

That I could get used to almost anything I found out about my roommate.

That home is a great place to visit.

That most of my education would be obtained outside of my classes.

That friendship is more than getting drunk together.

That I would be one of those people my parents warned me about.

That free food served until 10:00 is gone by 9:50.

That Sunday is a figment of the world's imagination.

That Psychology is really Biology, that Biology is really Chemistry, that Chemistry is really Physics, and Physics is really Math.

That my parents would become so much smarter in the last few years.

That it's possible to be alone even when I'm surrounded by friends.

That friends are what make college worthwhile!

I have a daughter who goes to SMU. She could've gone to UCLA, but it's one more letter she'd have to remember.

SHECKY GREENE

MATURITY:

Women mature much faster than men. Most 17-year-old females can function as adults. Most 17-year-old males are still trading baseball cards and giving each other wedgies after gym class. This is why high school romances rarely work out. A woman is fully capable of running a family and holding a job at age 18. Men start growing up sometime after age 40.

Don't trust anyone over 30 who used to say, "Don't trust anyone over 30."

I said "no" to drugs, but they just wouldn't listen!

Friends help you move. Real friends help you move bodies.

PROFESSOR (in engineering class): What's a dry dock?

STUDENT: A physician who won't give out prescriptions.

PROFESSOR: What do you know of the age of Elizabeth?

STUDENT: She will be nineteen next September.

THE TOP TEN PHILOSOPHY QUESTIONS OF ALL TIME, ANSWERED!!!

1. *How do I know anything really exists?*

Kick it really hard.

2. *What is the essence of being human?*

Not understanding the opposite sex.

3. *If a tree falls in the woods, and there's no one there to hear it, does it make a sound?*

Not if it lands on a bunch of pillows.

4. *How do I know I'm not just a brain in a vat, hooked up to a computer simulation of life?*

Look in the mirror. If you see a gray, spongy thing in a glass container, you are.

5. *Can our minds exist separately from our bodies?*

If they could, we'd just send our minds to class and sleep in every morning.

6. *Is there a God?*

A billion Hindus can't be wrong.

7. *What is the nature of Knowledge?*

I'm still trying to figure out the nature of college.

8. *What is the meaning of life?*

All evidence to date suggests chocolate.

9. *Why get a philosophy degree?*

It's more respectable than a theatre degree, but you still get to drink lots of espresso.

10. *So, was Kant on drugs or what?*

Probably.

Two junkies are sitting by the side of the road, happily shooting up whatever it is that happy junkies shoot up with, and generally having a good time. A socially conscious individual walks up and notices that they are sharing a needle. He lectures them about AIDS and the danger that comes from sharing dirty needles. One of the junkies looks up and says, "It's okay, we're wearing condoms."

The Web brings people together because, no matter what kind of twisted sexual mutant you happen to be, you've got millions of pals out there.

Type in "Find people that have sex with goats that are on fire" and the computer will ask, "Specify type of goat."

JASON ALEXANDER

Two college students, Frank and Matt, are riding on a New York City subway when a beggar approaches them asking for spare change. Frank adamantly rejects the man in disgust. Matt, on the other hand, whips out his wallet, pulls out a couple of singles and gladly hands them over to the beggar with a smile.

The beggar thanks him kindly and then continues on to the other passengers. Frank is outraged by his friend's act of generosity.

"What on earth did you do that for?" shouts Frank. "You know he's only going to use it on drugs or booze."

Matt replies, "And we weren't?"

If you yelled for eight years, seven months, and six days, you would have produced enough sound energy to heat up one cup of coffee.

(Hardly seems worth it.)

If you fart consistently for six years and nine months, enough gas is produced to create the energy of an atomic bomb.

(Now, that's more like it.)

The human heart creates enough pressure when it pumps out of the body to squirt blood 30 feet.

A pig's orgasm lasts for 30 minutes.

(In my next life I want to be a pig.)

Banging your head against a wall uses 150 calories an hour.

(Still not over that pig thing.)

Humans and dolphins are the only species that have sex for pleasure.

(Is that why Flipper is always smiling? And why isn't the pig included in this list?)

On average, people fear spiders more than they do death.

The strongest muscle in the body is the tongue.

(Hmmmmmmmmmmmmmm....)

A crocodile cannot stick out its tongue.

The ant can lift 50 times its own weight, can pull 30 times its own weight, and always falls over on its right side when intoxicated.

(From drinking little bottles of...? Did the government pay for this research?)

Polar bears are left handed.

(Who knew? Who cares? Did the government pay for this, too?)

The flea can jump 350 times its body length. It's like a human jumping the length of a football field.

A cockroach will live nine days without its head before it starves to death.

The male praying mantis cannot copulate while its head is attached to its body. The female initiates sex by ripping the male's head off.

(Hi, honey, I'm home. What the...?)

Some lions mate over 50 times a day.

(In my next life I still want to be a pig. Quality over quantity, you know.)

Butterflies taste with their feet.

(Oh, jeez!)

Elephants are the only animals that can't jump.

An ostrich's eye is bigger than its brain.

Starfish don't have brains.

Remember, when someone annoys you, it takes 42 muscles in your face to frown. BUT, it only takes four muscles to extend you arm and smack the fool upside the head.

After the college boy delivered the pizza to Bud's trailer house, Bud asked, "What is the usual tip?"

"Well," replied the youth, "this is my first trip here, but the other guys say if I get a quarter out of you, I'll be doing great."

"Is that so?" snorted Bud. "Well, just to show them how wrong they are, here's five dollars."

"Thanks," replied the youth, "I'll put this in my school fund."

"What are you studying?" asked Bud.

The lad smiled and said, "Applied psychology."

THE COLLEGE DICTIONARY

Cafeteria: From two Latin words, "cafe" meaning "place to eat" and "teria" meaning "to retch."

Major: Area of study that no longer interests you.

Student Athlete: See "oxymoron." (Or "oxy moron.")

Grade: Unrealistic and limited measure of academic accomplishment.

Summer School: A viable alternative to a summer job.

Quarter: The most coveted form of currency on campus.

Hunger: Condition produced by five minutes of continuous studying.

WAYS TO GET THROWN OUT OF CHEMISTRY LAB

Pretend an electron got stuck in your ear, and insist on describing the sound to others.

Give a cup of liquid nitrogen to a classmate and ask, "Does this taste funny to you?"

Consistently write three atoms of potassium as "KKK."

Mutter repeatedly, "Not again...not again...not again."

When it's very quiet, suddenly cry out, "My eyes!"

Deny the existence of chemicals.

Begin pronouncing everything your immigrant lab instructor says exactly the way he/she says it.

Casually walk to the front of the room and urinate in a beaker. (Especially effective for female students.)

Pop a paper bag at the crucial moment when the professor is about to pour the sulfuric acid.

Show up with a 55-gallon drum of fertilizer and express an interest in federal buildings.

A kid called up his mom from college and asked her for money. His mom said, "Sure, sweetie. I will send you some. You also left your calculus book here when you visited two weeks ago. Do you want me to send that up too?"

"Uh, oh yeah, okay," responded the kid.

So his mom wrapped up the book along with the money and went to the post office to mail the package.

When she got back, her husband asked, "Well how much did you give the boy this time?"

She said, "Oh, I wrote two checks, one for twenty dollars and the other for one thousand."

"That's $1020!" yelled her husband. "Are you crazy?"

"Don't worry, Hon," she said. "I taped the twenty-dollar check to the cover of his book, but I put the thousand-dollar one somewhere in Chapter 19!"

Wouldn't it be nice to tell the Dean of your college what you *really* think about him or her? Well, if you like your Dean as much as I like my Dean, then you'd better keep your mouth shut. I knew I'd get kicked out of college if I expressed my true feelings, so I remained silent for four years.

But yesterday was my graduation. And as I walked across the stage, the Dean handed me that certificate, nicely scrolled and tied with a ribbon.

Once she had handed it to me, I could finally tell that bitch what I *really* thought of her. So I leaned across the podium and looked her straight in the eye.

"Hey, bitch," I said. "You're so damn ugly, you could practice birth control just by leaving the lights on!"

And then I walked off the stage, and went home. I gotta tell you that it felt just as good as I had imagined it would for the last four years.

Today, I unwrapped my diploma, framed it, and hung it in the living room, where it proudly exclaims to the world, "In order to receive your diploma, please present this certificate to the Dean of your college after final grades have been posted."

TIPS FOR SURVIVING COLLEGE

Minimize food budget by scheduling classes around Happy Hour.

Enjoy being a sophomore—it will be the best three years of your life.

Wear an athletic cup to panty raids, because it's all fun and games until someone loses their 'nads.

Lemon juice and baking soda make an excellent bong water stain remover.

Earn extra cash by parlaying chemistry knowledge into a lucrative "home pharmaceuticals" business.

If an 8:00 A.M. class is required for your major, change your major.

Boring lecture? Start a wave!

College-level algebra: five returnable bottles = one delicious Ramen Noodle dinner.

"I Phelta Thi" is *not* a real fraternity—except at state colleges.

Remember, almost no one complains when you puke in a dumpster.

Clever margin manipulation can turn a four-page outline into a 100-page senior essay.

Football games were never meant to be observed by sober people.

Don't think of it as sleeping with your professor—think of it as "acing Biology."

In a pinch, milk can be used as a beer substitute in your breakfast cereal.

On the first day of college, the Dean addressed the students, pointing out some of the rules.

"The female dormitory will be out-of-bounds for all male students, and the male dormitory to the female students. Anybody caught breaking this rule will be fined twenty-five dollars the first time."

He continued, "Anybody caught breaking this rule the second time will be fined fifty dollars. Being caught a third time will incur a hefty fine of a hundred dollars. Are there any questions?"

At this point, a male student in the crowd inquired, "How much for a season pass?"

CHANGING THOSE LIGHTBULBS ... COLLEGE STYLE

How many college students does it take to change a lightbulb in the South?

At Vanderbilt, it takes two. One to change the bulb and one more to explain how they did it every bit as well as any Ivy Leaguer.

At Georgia, it takes three. One to change the bulb and two to phone a friend at Georgia Tech and get instructions.

At Florida, it takes four. One to screw in the bulb and three to figure out how to get high off the old one.

At Alabama, it takes five. One to change it, two to talk about how Bear would have done it, and two to throw the old bulb at Auburn students.

At Ole Miss, it takes six. One to change it, two to mix the drinks, and three to find the perfect J. Crew outfit to wear for the occasion.

At LSU, it takes seven. And each one gets credit for four semester hours for it.

At Kentucky, it takes eight. One to screw it in, and seven to discuss how much brighter it shines during the basketball season.

At Tennessee, it takes ten. Two to figure out how to screw it in, two to buy an orange lampshade, and six to phone a radio call-in show and talk about how Phillip Fulmer is too stupid to do it.

At Mississippi State, it takes fifteen. One to screw in the bulb, two to buy the Skoal, and twelve to shout, "GO TO HELL OLE MISS, GO TO HELL!!!"

At Auburn, it takes 100. One to change it, 49 to talk about how they do it better than 'Bama, and 50 who realize it's all a lie.

At South Carolina, it takes 80,000. One to screw it in and 79,999 to discuss how this will finally be the year they have a good football team.

At Arkansas, it takes none. There is no electricity in Arkansas.

The student—not necessarily a well-prepared student—sat in his life science classroom staring at a question on the final exam. It said, "Give four advantages of breast milk."

What to write? He sighed, and began to scribble whatever came into his head, hoping for the best:

1. No need to boil.

2. Cats can't steal it.

3. Available whenever necessary.

Um. So far so good—maybe. But the exam demanded a four-part answer. Again, what to write?

He sighed. He frowned. He scowled. But suddenly, he brightened. He grabbed his pen, and triumphantly scribbled his definitive answer:

4. Comes in attractive containers.

A grandfather went to visit his college-age grandson at the dorm. Grandpa was astonished to find that his grandson was living a life of sin and corruption, as shown by the very high-heeled lady's pump nailed over the doorway.

"In my day," grumbled Gramps, "we would hang a horseshoe over the door for luck and then study late into the night hoping to pass our classes."

"But Grandpa," replied the grandson, "This *is* a whore's shoe."

There once was an old man of Esser,
Whose knowledge grew lesser and lesser.
It at last grew so small
He knew nothing at all,
And now he's a college professor.

It had been snowing for hours when an announcement came over the intercom: "Will the students who are parked on University Drive please move their cars so that we may begin plowing."

Twenty minutes later there was another announcement: "Will the twelve hundred students who went to move 26 cars please return to class."

A college professor in an anatomy class asked his students to sketch a naked man. As the professor walked around the class checking the sketches he noticed that a sexy young coed had sketched the man with an erect penis.

The professor commented, "Oh, no, I wanted it the other way."

She replied, "What other way?"

The stunning blonde went to her student advisor to discuss some course problems, but seemed to be paying only half attention to his replies.

"Are you feeling okay?" he asked.

"Well to be honest, I have this compulsion to have sex with every man I meet," she admitted. "Is there a name for my condition?"

"Why yes, there is," he said, as he picked her up and began carrying her to the couch. "It's called 'Good News.'"

Optimist: A college student who opens his wallet and expects to find money.

I have three college degrees:

B.S.—Bull Shit

M.S.—More of the Same

Ph.D.—Piled Higher and Deeper

The graduate with a science degree asks, "Why does it work?"

The graduate with an engineering degree asks, "How does it work?"

The graduate with an accounting degree asks, "How much will it cost?"

The graduate with an art degree asks, "Do you want fries with that?"

A college student in a philosophy class was taking his first examination. On the paper there was a single line: "Is this a question? Discuss."

After a short time he wrote, "If that is a question, then this is an answer."

The student received an "A" on the exam.

A Boston brokerage house advertised for a "young Harvard graduate or the equivalent."

Among the inquiries received was one from a Yale grad. He said, "Do you mean two Princeton men, or a Yale man part-time?"

Theresa was studying public speaking when she was assigned to give a short speech on sex. She said, "It gives me great pleasure. Thank you."

"How was your blind date?" a college student asked her roommate.

"Terrible!" the roommate answered. "He showed up in his 1932 Rolls Royce."

"Wow! That's a very expensive car. What's so bad about that?"

"He was the original owner!"

A young man hired by a supermarket reported for his first day of work.

The manager greeted him with a warm handshake and a smile, gave him a broom and said, "Your first job will be to sweep out the store."

"But I'm a college graduate," the young man replied indignantly.

"Oh, I'm sorry. I didn't know that," said the manager. "Here, give me the broom...I'll show you how."

A student comes to a young professor's office hours. She glances down the hall, closes his door, kneels pleadingly. "I would do anything to pass this exam." She leans closer to him, flips back her hair, gazes meaningfully into his eyes. "I mean..." she whispers, "I would do...anything."

"Anything?" His voice turns to a whisper. "Would you... study?"

One day our professor was discussing a particularly complicated concept. A pre-med student rudely interrupted to ask, "Why do we have to learn this stuff?"

"To save lives," the professor responded quickly, and continued the lecture.

A few minutes later, the same student spoke up again. "So how does physics save lives?" he persisted.

"It keeps the ignoramuses out of medical school," replied the professor.

The instructor was demonstrating the wonder of static electricity to his class at MIT. While holding a plastic rod in one hand and a wool cloth in the other, he told the class, "You see that I get a large charge from rubbing my rod..."

That was pretty much the end of learning for that day.

In a foreign country, an Athens State priest, a University of Alabama lawyer and an Auburn engineer are about to be guillotined.

The priest puts his head on the block, they pull the rope and nothing happens. He declares that he's been saved by divine intervention, so he's let go.

The lawyer is put on the block, and again the rope doesn't release the blade. He claims he can't be executed twice for the same crime and he, too, is set free.

They grab the Auburn engineer and shove his head into the guillotine. He looks up at the release mechanism and says, "Wait a minute, I see your problem…"

Why are rectal thermometers banned at Auburn University?

They cause too much brain damage.

How do you break a Georgetown guy's finger?

Punch him in the nose.

Why did the Purdue student marry the cow?

He had to.

How can you tell when there's been a Michigan student in your backyard?

The garbage is gone and your dog's pregnant.

What is the definition of safe sex down at UConn?

Placing a sign on the animals that kick.

How do you castrate an Alabama football player?

You hit his sister in the jaw.

How do you compliment an Ohio State fan?

Nice tooth.

How can you tell you're getting close to University of Wisconsin?

If you stop to take a piss, the cows back up to the fence.

A Georgia Tech graduate was suffering from constipation, so his doctor prescribed suppositories.

A week later the grad complained to the doctor that they didn't produce the desired results. "Have you been taking them regularly? the doctor asked.

"What do you think I've been doing," the grad said, "shoving them up my ass?"

COLLEGE SEX SURVEY

A professor teaching a college sexuality class was discussing the frequency of sex that could still be considered normal. "Many people find that sex every other week is sufficient to satisfy, and that's fine. Yet others want to make love nightly, and there's nothing wrong with that either.

"Let's take an informal survey of this class. Don't be embarrassed. Please answer honestly. How many people here make love more than twice a week?"

A few hands shot up.

"Twice a week?"

A few more hands.

"Weekly, on average?"

Many hands.

"Once every two weeks?" he continued and, "Once a month?" and "Once every several months?" and finally, "Once a year?"

At this last category one hand shot up, waving most eagerly. "Pardon my curiosity," the professor asked, "But if you only make love once a year, why are you so excited over it?"

"Tonight's the night!" replied the student.

Who is Steven Wright?

"I was a peripheral visionary. I could see the future, but only way off to one side."

Steven Wright was born on December 6, 1955. One of four children, he was raised in Burlington, Massachusetts, and later attended Emerson College. After graduating, he held a series of odd jobs before landing a regular gig as a performer at Ding Ho's Comedy Club and Chinese Restaurant in Cambridge, Massachusetts, a gig he scored after attending an open-mike audition. Wright's deadpan delivery and monotone voice quickly made him a distinctive presence on the Boston-area comedy circuit.

"I made a chocolate cake with white chocolate. Then I took it to a potluck. I stood in line for some cake. They said, 'Do you want white cake or chocolate cake?' I said, 'Yes.'"

Around this time, in August of 1982, Wright got his first big break when he was booked on Johnny Carson's *Tonight Show.* He was such a hit with both Johnny and the audience that he was asked back again within the same week. His back-to-back appearances catapulted him into the highest ranks of the national comedy scene, instantly pushing his fledgling career into the stratosphere.

"I have an existential map. It has 'you are here' written all over it."

Soon, his offbeat anecdotes and monotone monologues could be heard everywhere, from *Saturday Night Live* to *Late Night with David Letterman.*

"I spilled spot remover on my dog. Now he's gone."

Wright received a Grammy nomination for his 1986 debut album, "I Have a Pony," and in 1988 he starred in his first HBO Special, "On Location: Steven Wright." In 1989, Wright received an Academy Award for Best Short Film for *The Appointments of Dennis Jennings*, a film that he co-wrote and starred in.

"I woke up the other day and all of my furniture had been stolen and replaced with exact replicas. I said to my roommate, 'Dave, what happened?' He said, 'Who the hell are you?'"

In 1990, Wright starred in his second HBO special, "Wicker Chairs and Gravity." He has also appeared in numerous Hollywood films, including *Desperately Seeking Susan*, Mike Meyers's *So I Married an Axe Murderer*, Oliver Stone's *Natural Born Killers*, and Nora Ephron's *Mixed Nuts*. In 1999, Wright was featured in Albert Brooks's film *The Muse*, alongside Sharon Stone, Andie MacDowell, and Jeff Bridges.

"If it's a penny for your thoughts and you put in your two cents' worth, someone, somewhere is making a penny."

Wright has continued his career in film, not surprisingly in the independent vein. His short film, *One Soldier*, which he wrote, directed, and starred in, was screened at numerous film festivals and can be seen on the Independent Film Channel. Fittingly, it is the story of a man who is obsessed with the unanswerable questions in life. Wright continues to tour the U.S., Canada, and Europe.

"Yesterday I saw a chicken crossing the road. I asked it why. It told me it was none of my business."

EXCHANGE STUDENT

At a local college, there was a dance. A guy from America asked a girl from Sweden to dance. While they were dancing, he gave her a little squeeze and said, "In America, we call this a hug."

She said, "Yaah, in Sveden, we call it a hug, too."

A little later, he gave her a peck on the cheek, and said, "In America, we call this a kiss."

She said, "Yaah, in Sveden, we call it a kiss, too."

Later that evening, after quite a few drinks, he took her out on the campus lawn and proceeded to screw her, and said, "In America, we call this a grass sandwich."

She said, "Yaaah, in Sveden we call it a grass sandwich too, but we usually put more meat in it."

WAYS TO ANNOY YOUR COLLEGE ROOMMATE

Smoke jimson weed. Do whatever comes naturally.

Switch the sheets on your beds with the next door neighbors'.

Twitch a lot.

Pretend to talk while pretending to be asleep.

Steal a fish tank. Fill it with beer and dump sardines in it. Talk to them.

Walk and talk backwards.

Spend all your money on Jolt Cola. Drink it all.

Ask your roommate if your family can move in "just for a couple of weeks."

Buy as many back issues of *Field and Stream* as you can. Pretend to masturbate while reading them.

Smile. All the time.

Collect dog shit in baby food jars. Sort them according to what you think the dog ate.

Hide a bunch of potato chips and Ho Hos in the bottom of a trash can. When you get hungry, root around in the trash. Find the food, and eat it. If your roommate empties the trash before you get hungry, demand that she/he reimburse you.

Paste boogers on the windows in occult patterns.

Shoot rubber bands at your roommate while his/her back is turned, and then look away quickly.

Hide your underwear and socks in your roommate's closet. Accuse him/her of stealing it.

Whenever your roommate walks in, wait one minute and then stand up and announce that you are going to take a shower. Do so. Keep this up for three weeks.

Paint your half of the room black. Or paisley.

Whenever he/she is about to fall asleep, ask questions that start with, "Didja ever wonder why..." Be creative.

Always flush the toilet three times.

Buy a copy of Weird Al Yankovic's "Pennyslvania Polka," and play it at least 6 hours a day. If your roommate complains, explain that it's an assignment for your primitive cultures class.

Listen to radio static.

Cover one of the walls with Polaroids of fire hydrants from all over the city. Tell your roommate that you think that you were a dog in a former life. Stare lovingly at the photos, and make frequent trips to the bathroom.

Get a small, battery-operated clock which ticks very loudly. Put it in a briefcase and put the briefcase next to your roommate's bed.

Expound upon the importance of good personal hygiene. Wear rubber gloves and a surgical mask in the room.

Eat an entire bag of cheese curls at once. When you are finished, see how many times you can make orange fingerprints from all of the cheese junk left on your fingers.

Walk around in circles all the time. Complain that your turn signal is stuck.

YOU KNOW YOU'VE BEEN IN COLLEGE TOO LONG WHEN...

You consider McDonalds "real food."

You actually like doing laundry at home.

4:00 A.M. is still early on the weekends.

It starts getting late on the weeknights.

Two miles is not too far to walk for a party.

You wear dirty socks three times in a row and think nothing of it.

You'd rather clean than study.

Half the time you don't wake up in your own bed and it seems normal.

Computer Solitaire is more than a game, it's a way of life.

You schedule your classes around sleep habits and soaps.

You know the pizza boy by name.

You go to sleep when it's light and get up when it's dark.

Looking out the window is a form of entertainment.

Prank phone calls become funny again.

Wal-Mart is the coolest store.

World War III could take place and you'd be clueless.

You start thinking and sounding like your roommate.

Blacklights and highlighters are the coolest things on earth.

Rearranging your room is your favorite pastime.

You find out milk crates have so many uses.

The weekend lasts from Thursday to Sunday.

TOP TEN REASONS STUDYING IS BETTER THAN SEX

1. You can usually find someone to do it with.

2. If you get tired, you can stop, save your place and pick up where you left off.

3. You can finish early without feelings of guilt or shame.

4. When you open a book, you don't have to worry about who else has opened it.

5. A little coffee and you can do it all night.

6. If you don't finish a chapter you won't gain a reputation as a "book teaser."

7. You can do it, eat, and watch TV all at the same time.

8. You don't get embarrassed if your parents interrupt you in the middle.

9. You don't have to put your beer down to do it.

10. If you aren't sure what you're doing, you can always ask your roommate for help.

Let schoolmasters puzzle their brain
With grammar and nonsense and learning;
Good liquor, I stoutly maintain,
Gives genius a better discerning.

OLIVER GOLDSMITH

Today is the biggest day of your life;
It's yours and yours alone.
Now go out and tackle the world my friend,
And pay back your student loan.

You've earned a Bachelor of Science,
By passing all of the tests.
But remember what your degree really means,
You're a specialist with B.S.

We have always believed in you, through and through;
Even though just last year, your grade point was 2.
But we knew that you'd graduate because you are scrappy,
Now go get a job and make us all happy.

A college education is like a car. You never know what to
do with it when you go to work.

Q: What's the definition of college?

A: A big bar with a $20,000 cover charge.

A COLLEGE STUDENT AND HIS CRICKET

A college student was doing a lab test. He took a pencil and laid it down on the table. Then he took a cricket and set it down in front of the pencil. Then he told the cricket to jump. The cricket jumped over the pencil. "Good," he thought. The student pulled off a front leg and said "Jump." The cricket made it over the pencil once again. He pulled off the other front leg and said "Jump." The cricket did just that and jumped over the pencil. He then pulled off a back leg and said "Jump." The cricket just makes it over the pencil. After he pulls off the last leg he tells the cricket to jump but the cricket just lays there. He shouts, "JUMP!!" once more, but nothing. In his paper the student writes, under conclusion: "After all legs are pulled off of the cricket, it goes deaf."

SORORITY SISTERS

Q: How many sorority sisters does it take to change a light bulb?

A: Just one. She calls Daddy to come fix it for her.

CHAPTER FOUR:
ROUGH TIMES

Life, besides giving us plenty to celebrate, often hits us with some zingers. There are tragedies and rough spots along the road of life, and instead of obsessing over "The Horror, The Horror" that is human existence, why not tell a funny story, make a joke and poke some fun at your suffering friend or dead relative? The Friars love that stuff—hell, they practically invented it. They will make fun of anyone and everyone. They'll make fun of their shortcomings, their maladies, and often their anatomy. It's important to laugh at the sad times and sometimes—take divorce, for instance—they're not so sad after all.

There is always a place for a light touch, a comic turn, or, believe it or not, a really inappropriate joke. A long and happy life is something to celebrate. One spent in prison is not. So at a funeral for someone who enjoyed life, lived it to its fullest, and was not in prison, feel free to tell a nice story, a joke, or make a toast. If they owed you a ton of money or once slept with your wife then you might even want to roast them—who gives a fuck at that point anyway?

You know I've reached an age where I wake up in the morning, look in the obituary column, and if I don't see my name, I call a hooker.

FRIAR AND ROASTMASTER GEORGIE JESSEL

JASON ALEXANDER—ROAST OF JERRY STILLER

For 95 years the Friars Club has had a long and distinguished tradition of paying tribute to the very finest entertainers in our nation. Tonight, they have broken with that tradition and we're honoring Jerry Stiller. I am here, as many of you are, to fulfill the Community Service portion of my sentence.

BRETT BUTLER—ROAST OF ROB REINER

I love Abe Vigoda. I feel like his cock tonight, we've both risen from the dead.

Get Well Soon
(Pass the chicken soup)

A Jewish woman had two chickens. One got sick, so the woman made chicken soup out of the other one, to help the sick one get well.

HENNY YOUNGMAN

A guy complains of a headache. Another guy says, "Do what I do. I put my head on my wife's bosom and the headache goes away." The next day, the man says, "Did you do what I told you to?" "Yes, I sure did. By the way, you have a nice house!"

HENNY YOUNGMAN

I used to be schizophrenic, but we're all right now.

A toothache is the pain that drives you to extraction.

One day, a man walks into a dentist's office and asks how much it will cost to extract wisdom teeth.

"Eighty dollars," the dentist says.

"That's a ridiculous amount," the man says. "Isn't there a cheaper way?"

"Well," the dentist says, "if you don't use an anesthetic, I can knock it down to $60."

"That's still too expensive," the man says.

"Okay," says the dentist. "If I save on anesthesia and simply rip the teeth out with a pair of pliers, I could get away with charging $20."

"Nope," moans the man, "it's still too much."

"Hmm," says the dentist, scratching his head. "If I let one of my students do it for the experience, I suppose I could charge you just $10."

"Marvelous," says the man, "book my wife for next Tuesday!"

A patient was waiting in a pre-op room for his vasectomy. A nurse walked in, lifted his robes, and gave him a blow job. The patient exclaimed, "Hey, that was great, but why?"

The nurse responded, "The doctor likes your tubes to be flushed prior to the operation."

As the patient was being wheeled into the operating room, he noticed other patients masturbating. He asked the attendant why they were doing this.

The attendant replied that they, too, were about to have vasectomies. The patient then inquired why he got a blow job, while they had to masturbate.

"Simple," said the attendant. "They have an HMO. You've got Blue Cross."

TOP TEN SIGNS YOU'VE JOINED A CHEAP HEALTH PLAN:

1. The annual breast exam is conducted at Hooters.

2. Directions to your doctor's office include "Take a right when you enter the trailer park."

3. The tongue depressors taste faintly like Fudgsicles.

4. The only proctologist in the plan is Gus from Roto-Rooter.

5. The only item listed under Preventive Care Coverage is "An apple a day."

6. Your primary-care physician is wearing the pants you gave to Goodwill last month.

7. "Patient responsible for 200 percent of out-of-network charges" is not a typo.

8. The only expense covered 100% is embalming.

9. With your last HMO, your Prozac didn't come in different colors with little *M*s on them.

10. You ask for Viagra, you get a Popsicle stick and duct tape!

A man goes into a restaurant and orders soup. When the waiter brings out the bowl he has his thumb stuck in the soup, but the customer decides to let it go.

"Would you like anything else?" the waiter inquires. "We have some very good beef stew today."

"Sounds good," says the customer. So the waiter goes off and comes back with a plate of stew, and his thumb is in the stew. The customer is getting angry now, but decides to hold his tongue.

"How about some hot apple pie?" asks the waiter.

"Fine," says the customer. The waiter returns with his thumb stuck in the pie. Now the customer is really getting furious.

"Coffee?" asks the waiter, and when the customer nods yes, he hurries off. He returns with his thumb stuck in the cup of coffee. By now the customer can no longer restrain himself.

"What the hell do you think you're doing? Every time you've come to the table you've had your thumb stuck in my food!"

"I've got an infection and my doctor told me to keep my thumb in a hot, moist place."

"Why don't you just stick it up your ass?"

"Where do you think I put it when I'm in the kitchen?"

DOCTOR: I don't like the looks of your husband.

WIFE: I don't either, but he's good to the children.

The only way to keep your health is to eat what you don't want, drink what you don't like, and do what you'd rather not.

MARK TWAIN

Death (No more soup for you)

THE FUNERAL

One fall day, Bill was out raking leaves when he noticed a hearse slowly drive by. Following the first hearse was a second hearse, which was followed by a man walking solemnly along, followed by a dog, and then about 200 men walking in single file.

Intrigued, Bill went up to the man following the second hearse and asked him who was in the first hearse.

"My wife," the man replied.

"I'm sorry," said Bill, "What happened to her?"

"My dog bit her and she died."

Bill then asked the man who was in the second hearse.

The man replied, "My mother-in-law. My dog bit her and she died as well."

Bill thought about this for a while. He finally asked the man, "Can I borrow your dog?"

The man replied, "Get in line."

THE WALL OF LIFE

A funeral service is being held in a synagogue for a woman who has just passed away.

At the end of the service, the pallbearers are carrying the casket out when they accidentally bump it into a wall.

They hear a faint moan. They open the casket and find that the woman is actually alive.

She lives for 10 more years and then dies. A ceremony is again held at the same synagogue and at the end of the service the pallbearers are again carrying out the casket.

As they are walking, the husband cries out, "Watch out for the wall!"

A man died and his wife called the newspaper to place an obituary. "This is what I want to print: Murray is dead."

The newspaper man said, "But for $45 you can print six words."

"All right, then print: Murray is dead. Toyota for sale."

Two Indians and a hillbilly were walking in the woods, when all of a sudden one of the Indians ran up a hill to the mouth of a small cave.

"Wooooo! Wooooo! Woooo!" he called into the cave and then he listened very closely until he heard answering, "Woooo! Woooo! Woooo!" He tore off his clothes and ran into the cave.

The hillbilly was puzzled and asked the other Indian what that was all about, was the first Indian crazy or what?

"No," said the second Indian. "It is our custom during mating season when Indian men see a cave, they holler 'Woooo! Woooo! Woooo!' into the opening. If they get an answer back, it means there is a girl in there waiting to mate."

Just then they saw another cave. The second Indian ran up to the opening of the cave, stopped, and hollered, "Woooo! Woooo! Woooo!" Immediately, there was an answering, "Woooo! Woooo! Woooo!" from deep within the cave. He tore off his clothes and ran into the cave.

The hillbilly wandered around in the woods alone for a while, and then he came upon a great big cave. As he looked in amazement at the size of the huge opening, he was thinking, "Hoo, man! Look at the size of this cave! It is bigger than those the Indians found. There must be some really big, fine women in this cave!"

He stood in front of the opening and hollered with all his might, "Woooo! Wooo! Woooo!" He grinned and closed his eyes with anticipation, and then he heard the answering call, "WOOOOOO! WOOOOOO! WOOOOO!" With a gleam in his eyes and a smile on his face, he raced into the cave, tearing off his clothes as he ran. The following day, the headline in the local newspaper read:

"NAKED HILLBILLY RUN OVER BY FREIGHT TRAIN."

A flea died and went to Heaven. St. Peter met it at the gate and explained that it could choose how to spend the rest of eternity.

St. Peter: "Have you thought about it? Do you know how you'd like to spend the rest of eternity?"

Flea: "Yes St. Peter, I have thought about it. I'd like to spend the rest of eternity on the back of a rich lady's dog."

St. Peter: "So be it, it's done."

A few weeks later, St. Peter was wondering about the flea and so he called.

St. Peter: "Flea, how are you doing?"

Flea: "Oh St. Peter, I made a terrible mistake. This old broad washes her dog two to three times a day, she perfumes it, and I'm nauseous and I have a headache from the smell."

St. Peter: "Well you know that you aren't supposed to get more than one chance to choose how to spend the rest of eternity, but I want you to be happy. Have you thought about what else you might like to do?"

FLEA: "Oh yes St. Peter! I have thought about it and I'm sorry I didn't bring it up before. I'd like to spend it in Willie Nelson's beard."

ST. PETER: "So be it, it's done."

Out of curiosity, St. Peter checked on the flea a few weeks later.

ST. PETER: "Hello, flea, how are you doing now?"

FLEA: "I'm sorry St. Peter, I'm not doing well at all. I get awakened up in the middle of the night, get drenched with beer, foul language all the time, and I keep getting woozy from this white powder that flies around. It's Hell, St. Peter, I'm miserable!"

ST. PETER: "You know, flea, you're not supposed to be able to change your mind about how you spend the rest of eternity, but you say this is Hell. Have you considered what else you might like to do?"

FLEA: "Oh St. Peter, YES! I HAVE thought about it and I have decided that I'd like to spend the rest of eternity in Dolly Parton's bush."

ST. PETER: "So be it, it's done."

Not being able to stand his curiosity, St. Peter decided to check on the flea again after a few weeks.

ST. PETER: "How's it going, flea?"

FLEA: "Oh hi St. Peter, well, it's kind of strange... You see there was this big party. There was lots of singing and dancing, I got bounced around a lot and there was this weird smoke in the air that made me dizzy. There were hands all over me and I don't quite remember all that happened, but would you believe it? I'm back in Willie Nelson's beard!"

I don't want to achieve immortality through my work. I want to achieve it through not dying.

WOODY ALLEN

I don't believe in an afterlife, although I am bringing a change of underwear.

WOODY ALLEN

Drink and dance and laugh and lie,
Love the reeling midnight through,
For tomorrow we may die!
(But, alas, we never do.)

DOROTHY PARKER

Three guys died at the same time and ended up in front of Peter at the Pearly Gates.

St. Peter says to the first guy, "Why should I let you in?"

The guy answers, "Well, I was a doctor, and I helped many people get well."

St. Peter says, "OK, you may come in."

St. Peter says to the second guy, "Why should I let you in?"

This guys says, "I was a lawyer, and I defended many innocent people."

St. Peter says, "OK, you may come in."

St. Peter says to the last guy, "And why should I let you in?"

The guy answers, "Well, I was a managed-care professional, and I helped to keep health-care costs down."

St. Peter thinks about this a moment. Then he says, "OK, you may come in. But you can only stay three days."

Death is just another way of saying, "Yesterday was the last day of the rest of your life."

Funeral (If you have nothing nice to say...)

I've drunk to your health in taverns,
I've drunk to your health in my home,
I've drunk to your health so damn many times,
I believe I've ruined my own!

Either he's dead or my watch has stopped.

GROUCHO MARX, *A DAY AT THE RACES*

I can't understand why you don't get any mail from me. Perhaps it's because I haven't been writing.

GROUCHO MARX

May our lives like the leaves of the maple, grow
More beautiful as they fade.
May we say our farewells, when it's time to go,
All smiling and unafraid.

LARRY E. JOHNSON

Here's to you,
And here's to me;
But as you're not here,
Here's two to me.

Mae West

The Original "Scandalous Broad"

"Oh, Miss West, I've heard so much about you."

"Yeah, honey, but you can't prove a thing."

"Is that a gun in your pocket, or are you just glad to see me?"

Mae West was born on August 17, 1893, in Brooklyn, New York. She was a child star in vaudeville, with an enormous and instinctive knowledge of comedic techniques that belied her years. As she grew up, she began writing plays, one of which, *Sex*, is notable for the scandal that surrounded it (she was even arrested during a performance). It was extremely racy for 1926—but typically audacious of Mae West.

"It is better to be looked over than overlooked."

She started working in films in 1932 when she played what was considered a bit part in *Night After Night*. Apparently she was unhappy with the role as written, so she rewrote all of her dialogue. As a result, she stole the show in every scene she was in, although the film was meant to be a vehicle for the actor George Raft.

"I'm a woman of very few words, but lots of action."

During the Depression, American filmgoers saw Mae West as a brazen, independent women, adorned in jewels and loving every minute of her scandalous life. Political conservatism and religious fervor were rampant during these days, though, and there were strong and successful efforts to censor her movies and her life. She was considered by these zealots to be a threat to the moral fiber of the entire nation.

"Between two evils, I always pick the one I never tried before. It ain't no sin if you crack a few laws now and then, just so long as you don't break any."

In her first starring role, in *She Done Him Wrong*, based on her hit play, *Diamond Lil*, West rode the tide against the film business' censors and emerged victorious. This film is generally considered her best. Unfortunately, every film she was in afterwards, was doggedly attacked by these "moral" censors. As a result, her racy comedic style was forcibly watered down and eventually, she lost interest and decided to abandon films completely.

"Virtue has its own reward, but has no sale at the box office."

By the time she quit the film business, Mae West had made nine movies. Out of those, she had a writing credit on five of them. Her power at the box office and her public appeal had successfully resurrected Paramount Studios, which had been on the verge of financial collapse.

"Goodness, what lovely diamonds."

"Goodness had nothing to do with it, dearie."

Mae West continued to work for most of her life, producing, writing, and starring in plays and musicals. The film director Billy Wilder personally offered Mae the part of Norma Desmond in *Sunset Boulevard*, but she turned it down, for creative reasons.

"Any time you got nothing to do—and lots of time to do it—come on up."

"It isn't what I do, but how I do it. It isn't what I say, but how I say it, and how I look when I do it and say it."

Memorial Service (... don't say these)

Best while you have it use your breath
There is no drinking after death.

Here's to us that are here, to you that are there, and the rest of us everywhere.

RUDYARD KIPLING

I drink as the fates ordain it.
Come fill it and have done with rhymes.
Fill up the lovely glass and drain it
In memory of dear old times.

WILLIAM MAKEPEACE THACKERAY

The pain of parting is nothing to the joy of meeting again.

CHARLES DICKENS

You're Caught (Get your hand out of the cookie jar)

Three nuns were talking. The first nun said, "I was cleaning the Father's room the other day and do you know what I found? A bunch of pornographic magazines."

"What did you do?" the other nuns asked.

"Well, of course, I threw them into the trash."

The second nun said, "Well, I can top that. I was in Father's room putting away laundry and I found a bunch of condoms."

"Oh, my," gasped the other nuns. "What did you do?"

"I poked holes in all of them."

The third nun said, "Oh, shit."

A fellow was visiting the Vatican and became separated from his tour group. After wandering for awhile, he needed to relieve himself. He finally found a bathroom and wandered in. You can imagine his surprise to discover the Pope sitting on the toilet masturbating.

Figuring that this would be an attraction few tourists ever saw, the man snapped a couple of pictures. The Pope managed to recover his composure and offered the fellow $10,000 for the camera. The photographer decided to take him up on the offer and an exchange was arranged.

The camera was a pretty nice unit so, after disposing of the film, the Pope decided he would use it on his world travels. One day while visiting a foreign country, one of the faithful noticed the Pope's camera and remarked that it was quite impressive. He then asked, "How much did you pay for it?"

"Ten thousand dollars."

"Wow, the guy who sold you that must have seen you coming!"

I know a gentleman who made a fortune by putting children on his lap and talking to them. I got an uncle did the same thing; now he is serving ten to twenty.

JOEY BISHOP

A man is holding his wife's hand as she lies on her death bed.

"Jerry, I…I have something to tell you before I pass on."

"No, no, dear. Everything is forgiven now. All is well."

"No, Jerry. I've been carrying this load for a year now, and I must tell you. I…I've been unfaithful to you. I slept with your best friend, Phil. I'm so terribly sorry."

"Yes, dear, I know. Why do you think I poisoned you?"

Divorce (Free at last!)

Here's to life—ain't it grand.
Just got divorced from my old man.
I laughed and laughed at the court's decision.
They gave him the kids and they ain't even his'n!

Why do Jewish divorces cost so much?

They're worth it.

HENNY YOUNGMAN

I'm an excellent housekeeper. Every time I get divorced, I keep the house.

ZSA ZSA GABOR

Alimony is the arrangement whereby two people make a mistake, but only one person pays for it.

A judge was interviewing a woman regarding her pending divorce and asked, "What are the grounds for your divorce?"

"About four acres and a nice little home in the middle of the property with a stream running by."

"No," he said, "I mean what is the foundation of this case?"

"It is made of concrete, brick and mortar."

"I mean," the judge continued, "What are your relations like?"

"I have an aunt and uncle living here in town, and so do my husband's parents."

He said, "Do you have a real grudge?"

"No," she replied, "We have a two-car carport and have never really needed one."

"Please," he tried again, "is there any infidelity in your marriage?"

"Yes, both my son and daughter have stereo sets. We don't necessarily like the music, but the answer to your questions is yes."

"Ma'am, does your husband ever beat you up?"

"Yes," she responded, "about twice a week he gets up earlier than I do."

Finally, in frustration, the judge asked, "Lady, why do you want a divorce?"

"Oh, I don't want a divorce," she replied. "I've never wanted a divorce. My husband does. He said he can't communicate with me."

My husband was delighted with the divorce settlement. He got custody of the money.

We had a lot in common. I loved him and he loved him.

SHELLEY WINTERS

She got a divorce on the grounds that her husband had only touched her three times in the course of a five-year marriage. She also got custody of the three kids.

My mother always said, don't marry for money, divorce for money.

My wife and I were considering a divorce. But when we looked into the cost of lawyers, we decided to put in a pool instead.

Many a man owes his success to his first wife and his second wife to his success.

JIM BACKUS

A woman drove me to drink and I never even had the courtesy to thank her.

W.C. FIELDS

CHAPTER FIVE:
OFF TO WORK

Let's face it, our fates are sealed the moment we squirm our way through the birth canal—we have to go to work. Even those who made it out with their proverbial silver spoon in place have to get out there and earn their keep. Whether it means scampering down a runway in scantily designed togs, flipping burgers at McDonald's, or telling jokes for a living, everybody works.

Work can be exciting, challenging, rewarding, and even thrilling (well, somebody has to clean the pigeon shit off the hands of Big Ben). It can also be a pain in the ass (okay, somebody still has to clean the pigeon shit off the hands of Big Ben). And let's face it, bosses don't help. They're the ones who either make us enjoy punching that clock or reduce us to tears, which is when we consider urinating in their morning coffee.

This chapter is filled with "Did you hear the one about the nurse and the donkey?" and "How many taxidermists does it take to screw in a light bulb?" jokes. The following toasts, jokes, quips and quotes often pertain to a specific profession but can usually be altered to fit your own needs. Whether it be a holiday party, a retirement celebration, a Lou-just-got-canned-so-let's get-drunk-and-Xerox-our-butts-party, or anything else, all the material you'll ever need is right here.

We're all in this together so read on and discover that your boss ain't the only prick on the page.

JACK CARTER:

A drunk in a bar yells, "Assholes, all lawyers are ass-holes."

Another guy pipes up, "Wait a minute, I resent that remark."

The first guy says, "Why? Are you a lawyer?"

The second guys says "No, I'm an asshole."

BILLY CRYSTAL—ROAST OF ROB REINER:

Rob, my friend, I love you and I'm delighted to be here to honor you and to say to you (pause) Fuck You.

BILLY CRYSTAL—ROAST OF ROB REINER:

I love you Rob, the way Dr. Ruth loves to hook-up her clapper to a vibrator.

JOB DESCRIPTIONS

An accountant is someone who knows the cost of every-thing and the value of nothing.

An actuary is someone who brings a fake bomb on a plane because that decreases the chances that there will be a real bomb on the plane.

A banker is a fellow who lends you his umbrella when the sun is shining and wants it back the minute it begins to rain.

MARK TWAIN

A consultant is someone who takes the watch off your wrist and tells you the time.

A diplomat is someone who can tell you to go to hell in such a way that you will look forward to the trip.

An economist is an expert who will know tomorrow why the things he predicted yesterday didn't happen today.

A lawyer is a person who writes a 10,000-word document and calls it a "brief."

FRANZ KAFKA

A mathematician is a blind man in a dark room looking for a black cat which isn't there.

CHARLES DARWIN

A professor is someone who talks in someone else's sleep.

A programmer is someone who solves a problem you didn't know you had in a way you don't understand.

A psychologist is a man who watches everyone else when a beautiful girl enters the room.

A schoolteacher is a disillusioned woman who used to think she liked children.

A statistician is someone who is good with numbers but lacks the personality to be an accountant.

A topologist is a man who doesn't know the difference between a coffee cup and a doughnut.

The Dreaded Job Interview

MANAGER (interviewing a job applicant): "For a man with no experience, you are certainly asking for a high wage."

JOB APPLICANT: "Well, sir, the work is so much harder when you don't know what you're doing!"

I used to be indecisive, now I'm not so sure.

My first job was working in an orange juice factory, but I got canned...couldn't concentrate. Then I worked in the woods as a lumberjack, but I just couldn't hack it, so they gave me the ax. After that I tried to be a tailor, but I just wasn't suited for it...mainly because it was a so-so job. Next I tried working in a muffler factory but that was too exhausting. Then I tried to be a chef—figured it would add a little spice to my life, but I just didn't have the time. I attempted to be a deli worker, but any way I sliced it, I couldn't cut the mustard. My best job was being a musician, but eventually I found I wasn't note-worthy. I studied a long time to become a doctor, but I didn't have any patience. Next was a job in a shoe factory; I tried but I just didn't fit in. I became a professional fisherman, but discovered that I couldn't live on my net income. I managed to get a good job working for a pool maintenance company, but the work was just too draining. So then I got a job in a workout center, but they said

I wasn't fit for the job. After many years of trying to find steady work, I finally got a job as a historian until I realized there was no future in it. My last job was working at Starbucks, but I had to quit because it was always the same old grind. So I retired and I found I am perfect for the job.

First Job (Who's this FICA, and why does he get more money than me?)

An Israeli soldier who just enlisted asks the Commanding Officer for a three-day pass.

The CO says, "Are you crazy? You just joined the Israeli army, and you already want a three-day pass? You must do something spectacular for the recognition!"

So the soldier comes back a day later in an Arab tank!

The CO is so impressed, he asks, "How did you do it?"

"Well, I jumped in a tank and went toward the border. As I approached the border, I saw an Arab tank. I put my white flag up, the soldier in the Arab tank put his white flag up. I said to the Arab soldier, 'Do you want to get a three-day pass?'

"So we exchanged tanks!"

HENNY YOUNGMAN

Anyone who has never made a mistake has never tried anything new.

ALBERT EINSTEIN

Anyone who lives within his means suffers from lack of imagination.

LIONEL STANDER

The trouble with experience is that you never have it until after you need it.

DIFFERENCES BETWEEN YOU AND YOUR BOSS

When you take a long time, you're slow. When your boss takes a long time, he's thorough.

When you don't do it, you're lazy. When your boss doesn't do it, he's too busy.

When you make a mistake, you're an idiot.

When your boss makes a mistake, he's only human.

When doing something without being told, you're overstepping your authority.

When your boss does the same thing, that's initiative.

When you take a stand, you're being bull-headed.

When your boss does it, he's being firm.

When you overlook a rule of etiquette, you're being rude.

When your boss skips a few rules, he's being original.

When you please your boss, you're ass-kissing.

When your boss pleases his boss, he's being co-operative.

When you're out of the office, you're wandering around.

When your boss is out of the office, he's on business.

When you have one too many drinks and get personal at a party, you're a drunken bum.

When your boss does the same, he appreciates women.

When you're on a day off sick, you're "always sick."

When your boss takes a day off sick, he must be very ill.

When you apply for leave, you must be going for an interview.

When your boss applies for leave, it's because he's overworked.

Some employees bought their boss a gift for his birthday. Before opening it, the boss shook it slightly, and noticed that it was wet in the corner. Touching his finger to the wet spot and tasting it, he asked, "A bottle of wine?"

His employees replied, "No."

Again, he touched his finger to the box and tasted the liquid. "A bottle of scotch?"

"His employees replied again, "No."

Finally the boss asked, "I give up. What is it?"

His workers responded, "A puppy."

The Work (Hi-ho, hi-ho ... oh, forget it)

THINGS YOU WISH YOU COULD SAY AT WORK

1. Ahhh...I see the fuck-up fairy has visited us again...

2. How about never? Is never good for you?

3. I see you've set aside this special time to humiliate yourself in public.

4. I'm really easy to get along with once you people learn to worship me.

5. I'll try being nicer if you'll try being smarter.

6. Won't call you back, but feel free to leave a message...

7. It sounds like English, but I can't understand a word you're saying.

8. I can see your point, but I still think you're full of shit.

9. I like you. You remind me of when I was young and stupid.

10. I have plenty of talent and vision. I just don't give a damn.

11. I'm already visualizing the duct tape over your mouth.

12. The fact that no one understands you doesn't mean you're an artist.

13. Any connection between your reality and mine is purely coincidental.

14. I'm not being rude. You're just insignificant.

15. Who me? I just wander from room to room.

One of the symptoms of an approaching nervous breakdown is the belief that one's work is terribly important.

BERTRAND RUSSELL

TOP 10 THINGS THAT SOUND DIRTY AT THE OFFICE, BUT AREN'T

1. I need to whip it out by five.

2. Mind if I use your laptop?

3. Just stick it in my box.

4. If I have to lick one more, I'll gag!

5. I want it on my desk, NOW!!!

6. Hmmmmmmmmmm. I think it's out of fluid!

7. My equipment is so old, it takes forever to finish.

8. It's an entry-level position.

9. When do you think you'll be getting off today?

10. It's not fair...I do all the work while he just sits there!

The following is a list of preferred new phrases provided so that proper exchange of ideas and information can continue in an effective manner without risk of offending our more sensitive employees:

TRY SAYING...Perhaps I can work late.

INSTEAD OF...When the fuck do you expect me to do this?

TRY SAYING...I'm certain that this is not feasible.

INSTEAD OF...No fucking way!!

TRY SAYING...Really?

INSTEAD OF...You've got to be shitting me.

TRY SAYING...Perhaps you should check with...

INSTEAD OF...Tell someone who gives a shit.

TRY SAYING...Of course I'm concerned.

INSTEAD OF...Ask me if I give a shit.

TRY SAYING...I wasn't involved in the project.

INSTEAD OF...It's not my fucking problem.

TRY SAYING...That's interesting.

INSTEAD OF...What the fuck?!?!

TRY SAYING...I'm not sure if I can implement this.

INSTEAD OF...Fuck it, it won't work.

TRY SAYING...I'll try to schedule that.

INSTEAD OF...Why the hell didn't you tell me sooner?

TRY SAYING...Are you sure this is a problem?

INSTEAD OF...Who the fuck cares?

TRY SAYING...He's not familiar with the problem.

INSTEAD OF...He's got his head up his ass.

TRY SAYING...Excuse me sir?

INSTEAD OF...Eat shit and die motherfucker.

TRY SAYING...So you weren't happy with it?

INSTEAD OF...Kiss my ass.

TRY SAYING...I'm a bit overloaded at this moment.

INSTEAD OF...Fuck it, I'm on salary.

TRY SAYING...I don't think you understand.

INSTEAD OF...Shove it up your ass.

TRY SAYING...I love a challenge.

INSTEAD OF...This job sucks.

TRY SAYING...You want me to take care of that?

INSTEAD OF...Who the hell died and made you boss?

TRY SAYING...I see.

INSTEAD OF...Blow me.

TRY SAYING...Yes, we really should discuss it.

INSTEAD OF...Another fucking meeting!!!

TRY SAYING...I don't think this will be a problem.

INSTEAD OF...I really don't give a shit.

TRY SAYING...He's somewhat insensitive.

INSTEAD OF...He's a fucking prick.

TRY SAYING...She's an aggressive go-getter.

INSTEAD OF...She's a ball-busting bitch.

THE WORST JOBS

Photographer for the "Miss Nude Octogenarian" pageant.

Laxative tester.

Internet spelling/grammar corrector.

Certified Public Accountant.

Any job in the White House if you're wearing a skirt. And that includes the poor bagpipe players.

Depends Undergarment maximum load tester.

Jessie Ventura's press secretary.

Restroom attendant at the Texas Chili Competition.

TOP 22 SIGNS YOU'RE A WORKAHOLIC

1. You hear most of your jokes via e-mail instead of in person.

2. You think a "half-day" means leaving at 5 o'clock.

3. You think Einstein would have been more effective had he put his ideas into a matrix.

4. You ask your friends to "think out of the box" when making Friday night plans.

5. You know the people at the airport hotels better than you know your next-door neighbors.

6. You think that "progressing an action plan" and "calendarizing a project" are acceptable English phrases.

7. You normally eat out of vending machines and at the most expensive restaurant in town within the same week.

8. You find you really need PowerPoint to explain what you do for a living.

9. You refer to the tomatoes you grow in your garden as deliverables.

10. You get all excited when it's Saturday and you can wear sweats to work.

11. You lecture the neighborhood kids selling lemonade on ways to improve their profits.

12. Your grocery list has been on your refrigerator so long some of the products don't even exist any more.

13. Your idea of being organized is multiple-colored Post-it notes.

14. You refer to your dining room table as the flat filing cabinet.

15. You assume the question to valet park or not is rhetorical.

16. You consider 2nd-day Air delivery painfully slow.

17. Pick-up lines now include a reference to liquid assets and capital gains.

18. You have actually faxed your Christmas list to your parents.

19. You have a "to-do list" that includes entries for lunch and bathroom breaks, and they are the ones that never get crossed off.

20. Keeping up with sports entails adding ESPN's home page to your bookmarks.

21. Your reason for not staying in touch with family is that they do not have e-mail addresses.

22. Cleaning up the dining area means getting the fast food bags out of the back seat of your car.

YOUR PROFESSION AND YOU

What does your profession say about you?

Marketing: You are ambitious yet stupid. You chose a marketing degree to avoid having to study in college, concentrating instead on drinking and socializing, which is pretty much what your job responsibilities are now. Least compatible with sales.

Sales: Laziest of all jobs, referred to as "marketing without a degree." You are also self-centered and paranoid. Unless someone calls you and begs you to take their money, you avoid contact with customers so you can "concentrate on the big picture." You seek admiration for your golf game throughout your life.

Technology: Unable to control anything in your personal life, you are instead content to completely control everything that happens at your workplace. Often even *you* don't understand what you are saying but who the hell can tell? It is written that geeks shall inherit the earth.

Engineering: Actually studied in school. It is said that ninety percent of all Personal Ads are placed by engineers. You can be happy with yourself; your office is full of all the latest ergonomic gadgets, but you don't really know what is causing your "carpal tunnel syndrome."

Accounting: Also studied in school. You are mostly immune from office politics. You are the most feared person in the organization; combined with your extreme organizational traits, the majority of rumors concerning you say that you are completely insane.

Human Resources: Ironically, given your access to confidential information, you tend to be the biggest gossip in the organization. Possibly the only other person that does less work than marketing, you are unable to return any calls today because you have to get a haircut, have lunch **AND** mail a letter.

Middle Management: Catty, cutthroat, yet completely spineless, you are destined to remain at your current job for the rest of your life. Unable to make a single decision, you tend to measure your worth by the number of meetings you can schedule for yourself. Best suited to marry other "middle managers," as everyone in your social circle is called.

Senior Management: (see above, different title)

Customer Service: Bright, cheery, positive you are a fifty-cent cab ride from taking your own life. As children, very few of you asked your parents for a little cubicle for your room and a headset so you could pretend to play "customer service." Continually passed over for promotions, your best bet is to sleep with your manager.

Consultant: Lacking any specific knowledge, you use acronyms to avoid revealing your utter lack of experience. You have convinced yourself that your skills are in demand and that in a heartbeat you could get a higher paying job with any other organization. You will spend an eternity contemplating these career opportunities without ever taking direct action.

Recruiter, "Headhunter": As a "person" who profits from the success of others, you are disdained by most people who actually work for a living. Paid on commission and susceptible to alcoholism, your ulcers and frequent heart attacks correspond directly with fluctuations in the stock market.

Partner, CEO: You are either brilliant or lucky. Your inability to figure out complex systems such as the fax machine suggests the latter.

Government Worker: Paid to take days off. Government workers are genius inventors, specializing in the invention of new holidays. They usually suffer from deep depression or anxiety and usually commit serious crimes while on the job. Thus the term "going postal."

It's been a rough day. I got up this morning...put on a shirt and a button fell off. I picked up my briefcase and the handle came off. I'm afraid to go to the bathroom!

Stress is when you wake up screaming and then you realize that you haven't fallen asleep yet.

47.5 percent of all statistics are made up on the spot.

No one is listening until you make a mistake.

Success always occurs in private and failure in full view.

We work in the trenches
Day after day.
Your friendship makes it worthwhile,
It's certainly not the pay.

There was once a young man who, in his youth, had the desire to become a "great" writer. When asked to define "great," he said: "I want to write something that the whole world will read, something that people will react to on a truly emotional level, something that will make them scream, cry, wail, howl in pain, desperation, and anger!"

He now works for Microsoft writing error messages.

A boss is someone who delegates all the authority, shifts all the blame, and takes all the credit.

"I finally got my boss to laugh out loud."

"Did you tell him a joke?"

"No, I asked for a raise!"

I made my money the old-fashioned way. I inherited it!

My boss had to do it the hard way. He had to be nice to his father.

When I say he's a born executive, I mean his father owns the business.

Accountants (Count those beans)

There's no business like show business, but there are several businesses like accounting.

DAVID LETTERMAN

What does the IRS have in common with a rubber?

Both stand for inflation, half productivity, cover up pricks, and most people can see right through them.

Did you hear the one about the constipated accountant?

He couldn't budget so he worked it out with a pencil.

Barry came to work looking more bedraggled than any of his coworkers had ever seen him. Finally his boss took him aside.

"Barry, " he said, "you look like hell. What's wrong?"

"Sorry," Barry replied, "I just couldn't get to sleep last night."

Trying to be helpful, his boss said, "Why didn't you try counting sheep?"

"I did," Barry answered, "and that was the problem. I made a mistake, and it took me the rest of the night to find it."

My accountant called me. He said, "I've got some terrible news for you. Last year was the best year you've ever had."

A company was looking to employ a new accountant and had called in the last three candidates for their final interviews. The first candidate was invited into the chairman's office and asked, "What's two plus two?"

"Four," he replied.

The second candidate was invited in and she was asked, "What's two plus two?"

She replied, "Four."

Finally, the third candidate was invited in and he was asked, "What's two plus two?"

He said, "What do you want it to be?"

The chairman said, "You've got the job."

APRIL 15TH

We know it is true that we're wicked,
That our criminal laws are lax;
But here's to punishment for the man
Who invented our income tax.

Actors (Is this any way for a grown person to make a living?)

The actor got home to find his house ablaze with flames, fire trucks lining the street, his children crying, and his wife frantic.

She ran up to him, "Honey, it was awful. I was making tea, your agent called, I picked up the phone, I must have left the burner on, the curtains caught fire, then the whole place started burning. I think we lost every-thing.... Thank god the children are okay...."

The husband looked at her, "My agent called?"

***

For him, the advent of television opened up a whole new area of unemployment.

***

You can always tell an actor, but you can't tell him much.

***

A celebrity is simply an actor with a publicity agent.

Advertising (New and improved)

Advertising is what makes you think you've longed all your life for something you've never heard of before.

Agents (Fifteen percent of your ass is mine)

An agent is someone who believes that an actor takes 85% of his money.

***

I've got a very ambitious agent. He's always opening offices overseas. At the moment, I'm out of work in seventeen countries.

Construction (If you build it...)

Contractor: A gambler who never gets to shuffle, cut or deal.

Bid Opening: A poker game in which the losing hand wins.

Bid: A wild guess carried out to two decimal places.

Low Bidder: A contractor who is wondering what he left out.

Engineer's Estimate: The cost of construction in heaven.

Project Manager: The conductor of an orchestra in which every musician is in a different union.

Critical Path Method: A management technique for losing your shirt under perfect control.

OSHA: A protective coating made by half-baking a mixture of fine print, red tape, split hairs, and baloney—usually applied at random with a shotgun.

Strike: An effort to increase egg production by strangling the chicken.

Delayed Payment: A tourniquet applied at the pockets.

Completion Date: The point at which liquidated damages begin.

Liquidated Damages: A penalty for failing to achieve the impossible.

Auditor: Person who goes in after the war is lost and bayonets the wounded.

Lawyer: Person who goes in after the auditors to strip the bodies.

Four workers are discussing how smart their dogs are.

The first is an engineer, who says his dog can do math calculations. His dog is named T-square, and the engineer tells him to get some paper and draw a square, a circle, and a triangle, which the dog does with no sweat.

The accountant says his dog is better. His dog is named Slide Rule. The accountant tells him to fetch a dozen cookies, bring them back, and divide them into piles of three, which the dog does without difficulty.

The chemist says that's good, but his dog is better. He tells his dog, Measure, to get a quart of milk and to pour 7 ounces into a 10-ounce glass. The dog does this with no problem.

All three men agree this is very good and that all the dogs are equally smart. They then turn to the union member and say, "What can your dog do?"

The Teamster calls his dog, whose name is Coffee Break, and says, "Show the fellas what you can do." Coffee Break goes over and eats the cookies, drinks the milk, shits on the paper, screws the other three dogs and claims he injured his back while doing so, files a grievance for unsafe working conditions, applies for worker's compensation, and goes home on sick leave.

Dentists (Open wide … your wallet, that is)

Q: What do you call a gay dentist?

A: A tooth-fairy.

I see my dentist twice a year, once for each tooth.

She's got so much bridgework that, if you want to kiss her, you have to pay a toll.

Nothing gets an old dental bill paid like a new toothache.

So the dentist didn't hurt a bit?

Not 'til I saw the bill.

Dentists are different from other people. For one thing, they are the only people who will invite you to spit in their sink.

I like my dental hygienist. I think she is very pretty. So when I go to have my teeth cleaned, while I'm in the waiting room, I eat an entire box of Oreo cookies.

STEVEN WRIGHT

'Twould make a suffering mortal grin,
And laugh away dull care,
If he could see his dentist in
Another dentist's chair.

Congrats, you are a dentist now,
We're filled with lots of pride.
'Cause now we have some place to go,
To get nitrous oxide.

"Open wide," my dentist said,
"Let's have a look around."
Then he picked up his drilling tool
Which made that awful sound.

So I reached out and grabbed him hard,
And he started to turn blue.
I said, "Hey doc I got a deal,
Don't hurt me and I won't hurt you."

Doctors (This won't hurt a bit... except your wallet, that is)

She got her good looks from her father. He's a plastic surgeon.

GROUCHO MARX

A specialist is a doctor with a smaller practice but a bigger house.

I finally found a way to get my doctor to make house-calls—I bought a house on the golf course.

"Doctor, I have a ringing in my ears."

"Don't answer!"

HENNY YOUNGMAN

An American tourist goes on a trip to China. While in China, he is very sexually promiscuous and does not use a condom. A week after arriving back home in the States, he awakes one morning to find his penis covered with bright green and purple spots. Horrified, he immediately goes to see his doctor.

The doctor, never having seen anything like this before, orders some tests and tells the man to return in two days for the results.

The man returns and the doctor says, "I've got bad news for you. You've contracted Mongolian VD. It's very rare and almost unheard of here. We know very little about it."

The man looks a little perplexed and says, "Well, give me a shot or something and fix me up, doc."

The doctor answers, "I'm sorry, there's no known cure. We're going to have to amputate your penis."

The man screams in horror, "Absolutely not! I want a second opinion!"

The doctor replies, "Well, that's you're prerogative. Go ahead if you want, but surgery is your only choice."

The next day, the man seeks out a Chinese doctor, figuring that he'll know more about the disease. The Chinese doctor examines his penis and proclaims, "Ah yes, Mongolian VD. Very rare disease."

The guys says to the doctor, "Yeah, yeah, I already know that, but what can you do? My American doctor wants to amputate my penis!"

The Chinese doctor shakes his head and laughs, "Stupid American doctor! American doctor, always want to operate. Make more money, that way. No need to operate!"

"Oh thank God!" the man replies.

"Yes!" says the Chinese doctor, "You no worry! Wait two weeks. Dick fall off by itself!"

A 75-year-old man went to his doctor's office to get a sperm count. The doctor gave the man a jar and said, "Take this jar home and bring me back a semen sample tomorrow."

The next day the 75-year-old man reappeared at the doctor's office and gave him the jar, which was as clean and empty as on the previous day.

The doctor asked what happened and the man explained; "Well, doc, it's like this: First I tried with my right hand, but nothing. Then I tried with my left hand, but still nothing. Then I asked my wife for help.

"She tried with her right hand, then her left, still nothing. She even tried with her mouth, first with her teeth in, then with her teeth out, still nothing. We even called up Earleen, the lady next door, and she tried too, first with both hands, then an armpit and she even tried squeez'n it between her knees, but still nothing."

The doctor was shocked! "You asked your neighbor?"

The old man replied, "Yep, but no matter what we tried, we still couldn't get that damned jar open."

In the beginning, God created the heavens and the Earth. And the Earth was without form, and void, and there was darkness. And Satan said, "It doesn't get any better than this." And God said, "Let there be light," and there was light. And God said, "Let the earth bring forth grass, the tree yielding seed, and the fruit tree yielding fruit," and God saw that it was good. And Satan said, "There goes the neighborhood." And God said, "Let us make Man in our image, after our likeness, and let him have dominion over the fish of the sea, and over the fowl of the air and over the cattle, and over all the Earth."

And so God created Man in his own image; male and female created he them. And God looked upon Man and Woman and saw that they were lean and fit. And Satan said, "I know how I can get back in this game." And God populated the earth with broccoli and cauliflower and spinach, green and yellow vegetables of all kinds, so Man and Woman would live long and healthy lives. And Satan created McDonald's. And McDonald's brought forth the 99-cent double cheeseburger. And Satan said to Man, "You want fries with that?" And Man said, "Super size them."

And Man gained five pounds. And God created the healthful yogurt, that woman might keep her figure that man found so fair. And Satan brought forth chocolate. And Woman gained five pounds. And God said, "I have sent thee heart-healthy vegetables and olive oil with which to cook them." And Satan brought forth chicken-fried steak so big it needed its own platter. And Man gained ten pounds and his bad cholesterol went through the roof.

And God brought forth running shoes and Man resolved to lose those extra pounds. And Satan brought forth cable TV with remote control so Man would not have to toil to change channels between ESPN and ESPN2. And Man gained another twenty pounds. And God said, "You're running up the score, Devil." And God brought forth the potato, a vegetable naturally low in fat and brimming with nutrition. And Satan peeled off the healthful skin and sliced the starchy center into chips and deep-fried them. And Man clutched his remote control and ate potato chips swaddled in cholesterol. And Satan saw and said, "It is good." And Man went into cardiac arrest. And God sighed and created quadruple bypass surgery. And Satan created HMOs.

The thing that bothers me about doctors is they give you an appointment six weeks ahead, then they examine you, then they ask, "Why did you wait so long to see me?

JOEY ADAMS

Q: What do you get when you cross the anti-baldness pill Rogaine with the anti-impotence pill Viagra?

A: Don King.

At the hospital, the relatives gathered in the waiting room, where beloved Uncle Sidney lay gravely ill. Finally, the doctor came in looking tired and somber. "I'm afraid I'm the bearer of bad news," he said as he surveyed the worried faces. "The only hope left for Sidney at this time is a brain transplant. It's an experimental procedure, semi-risky, and you will have to pay for the brain yourselves."

The family members sat silently as they absorbed the news. After a long time, someone asked, "Well, how much does a brain cost?"

The doctor quickly responded, "Five thousand dollars for a male brain, and two hundred dollars for a female brain."

The moment turned awkward. Men in the room tried not to smile, avoiding eye contact with the women. One man, unable to control his curiosity, blurted out the question everyone wanted to ask, "Why does the male brain cost so much more?"

The doctor smiled at the childish innocence and said, "It's just standard pricing procedure. We have to mark down the price of the female brains because they've been used."

An eighty-year-old man is having his annual checkup. The doctor asks him how he is feeling.

"I've never been better!" he replies. "I've got an eighteen-year-old bride who's pregnant with my child! What do you think about that?"

The doctor considers this for a moment, then says, "Well, let me tell you a story. I know a guy who is an avid hunter. He never misses a season. But one day he is in a bit of a hurry and he accidentally grabs his umbrella instead of his rifle.

"So he is walking in the woods near a creek and suddenly spots a beaver in some brush in front of him. He raises up the umbrella, points it at the beaver and squeezes the handle. BAM! The beaver drops dead in front of him."

"That's impossible!" says the old man in disbelief. "Someone else must have shot that beaver."

"Exactly."

Medical science has made a lot of progress with new miracle drugs. No matter what illness you have, the doctor can keep you alive long enough to pay your bill.

JOEY ADAMS

There was this world-famous painter. In the prime of her career, she started losing her eyesight. Fearful that she might lose her livelihood, she went to see the best eye surgeon in the world. After several weeks of delicate surgery and therapy, her eyesight was restored.

The painter was so grateful that she decided to show it by repainting the doctor's office. Part of her work included painting a gigantic eye on the wall. When she had finished the project, she held a press conference to unveil her latest work of art: the doctor's office.

During the press conference, one reporter noticed the eye on the wall, and asked the doctor, "What was your first reaction upon seeing your newly painted office, especially that large eye on the wall?"

To this, the eye doctor responded, "I said to myself, 'Thank God I'm not a gynecologist.'"

A BAD DAY

Upon arriving home, a husband was met at the door by his sobbing wife.

Tearfully she explained, "It's the druggist. He insulted me terribly this morning on the phone."

Immediately the husband drove downtown to confront the druggist and demand an apology. Before he could say more than a word or two, the druggist told him, "Now, just a minute, listen to my side of it. This morning the alarm failed to go off, so I was late getting up. I went without breakfast and hurried out to the car, just to realize that I locked the house with both house and car keys inside. I had to break a window to get my keys. Then, driving a little too fast, I got a speeding ticket. Later, when I was about three blocks from the store, I had a flat tire. When I finally got to the store there was a bunch of people waiting for me to open up. I got the store opened and started waiting on these people, and all the time the darn phone was ringing off the hook."

He continued, "Then I had to break a roll of nickels against the cash register drawer to make change, and they spilled all over the floor. I got down on my hands and knees to pick up the nickels; the phone was still ringing. When I came up I cracked my head on the open cash drawer, which made me stagger back against a showcase with a bunch of perfume bottles on it...half of them hit the floor and broke. Meanwhile, the phone is still ringing with no let up, and I finally got back to answer it. It was your wife. She wanted to know how to use a rectal thermometer...and believe me mister, as God is my witness, all I did was tell her!"

A fellow went to the doctor who told him that he had a bad illness and only a year to live. So he decided to talk to his best friend, Steve. After the man explained his situation, he asked Steve if there was any advice he could give him.

"What you should do is go out and buy a late '70 Dodge Pickup," said Steve. "Then go get married to the ugliest woman you can find, and buy yourselves an old trailer house some place in Alabama."

The fellow asked, "Will this help me live longer?"

"No," said Jim, "but it will make what time you do have left seem like forever."

A middle-aged woman had a heart attack and was taken to the hospital. While on the operating table she had a near-death experience. Seeing God, she asked, "Is my time up?" God said, "No, you have another 43 years, 2 months and 8 days to live."

Upon recovery, the woman decided to stay in the hospital and have a facelift, liposuction, and tummy tuck. She even had someone come and change the color of her hair. Since she had so much time to live, she figured she might as well make the most of it.

After her last operation, she was released from the hospital. While crossing the street on her way home, she was killed by an ambulance.

Arriving in front of God, she said, "I thought you said I had another 40+ years? Why didn't you pull me from the path of the ambulance?"

God replied, "I didn't recognize you."

Travel is very educational. I can now say "Kaopectate" in seven different languages.

A doctor had just finished a marathon sex session with one of his patients. He was resting afterwards and was feeling a bit guilty because he thought it wasn't ethical to screw a patient.

He went to his shrink and confessed. The shrink said, "Lots of other doctors have sex with their patients, you're not the first."

He replied, "Yeah, but they probably weren't veterinarians."

A guy goes to his doctor and says, "Doctor, you've got to help me. My penis is orange."

The doctor pauses to think and asks the guy to drop his pants so he can check. Damned if the guy's penis isn't orange. The doctor tells the guy, "This is very strange. Sometimes things like this are caused by stress."

Probing into the causes of possible stress, the doctor asks, "How are things going at work?"

The guy responds that he was fired about six weeks ago. The doctor tells him that this must be the cause of the stress.

The guy responds, "No. The boss was a real asshole, I had to work 20–30 hours of overtime every week, and I had no say in anything that was happening. I found a new job a couple of weeks ago where I can set my own hours, I'm getting paid double what I got on the old job, and the boss is really great."

So the doctor rules out stress as the cause and asks, "How is your home life?"

The guy says, "Well, I got divorced about six months ago."

The doctor figures that this has to be the reason for the stress. But the guy tells him, "I hated the bitch, I'm so much happier since she left, all she did was nag, nag, nag."

The guy is frustrated now. He says to the doctor, "Come on, man, you gotta help me, I need to know why my dick is orange."

The doctor thinks and thinks and finally asks, "Do you have any hobbies or a social life?"

The guy replies, "No, not really. Most nights I just sit at home, watch some porn flicks, and munch on Cheetos!"

Q: What's the good part about Alzheimer's Disease?

A: You keep meeting new friends!

THOUGHTS ABOUT DOCTORS—BY HENNY YOUNGMAN

A doctor gave a man six months to live. The man couldn't pay his bill, so he gave him another six months.

My doctor grabbed me by the wallet and said, "Cough!"

The doctor called Mrs. Cohen saying, "Mrs. Cohen, your check came back." Mrs. Cohen answered, "So did my arthritis!"

The doctor says, "You'll live to be 60!"

"I *am* 60!"

"See, what did I tell you?"

A doctor says to a man, "You want to improve your love life? You need to get some exercise. Run ten miles a day."

Two weeks later, the man called the doctor. The doctor says, "How is your love life since you have been running?"

"I don't know, I'm 140 miles away!"

The patient says, "Doctor, it hurts when I do this."

"Then don't do that!"

The doctor says to the patient, "Take your clothes off and stick your tongue out the window."

"What will that do?" asks the patient.

The doctor says, "I'm mad at my neighbor!"

A doctor has a stethoscope up to a man's chest. The man asks, "Doc, how do I stand?"

The doctor says, "That's what puzzles me!"

"Doctor, my leg hurts. What can I do?"

The doctor says, "Limp!"

A man goes to a psychiatrist. "Nobody listens to me!"

The doctor says, "Next!"

A man goes to a psychiatrist. The doctor says, "You're crazy."

The man says,"I want a second opinion!"

"Okay, you're ugly too!"

A guy walks into the psychiatrist's office wearing only shorts made from Glad Wrap.

The psychiatrist says, "Well, I can clearly see your nuts."

A man rushed into the doctor's office and shouted, "Doctor! I think I'm shrinking!"

The doctor calmly responded, "Now, settle down. You'll just have to be a little patient."

The colder the X-ray table, the more of your naked body is required on it.

Unto our doctors let us drink,
Who cure our chills and ills,
No matter what we really think
About their pills and bills.

PHILIP MCALLISTER

Here's to the psychiatrist.
He finds you cracked and leaves you broke.

You've sewn up flesh,
You've cast out germs,
You've even reset bones.
Now your last challenge
Before you rest,
Is paying your student loans.

Here's to the new doctor—may the rest of us never need your services.

Lawyers (Dewey, Cheatham, and Howe)

A new client had just come in to see a famous lawyer. "Can you tell me how much you charge?" said the client.

"Of course," the lawyer replied, "I charge two hundred dollars to answer three questions!"

"Well that's a bit steep, isn't it?"

"Yes it is," said the lawyer. "And what's your third question?"

Q: What happens when a lawyer is covered up to his neck in sand?

A: It means you don't have enough sand.

"I'm beginning to think that my lawyer is too interested in making money."

"Why do you think that?"

"Listen to this from his bill: 'For waking up at night and thinking about your case: twenty-five dollars.'"

Q: What's the difference between a good lawyer and a bad lawyer?

A: A bad lawyer can let a case drag out for several years. A good lawyer can make it last even longer.

A lawyer opened the door of his BMW, when suddenly another car came along and hit the door, ripping it off completely. When the police arrived at the scene, the lawyer was complaining bitterly about the damage to his precious BMW.

"Officer, look what they've done to my Beeeemer!!!" he whined.

"You lawyers are so materialistic, you make me sick!" retorted the officer, "You're so worried about your stupid BMW, that you didn't even notice that your left arm was ripped off!"

"Oh my gaaad…" replied the lawyer, finally noticing the bloody left shoulder where his arm once was, "Where's my Rolex?!"

An airliner was having engine trouble, and the pilot instructed the cabin crew to have the passengers take their seats and prepare for an emergency landing. A few minutes later, the pilot asked the flight attendants if everyone was buckled in and ready.

"All set here, Captain," came the reply, "except one lawyer who is still going around passing out business cards."

Q: What do you call one lawyer thrown off a bridge?

A: Pollution.

Q: What do you call all lawyers thrown off the bridge?

A: Solution.

In the USA, everything that is not prohibited by law is permitted.

In Germany, everything that is not permitted by law is prohibited.

In Russia, everything is prohibited, even if permitted by law.

In France, everything is permitted, even if prohibited by law.

In Switzerland, everything that is not prohibited by law is obligatory.

A junior partner in a firm was sent to a far-away state to represent a long-term client accused of robbery. After days of trial, the case was won, the client acquitted and released.

Excited about his success, the attorney telegraphed the firm: "Justice prevailed."

The senior partner replied in haste: "Appeal immediately."

Q: What happens to lawyers when they take Viagra?

A: They get taller.

Q: What can a goose do, a duck can't, and a lawyer should?

A: Stick his bill up his ass.

And God said, "Let there be Satan, so people don't blame everything on me. And let there be lawyers, so people don't blame everything on Satan."

GEORGE BURNS

I broke a mirror in my house and I am supposed to get seven years bad luck, but my lawyer thinks he can get me five.

STEVEN WRIGHT

Ninety-nine percent of all lawyers give the rest a bad name.

Q: How do you save a drowning lawyer?

A: Throw him a rock.

If law school is so hard to get through, how come there are so many lawyers?

CALVIN TRILLIN

The laws of God, the laws of man,
He may keep that will and can;
Not I, let God and man decree,
Laws for themselves and not for me.

A.E. HOUSEMAN

An old man was critically ill. Feeling that death was near, he called his lawyer. "I want to become a lawyer. How much is it for that express degree you told me about?"

"It's fifty thousand dollars," the lawyer said. "But why? You'll be dead soon, why do you want to become a lawyer?"

"That's my business! Get me the course!"

Four days later, the old man got his law degree. His lawyer was at his bedside, making sure his bill would be paid.

Suddenly the old man was wracked with fits of coughing, and it was clear that this would be the end. Still curious, the lawyer learned over and said, "Please, before it's too late, tell me why you wanted to get a law degree so badly before you died?"

In a faint whisper, as he breathed his last, the old man said, "One less lawyer."

For certain people after fifty, litigation takes the place of sex.

GORE VIDAL

Models (Can you spell gorgeous? I guess not. So what.)

On courage: They were doing a full back shot of me in a swimsuit and I thought, "Oh my God, I have to be so brave. See, every woman hates herself from behind."

CINDY CRAWFORD

On self-knowledge: Everywhere I went, my cleavage followed. But I learned I am not my cleavage.

CAROLE MALLORY

On poverty: Everyone should have enough money to get plastic surgery.

BEVERLY JOHNSON

On fate: I wish my butt did not go sideways, but I guess I have to face that.

CHRISTIE BRINKLEY

On psychology: I loved making *Rising Sun*. I got into the psychology of why she liked to get strangled and tied up in plastic bags. It has a lot to do with low self-worth.

TATJANA PATITZ

On arriving: Because modeling is lucrative, I'm able to save up and be more particular about the acting roles I take.

KATHY IRELAND

On career choices: My boyfriend thinks I lost my true calling to be a librarian.

PAULINA PORIZKOVA

On priorities: I would rather exercise than read a newspaper.

KIM ALEXIS

On geopolitics: Mick Jagger and I just really liked each other a lot. We talked all night. We had the same views on nuclear disarmament.

JERRY HALL

On inner strength: I love the confidence that makeup gives me.

TYRA BANKS

On death: Richard [Gere] doesn't really like me to kill bugs, but sometimes I can't help it.

CINDY CRAWFORD

On travel: I haven't seen the Eiffel Tower, Notre Dame, the Louvre. I haven't seen anything. I don't really care.

TYRA BANKS

On breakthroughs: Once I got past my anger toward my mother, I began to excel in volleyball and modeling.

GABRIELLE REECE

On epiphany: I just found out that I'm one inch taller than I thought.

CHRISTIE BRINKLEY

On heredity: My husband was just okay-looking. I was in labor and I said to him, "What if she's ugly? You're ugly."

BEVERLY JOHNSON

On the basics: It's very important to have the right clothing to exercise in. If you throw on an old T-shirt and sweats, it's not inspiring for your workout.

CHERYL TIEGS

On introductions: I think most people are curious about what it would be like to be able to meet yourself—it's eerie.

CHRISTY TURLINGTON

On courtship: The soundtrack to *Indecent Exposure* is a romantic mix of music that I know most women love to hear, so I never keep it far from me when women are nearby.

FABIO

On paradox: Sometimes I get lonely, but it's nice to be alone.

TATJANA PATITZ

On the conservation of matter: I've looked in the mirror everyday for twenty years. It's the same face.

CLAUDIA SCHIFFER

On tragedy: The worst was when my skirt fell down to my ankles—but I had on thick tights underneath.

NAOMI CAMPBELL

On instinct: If I'm making a movie and I get hungry, I call time-out and eat some crackers.

CAROL ALT

On the caste system: We're not Prince Charles and Princess Di. We don't think of ourselves as royalty. We happen to be working people.

CHRISTIE BRINKLEY

On occupational hazards: I tried on two hundred and fifty bathing suits in one afternoon and ended up having little scabs up and down my thighs, probably from some of those with sequins all over them.

CINDY CRAWFORD

On economics: I don't wake up for less than ten thousand dollars a day.

LINDA EVANGELISTA

On thinking: When I model I'm pretty blank. You can't think too much or it doesn't work.

PAULINA PORIZKOVA

On logic: I think, if my butt's not too big for them to be photographing it, then it shouldn't be too big for me.

CHRISTY TURLINGTON

On body parts: I don't know what to do with my arms. It just makes me feel weird and I feel like people are looking at me and that makes me nervous.

TYRA BANKS

On body language: You can usually tell when I'm happy by the fact that I've gained weight.

CHRISTY TURLINGTON

On deprivation: If they had Nautilus on the Concorde, I would work out all the time.

LINDA EVANGELISTA

On motivation: It was kind of boring for me to have to eat. I would know that I had to, and I would.

KATE MOSS

On versatility: I can do anything you want me to do so long as I don't have to speak.

LINDA EVANGELISTA

On the grief process: When my Azzedine Alaia jacket from 1987 died, I wrapped it up in a box, attached a note saying where it came from and took it to the Salvation Army. It was a big loss.

VERONICA WEBB

On vengeance: Girls are always getting mad at each other and they tell their hairdressers to purposely mess up another girl's hair.

TASHA

STRANDED WITH CINDY CRAWFORD

This guy was stranded on a desert island with Cindy Crawford. He was cool and he didn't make any moves towards her for several weeks.

Finally, one day, he asked her if maybe they could start up a physical relationship, so as to attend to each other's needs. Cindy said she was game and a very nice sexual relationship began.

Everything was great for about four months. One day the guy went to Cindy and said, "I'm having this problem... It's kind of a guy thing, but I need to ask you a favor."

Cindy replied, "Okay."

So he said, "Can I borrow your eyebrow pencil?"

Cindy looked at him a little funny, but answered, "Sure, you can borrow my eyebrow pencil."

The guy then said, "Do you mind if I use the eyebrow pencil to draw a mustache on you?"

Cindy was getting a little worried, but said, "Okay."

And so the guy drew a moustache on her.

Then the guy said, "Can you wear some of my guy clothing? I need for you to look more like a man."

Cindy was getting a little disappointed at this point, but said, "I guess so."

Then, she put on some of his clothes.

Then the guy said to Cindy, "Do you mind if I call you Fred?"

Cindy was now getting very dejected, but said, "No, I guess it's okay, you can call me Fred."

So then the guy reached out and grabbed Cindy by the arms and shouted, "Fred! You won't believe who I have been sleeping with these past four months!"

Nurses (Hey, that thing is cold!)

YOU MIGHT BE A GOOD NURSE IF...

You avoid unhealthy-looking people in the mall for fear that they'll drop near you and you'll have to do CPR on your day off.

It doesn't bother you to eat a candy bar in one hand while performing digital stimulation on your patient with another.

You've had a patient with a nose ring, a brow ring, and twelve earrings say, "I'm afraid of shots."

You've ever bet on someone's blood alcohol level.

You plan your next meal while performing gastric lavage.

You believe every waiting room should have a Valium salt lick.

You have your weekends off planned a year in advance.

You know it's a full moon without having to look at the sky.

A woman enrolled in nursing school is attending an anatomy class. The subject of the day is involuntary muscles. The instructor, hoping to perk up the students a bit, asks the woman if she knows what her asshole does when she has an orgasm.

"Sure!" she says, "He's at home taking care of the kids."

Q: How can you tell when you have the head nurse?

A: She has dirty knees.

Salesperson (Come out, come out, wherever you are)

A software manager, a hardware manager, and a marketing manager are driving to a meeting when a tire blows. They get out of the car and look at the problem.

The software manager says, "I can't do anything about this—it's a hardware problem."

The hardware manager says, "Maybe if we turned the car off and on again, it would fix itself."

The marketing manager says, "Hey, seventy-five percent of it is working—let's ship it!"

A salesman who was out on his territory had a heart attack in his motel room and died.

The motel manager called the salesman's company and related the tragedy to the sales manager.

The sales manager received the news in a nonchalant manner and told the motel manager, "Return his samples by freight and search his pants for orders."

Q: How can you tell when a salesman is lying?

A: His lips are moving.

A golfer, playing a round by himself, is about to tee off when a salesman runs up to him and yells, "Wait! I have something really amazing to show you!"

The golfer, annoyed, says, "What is it?"

"It's a special golf ball," says the salesman. "You can never lose it!"

"Whattaya mean," scoffs the golfer, "you can never lose it? What if you hit it into the water?"

"No problem," says the salesman. "It floats, and it detects where the shore is, and spins towards it."

"Well, what if you hit it into the woods?"

"Easy," says the salesman. "It emits a beeping sound, and you can find it with your eyes closed."

"Okay," says the golfer, impressed. "But what if your round goes late and it gets dark?"

"No problem, this golf ball glows in the dark! I'm telling you, you can never lose this golf ball!"

The golfer buys it at once. "Just one question," he says to the salesman. "Where did you get it?"

"I found it."

The more cordial the buyer's secretary, the greater the odds that the competition already has the order.

Productivity (More work for me)

YOU WORK IN CORPORATE AMERICA IF...

1. You've sat at the same desk for four years and worked for three different companies.

2. Your company's welcome sign is attached with Velcro.

3. Your resume is on a diskette in your pocket.

4. Your biggest loss from a system crash is your best jokes.

5. You sit in a cubicle smaller than your bedroom closet.

6. Salaries of the members on the Executive Board are higher than all the Third World countries' annual budgets combined.

7. You think lunch is just a meeting to which you drive.

8. It's dark when you drive to and from work.

9. You see a good-looking person and know it is a visitor.

10. Free food left over from meetings is your main staple.

11. Weekends are those days your spouse makes you stay home.

12. Being sick is defined as can't walk or you're in the hospital.

13. You're already late on an assignment you just got.

14. You work 200 hours for the $100 bonus check and jubilantly say, "Oh wow, thanks!"

15. Dilbert cartoons hang outside every cube.

16. Your boss's favorite lines are, "When you get a few minutes," "In your spare time," "When you're freed up," and "I have an opportunity for you."

17. Vacation is something you roll over into next year, or a check you get every January.

18. Your relatives and family describe your job as, "works with computers."

19. The only reason you recognize your kids is because their pictures are hanging in your cube.

Q: The difference between ignorance and apathy?

A: I don't know, and I could care less.

HOW TO LOSE WEIGHT WITHOUT DOING MUCH

Here's a guide to calorie-burning activities and the number of calories per hour they consume.

Beating around the bush	75
Jumping to conclusions	100
Climbing the walls	150
Swallowing your pride	50
Passing the buck	25
Throwing your weight around (depending on your weight)	50–300
Dragging your heels	100
Pushing your luck	250
Making mountains out of molehills	500
Hitting the nail on the head	50
Wading through paperwork	300
Bending over backwards	75
Jumping on the bandwagon	200
Balancing books	25
Running around in circles	350
Eating crow	225
Tooting your own horn	.25
Climbing the ladder of success	750
Pulling out the stops	75
Adding fuel to the fire	160
Wrapping it up at the days end	12

To which you may want to add your own favorite activities, including:

Opening a can of worms	50
Putting your foot in your mouth	300
Starting the ball rolling	90
Going over the edge	25
Picking up the pieces	350
Counting eggs before they hatch	6
Calling it quits	2

PUT MORE STRESS INTO YOUR LIFE

Refuse to take action on nagging problems. Procrastinate, brood, and if possible, lose some sleep over them.

Make a concerted effort to take note of irritations in your life and blow them out of proportion.

Consider the power of negative thinking.

Hide your sense of humor. Erase the words smile, joke, and laugh from your vocabulary; concentrate on frowning.

If you've been working a 60-hour week, try 65 or 70 or 75! Spending more time at work will give you less time to consider how stressed you are.

Consume vast quantities of caffeine. As a stimulant it will ensure that you are awake day and night.

Practice the art of "hurry up and wait." This means dashing off to join a queue somewhere—like the bank, cinema, or ticket outlet.

Make sure you drive no farther than two feet from the car in front.

To relieve boredom while waiting for traffic lights, pretend you are on the starting grid for the Indy 500.

Never read a book or listen to music.

Play hide-and-seek by concealing important documents from yourself.

Delegate nagging problems. You've proved that you can't deal with them.

Tell yourself that your abilities are unlimited. Do not waver from this conviction until you are fired for lack of competence.

Giggle nervously. It will make other people nervous, meetings will be unproductive and you won't come away with a long list of things to do.

Find a disagreeable tennis partner. Perhaps your spouse.

When feeling stressful, breathe deeply and hyperventilate until you pass out.

When things are going badly, knock your head against the wall. The resulting headache will supersede the original problem.

I just got lost in thought. It was unfamiliar territory.

If at first you don't succeed, destroy all evidence that you tried.

A conclusion is the place where you got tired of thinking.

For every action there is an opposite and equal criticism.

The sooner you fall behind, the more time you'll have to catch up.

Announcing Great Results (Like I care)

A start of a toast: We received a number of congratulatory telegrams for this event—from people congratulating themselves for not being here.

A successful manager is one who believes in sharing the credit with the man who did the work.

Motivational Speech (Did you say something?)

Don't look back—something might be gaining on you.

SATCHEL PAIGE

It is not enough to succeed. Others must fail.

GORE VIDAL

This is a test. It is only a test. Had it been an actual job, you would have received raises, promotions, and other signs of appreciation.

If you can't convince them, confuse them.

HARRY S TRUMAN

Goodman was a moderately successful stockbroker who dreamed of making the big money someday. He took his friend out for a drive, and chose the route carefully in order to impress on his friend the possibilities of the brokerage business.

"Look at that yacht," he said as they drove slowly past the marina. "That belongs to the senior partner at Merrill Lynch. That one over there is owned by the head of Goldman, Sachs. And look at that huge yacht out there. That's the pride and joy of the top seller at Prudential-Bache."

His friend was silent.

Goodman turned to look at him and saw a pained look on his face. "What's the matter?" Goodman asked.

"I was just wondering," his friend said. "Are there any customers' yachts?"

Many a man has finally succeeded only because he has failed after repeated efforts. If he had never met defeat, he would never have known great victory.

You're never going to get anywhere if you think you're already there.

Rodney Dangerfield
Lovable Loser

Rodney "I Get No Respect" Dangerfield started his life in the world of comedy at the age of 15, as a joke writer. By the age of 17 he was already performing his routine at amateur nights. At 19 he had two jobs, one as a comic who couldn't earn a living, and the other as a singing waiter. Yes, believe it. Rodney Dangerfield would actually sing, and people threw money at him. Big surprise.

"Geez, I haven't been this popular since I owed money."

Rodney worked and traveled the comedy circuit for ten years but reluctantly gave up his first love for a regular income. When he turned 40, he made the decision to relaunch his career as a standup comedian and comedy writer. He continued to work days in an office while spending his nights in New York City comedy clubs.

Not happy with the way the clubs were being run, Rodney decided to open his own, the now famous Dangerfield's on First Avenue in Manhattan. Both the club and the owner became huge successes.

"My life today is tough. My wife, she's attached to a machine that keeps her alive—the refrigerator!"

Rodney became a hit with audiences portraying a lovable loser. He became the master of the classic premise-setup-punchline school of comedy.

"At my house we pray after we eat. Hey, I don't think toast should have bones!"

Dangerfield's became the place to discover rising young comedians. Rodney hosted an HBO show from the club that introduced some very funny people to television audiences for the first time.

Among them were Tim Allen, Roseanne Barr, Jim Carrey, Jeff Foxworthy, Sam Kinison, Bob Saget, Jerry Seinfeld, Rita Rudner, Robert Townsend, and Louie Anderson, to name a few.

No one can forget Rodney's star turn in the classic hit comedy film *Caddyshack*, or his role in *Easy Money*, which he co-wrote. Then there was the mega-hit *Back to School* (one of the first comedies to gross over $100 million). Rodney also played a dramatic role offered to him by Oliver Stone in *Natural Born Killers*, for which he received critical acclaim across the board.

"What am I sweating for? I got the job."

Aside from being a premiere Las Vegas entertainer for over 20 years, Dangerfield has also made countless appearances on television. His first big break was *The Ed Sullivan Show*, on which he appeared 16 times. Rodney also appeared on *This Is Your Life*, *What's My Line*, *The Dean Martin Show*, *Saturday Night Live*, and a record 70 times on *The Tonight Show with Johnny Carson*. More recently, Dangerfield has shown up on *Mad TV*, *Suddenly Susan*, *Late Night with Conan O'Brien*, *The Single Guy*, and *The Tonight Show with Jay Leno*.

"Hey, I'm not going to let you fuck up my timing; joke 2-3-4...joke 2-3-4."

Rodney was also the first comedian to launch his own website on the Internet. Started up in February 1995, http://www.rodney.com, has won many awards and distinctions as a popular comedy destination on the Web, securing his appeal to yet another generation.

Getting a Promotion
(That brown-nosing paid off)

A handicapped golfer is one who plays his boss.

Destiny is not a matter of chance, but a matter of choice. It is not a thing to be waited for, it is a thing to be achieved.

WILLIAM JENNINGS BRYANT

Three women are up for a promotion but the company only has one position available. The boss decides to put an extra hundred dollars in each one's envelope to see how they react.

The first woman says, "Wow, an extra hundred dollars! I'm going to buy more company stock!" The boss notes this.

The second says, "An extra hundred dollars! I'm going shopping!" The boss notes this.

The third says, "An extra hundred dollars! Payroll must have made an error. I'll go straighten this out right away."

Which one got the promotion?

The one with the biggest tits.

Getting Fired
(Not enough brown-nosing)

Forgive your enemies, but never forget their names.

JOHN F. KENNEDY

A young man was called into the personnel director's office. "What is the meaning of this?" the director asked. "When you applied for this job, you told us that you had five-years' experience. Now we discover that this is the first job you've ever had."

"Well," the young man replied, "in your advertisement you said that you wanted somebody with imagination."

Ambition is a poor excuse for not having enough sense to be lazy.

Hard work pays off in the future. Laziness pays off now.

STEVEN WRIGHT

Some people hate waking up and getting out of bed. I enjoy it. I do it three or four times a day.

He who laughs last has not yet heard the bad news.

BERTOLT BRECHT

I don't know the key to success, but the key to failure is trying to please everybody.

BILL COSBY

Retirement/Going Away Party (I gave you my life, and all I got was this watch)

May you taste the sweetest pleasures that fortune ere bestowed,
And may all your friends remember all the favors you are owed.

I didn't realize just how long you had been with the company until we were cleaning out your desk and found a stagecoach ticket.

What can you say about a man who is admired, revered, and loved by everyone? I can start by saying he's not the man we're honoring tonight.

He doesn't put on airs. After all the holiday eating, he has enough trouble just putting on his pants.

He's afraid nobody will remember him when he's gone. Gee, I can think of several reasons he'll be remembered. He wouldn't like any of them, but I can think of them.

With most people, the left side of the brain does some things, and the right side does others. In his case, however, neither side seems to do a whole lot.

There's no middle ground with this guy—you either hate him or detest him.

Before I introduce our guest of honor, I'd like to introduce several people who admire and revere him. And since there's no one here like that, I'll introduce him.

Learn to live well, or fairly make your will.
You've played, and loved, and ate, and drunk your fill;
Walk sober off; before a sprightlier age
Comes titering on, and shoves you from the stage;
Leave such to trifle with more grace and ease,
Whom Folly pleases, and whose follies please.

ALEXANDER POPE

A toast to you as you move onward and upward to bigger and better endeavors. We hated to lose you to retirement but it was the only way we could get rid of you.

Congratulations on your retirement. It could not have happened to a nicer person. More deserving maybe, but none nicer.

Our guest of honor is retiring. No longer will we see his smiling face around the office. No more will we hear his silly laugh or have him around to help us with our problems. On the other hand, I think this is a great time to buy stock in the company.

Not to say you are old, but, when you were a kid, the Dead Sea was only slightly ill.

CHAPTER SIX:

HOLIDAYS

Overeating. Seeing people you hate and having to be nice to them. Drinking too much. Drinking too little. Getting bad presents. Getting good presents. Holidays are milestones. Ever sit down at Thanksgiving and can't believe an entire year has passed? It's amazing. You used to read the Four Questions at Passover, now you need your glasses to figure out which is the Hebrew writing and which the English. Years pass, family dynamics change (did she have to marry that idiot?) but the holidays themselves are constants. Every year they show up like clockwork.

If you live in a warm climate, holidays are the only way you know the seasons have changed. It's an odd feeling to be driving down Sunset Boulevard in a convertible and see Santa and his Ralph Lauren-clad reindeer on the lawn of a giant mansion with a Star of David on the chimney—but hey, that's holidays for you. All for one and one for all.

PAUL SHAFFER—ROAST OF RICHARD BELZER:

I met Richard Belzer 27 years ago. That's when he still considered heroin one of the four basic food groups.

BILLY CRYSTAL—ROAST OF ROB REINER:

Rob, "roast" is such a perfect word for you. Look at you, you're a brisket in a suit. Sit back down, go on, grease up your sides, and get back in the chair.

New Years (A license to kiss)

Are you sick of making the same resolutions year after year that you never keep? Why not promise to do something you can actually accomplish?

1. I want to gain weight. Put on at least thirty pounds.

2. Stop exercising. Waste of time.

3. Read less.

4. Watch more TV. I've been missing some good stuff.

5. Procrastinate more.

6. Drink. Drink some more.

7. Take up a new habit: smoking.

8. Spend at least $1,000 a month on hookers.

9. Spend more time at work.

10. Take a vacation to someplace important—like, to see the largest ball of twine.

11. Stop bringing lunch from home. I should eat out more.

12. Quit giving money and time to charity.

13. Start being superstitious.

14. Have my car lowered and invest in a really loud stereo system. Get the windows tinted. Buy some fur for the dash.

15. Speak in a monotone voice and only use monosyllabic words.

16. Only wear jeans that are two sizes too small, and use a chain or rope for a belt. Only wear T-shirts with those fashionable yellow stains under the arms.

18. Personal goal: Bring back disco.

Here's to you a New Year's toast
May your Joy ne'er see a Sorrow's Ghost.

In the New Year, may your right hand always be stretched out in friendship, but never in want.

NEW YEAR'S RESOLUTION

Whatever you resolve to do,
On any New Year's Day,
Resolve to yourself to be true
And live—the same old way.

Ring out the old, ring in the new,
Ring happy bells across the snow;
The year is going, let him go.

ALFRED, LORD TENNYSON

Welcome be ye that are here,
Welcome all, and make good cheer,
Welcome all, another year.

Here's to a bright New Year
And a fond farewell to the old;
Here's to the things that are yet to come
And to the memories we hold.
A song for the old, while its knell is tolled,
And it parting moments fly!
But a song and a cheer for the glad New Year,
While we watch the old year die!

GEORGE COOPER

New Year's Eve, "when auld acquaintance be forgot"—
unless those tests come back positive.

JAY LENO

New Year's Eve is a night when we all sing, "Auld Lang
Syne" from the heart—which isn't easy, since none of us
knows what it means.

The morning after the New Year's Eve party is when you
wake up to find the old year erased from your memory...
along with your name and where you left your car.

The nice thing about wild New Year's Eve parties is that
when you wake up the next morning, you know that
from that point on, the year has got to get better.

Valentine's Day (Blissfully happy, or lonely loser?)

I'd like to play a game with you—
I'm thinking Naked Twister.
I'll bring the board and lots of wine
Could you please bring your sister?

Let's plan a trip to the falls of Niagara!
Just me and you and my Viagra.

Roses are red,
Politicians are sleazy.
Will you be mine?
I hear that you're easy.

My sugar-lumps, I love you so—
You fill me with desire.
I'll still love you even though
Your hourly rate got higher.

Roses are red
I like Spaghetti-O's,
Now what in the world
Rhymes with "fellatio"?

We're both white trash,
Bred by the dozen,
And now it's time,
To do my cousin.

Phyllis Diller
What a Face

Phyllis Diller is really very different from her stage persona. With the help of a hair dresser and a stylist, Phyllis cuts quite a striking and lovely figure.

She is also a talented chef, an established painter, and a devoted mother and grandmother. Masking her natural beauty under fright wigs and unflattering attire, she has always made a living making fun of her ugliness, skinniness, ineptitude, and just about every defect a woman can have.

"You can say the nastiest things about yourself without offending anyone."

Phyllis is loved and admired by millions as an irrepressible woman with a world-famous laugh. She has headlined in virtually every major supper club in the U.S. and around the world; she writes her own rapid-fire comedy routines; and she recently celebrated 35 years in show business.

"We spend the first twelve months of our children's lives teaching them to walk and talk, and the next twelve telling them to sit down and shut up."

Phyllis heard the call of show business later than most, not starting her career until the age of 37. Until then, she'd been a housewife and mother of five children, while working at radio station KSFO, San Francisco, as a publicist, newspaper reporter, and columnist.

At the insistence of her husband, Sherwood Diller, Phyllis created an act for herself and got booked into the famous Purple Onion in San Francisco. She snaked around the piano, made fun of current celebrities, used her ever-present cigarette holder, and had a ball at the expense of high fashion and life in general. Her first performance was on March 7, 1955. She had been booked for only two weeks but she stayed for 89. It was the birth of a legend.

"Women want men, careers, money, children, friends, luxury, comfort, independence, freedom, respect, love, and three-dollar pantyhose that won't run."

She followed up this debut with a cross-country tour, perfecting the housewife and daily life routines that have made her the "high priestess of the ridiculous." She played in small clubs like the Blue Angel in New York and appeared on *The Jack Paar Show*. From that point on her career took off. In only five years she was performing at Carnegie Hall.

"A smile is a curve that sets everything straight."

Phyllis Diller has appeared in 16 movies, scores of television specials and shows, recorded 5 major comedy albums, written four best-selling books, and found time to help thousands throughout the world with charity work. She has appeared as a piano soloist with 100 symphony orchestras across the country.

Recently, she launched several new endeavors: she has marketed her own chili, Phyllis Diller's Original Recipe; a line of La Vie beauty products; and Phyllis Diller Creations, a collection of jewelry. She did all this after raising five children.

"I buried a lot of my ironing in the back yard."

We've a date tonight,
Oh, Valentine!
I hope I can stay calm!
'Cause recently,
I've only dated
The lovely Mrs. Palm.

Time to choose your Valentine!
If I don't seem up to snuff,
Another case of Ballantine
And I'll look good enough.

Here's to this water,
Wishing it were wine,
Here's to you my darling,
Wishing you were mine.

Here's to the love that I hold for thee;
May it day by day grow stronger;
May it last as long as your love for me,
And not a second longer!

Here's to the red and sparkling wine,
I'll be your sweetheart, if you'll be mine,
I'll be constant, I'll be true,
I'll leave my happy home for you.

St. Patrick's Day
(Start drinking at 9:00 A.M...)

May your blessings outnumber
The shamrock that grow,
And may trouble avoid you
Wherever you go.

May the Irish hills caress you.
May her lakes and rivers bless you.
May the luck of the Irish enfold you.
May the blessings of Saint Patrick behold you.

AN OLD IRISH RECIPE FOR LONGEVITY

Leave the table hungry.
Leave the bed sleepy.
Leave the table thirsty.

May the leprechauns be near you,
To spread luck along your way.
And may all the Irish angels,
Smile upon you St. Patrick's Day.

Gays are not allowed to march in the St. Patrick's Day parade, but someone from the Irish Republican Army did. Now I ask you, who is more dangerous? A group who has been known to blow up buses, or people who know all the lyrics to Stephen Sondheim musicals?

JOY BEHAR

A little boy was in the school's bathroom. He found there was no toilet paper so he used his hand. When he got back to his classroom the teacher asked what he had in his hand.

"A little leprechaun, and if I open my hand he'll get scared away."

The teacher couldn't get him to open his hand and sent him to the principal who also asked what he had in his hand.

"A little leprechaun, and if I open my hand he'll get scared away."

He was sent home with a note asking to see his parents, so his mom asked him what he had in his hand.

"A little leprechaun, and if I open my hand he'll get scared away."

He was sent to his room. In a while his dad came in and asked, "What do you have in your hand?"

Again came the reply, "It's a little leprechaun, and if I open my hand he'll get scared away."

His dad ordered him to open his hand, and as he did so the boy said, "Oh no, Dad, look; you scared the shit out of him!"

Fourth of July (I saw fireworks)

It's a funny thing about our nation. July 4th is its birthday, but April 15th is when it collects the presents.

Halloween (Yes, you can wear ladies' clothes)

HALLOWEEN COSTUME PARTY

A couple was invited to a swanky masked Halloween party. The wife got a terrible headache and told her husband to go to the party alone. He, being a devoted husband, protested, but she argued and said she was going to take some aspirin and go to bed, and that there was no need for his good time to be spoiled by not going. So he took his costume and away he went.

The wife, after sleeping soundly for about an hour, awakened without pain; and, as it was still early, she decided to go to the party. In as much as her husband did not know what her costume was, she thought she would have some fun by watching him to see how he acted when she was not around.

She joined the party and soon spotted her husband cavorting around on the dance floor, dancing with every pretty girl he could, and copping a little feel here and a little kiss there. His wife went up to him and, being a rather seductive babe herself, he left his partner high and dry and devoted his time to the new stuff who had just arrived.

She let him go as far as he wished, naturally, since he was her husband. Finally he whispered a little proposition in her ear and she agreed, so off they went to one of the cars and had a little bang. Just before unmasking at midnight, she slipped away and went home, put the costume away, and got into bed, wondering what kind of explanation he would make for his behavior.

She was sitting up reading when he came in and asked what kind of a time he had.

He said, "Oh, the same old thing. You know I never have a good time when you're not there."

Then she asked, "Did you dance much?"

He replied, "I'll tell you, I never even danced one dance. When I got there, I met Pete, Bill Brown, and some other guys, so we went into the den and played poker all evening. But I'll tell you...the guy I loaned my costume to sure had a real good time!"

WHY TRICK-OR-TREATING IS BETTER THAN SEX

1. Guaranteed to get at least a little something in the sack.

2. If you get tired, wait ten minutes and go at it again.

3. The uglier you look, the easier it is to get some.

4. You don't have to compliment the person who gave you candy.

5. It's okay when the person you're with fantasizes you're someone else, because you ARE someone else.

6. Forty years from now, you'll still enjoy candy.

7. If you don't get what you want, you can always go next door.

8. Doesn't matter if kids hear you moaning and groaning.

9. Less guilt the next morning.

10. You can do the whole neighborhood!!!

Q: Do witches stay home on weekends?

A: No. They go away for a spell.

Q: How can you tell that Dr. Frankenstein had a good sense of humor?

A: He kept his monster in stitches.

Q: How do mummies hide?

A: They wear masking tape.

"Mommy, Mommy, the kids all call me a werewolf."

"Never mind, dear, now go and comb your face."

Mother vampire to son:

"Hurry up and eat your breakfast before it clots."

Q: What did the policeman say when a black widow spider ran down his back?

A: "You're under a vest!"

Q: What did the bat say to the witch's hat?

A: You go on ahead. I'll hang around for a while.

Q: What did the mother ghost say to the baby ghost?

A: Put your boos and shocks on.

Q: What did the Mommy Vampire say to the Baby Vampire?

A: "You are driving me batty."

Q: What do little ghosts drink?

A: Evaporated milk.

Q: What do you say to a two-headed monster?

A: Hello, hello.

Q: What happened to the monster children who ate all their vegetables?

A: They gruesome.

Q: What kind of dog does Dracula have?

A: A bloodhound!

Thanksgiving (Start by being grateful for St. Patrick's Day)

He laid her on the table
So white, clean and bare.
His forehead wet with beads of sweat
He rubbed her here and there.
He touched her neck and then her breast
And then, drooling, felt her thigh.
The slit was wet and all was set,
He gave a joyous cry.
The hole was wide...he looked inside
All was dark and murky.
He rubbed his hands and stretched his arms...
And then he stuffed the turkey.

TOP 10 THINGS THAT SOUND DIRTY AT THANKSGIVING

1. "Just reach in and grab the giblets."

2. "Whew...that's one terrific spread!"

3. "I am in the mood for a little dark meat!"

4. "Tying the legs together will keep the inside moist."

5. "Talk about a *huge* breast!"

6. "And he forces his way into the end zone!"

7. "She's five thousand pounds fully inflated and it takes 15 men to hold her down."

8. "It's cool whip time!"

9. "If I don't unbutton my pants, I am going to burst!"

10. "It must be broken 'cause when I push on the tip, nothing squirts out."

I celebrated Thanksgiving in the traditional way. I invited everyone in my neighborhood to my house, we had an enormous feast. And then I killed them and took their land.

JON STEWART

Here's to the blessings of the year,
Here's to the friends we hold so dear,
To peace on earth, both far and near.

Here's to the good old turkey
The bird that comes each fall
And with his sweet persuasive meat
Makes gobblers of us all.

Christmas (Deck those halls)

Now, thrice welcome, Christmas!
Which brings us good cheer,
Mince pies and plum pudding—
Strong ale and strong beer!

Q: What does the pope have in common with a Christmas tree?

A: Both have balls just for decoration?

At Christmas time I sat on Santa's lap. His fly was open. Boy...what a present he gave me!

RODNEY DANGERFIELD

Q: What do female reindeer do at Christmas?

A: They blow a few bucks.

Q: Why are Santa Claus's balls so big?

A: Because he only comes once a year.

A THOUGHT FOR CHRISTMAS

Do you know what would have happened if it had been Three Wise Women instead of Three Wise Men?

They would have asked directions,
Arrived on time,
Helped deliver the baby,

Cleaned the stable,
Made a casserole,
Brought practical gifts, and
There would be Peace on Earth.

Q: Why is Santa so jolly?

A: Because he knows where all the naughty girls live.

As fits the holy Christmas birth,
Be this, good friends, our carol still—
Be peace on earth, be peace on earth,
To men of gentle will.

WILLIAM MAKEPEACE THACKERAY

Here's to the holly with its bright red berry.
Here's to Christmas, let's make it merry.

I love Christmas. I receive a lot of wonderful presents I
can't wait to exchange.

HENNY YOUNGMAN

Santa Claus has the right idea. Visit people once a year.

VICTOR BORGE

Most people go through three Santa Claus stages.

First, you believe in Santa Claus.

Then, you don't believe in Santa Claus.

Finally, you are Santa Claus.

CHAPTER SEVEN:
THE MEDIA CIRCUS

Ever since early man sketched pictures of woolly mammoth hunts in his cave—and early woman got pissed off at him for ruining the walls—the media has taken over our lives. Your kids may not know who Patrick Henry was but they sure as hell can tell you all about N'Sync. (Okay, so you probably don't remember who Patrick Henry was either, but you're well aware of Oprah!).

But the media is fascinating and often, it is worthy of a good joke or a funny story, or a bad joke and a sad story. The movie business is more popular than ever—ten-year-olds all over the country discuss the weekend grosses. Movies are not what they used to be but there are certainly more of them. And TV—it's out of control. When we were kids, there were cartoons and a test pattern. Now, kids have 500 channels and their own DVD players.

Television used to be what you watched when there was nothing else to do. Now it's an activity. Weird, but true. Sad, but a fact. So, there's a lot to say about the media, and we've got most of it here. Movies, books, the dreaded television, and everything else that goes with it.

This is the twenty-first century and it's time to get on board, turn on and tune in (get it?). Read the chapter. Be funny and witty, know more than your friends and less than you think.

SAL RICHARDS—ROAST OF FREDDIE ROMAN:

When I look at Freddie I think there must be an opening in the Keebler forest.

FREDDIE ROMAN AT HIS ROAST:

To my dear friend Alan King, many thanks for presenting me with this honor—I realize how hard it is for you to do something nice for someone else.

FREDDIE ROMAN AT HIS ROAST:

For most people the onset of senility is a tragedy, for Irwin Corey, it's the realization of a dream.

FREDDIE ROMAN AT HIS ROAST:

Joy Behar was not named for a happy emotion or a feeling of gladness. She was named for a kitchen soap!

STEVEN SCOTT—ROAST OF FREDDIE ROMAN:

If I can be half as successful as this man has been, I'm fucked.

I love the Friars. It's the only place I get called a cunt and it's a compliment.

JOY BEHAR

JOY BEHAR—ROAST OF FREDDIE ROMAN:

We're here to honor a man, who, even though he's impotent, is the biggest prick I know.

DICK CAPRI—ROAST OF FREDDIE ROMAN:

Freddie saved himself from a pit bull that was humping his leg by faking an orgasm.

There was a bomb scare at the Friars. Someone threatened to show Howie Mandel's pilot episode.

SOUPY SALES

SOUPY SALES—ROAST OF FREDDIE ROMAN:

Tonight you'll hear a lot of blue words such as hump, screw, and crap—these are the few things left the people on this dais can still do!

JEFFREY ROSS—ROAST OF KELSEY GRAMMAR:

He's just out of rehab. He's been in and out of Betty Ford more times than Gerry Ford.

Mr. Martin, Mr. Toastmaster, fellow Friars, Ladies and Gentlemen, [sigh], I have to go to the bathroom.

FRANK SINATRA

ALAN KING—ROAST OF ROB REINER:

Who can forget that scene in *When Harry Met Sally*, in Katz's deli, where Meg Ryan fakes an orgasm. Rob got that idea from his first wife, Penny Marshall.

When Rob and I were working together on his debut film *This is Spinal Tap*, he said to me, "Michael, I have a dream," and I said, "Rob, if you believe in that dream, I think you should go for it." Well Rob never did fuck Mitzi Gaynor.

BRETT BUTLER—ROAST OF ROB REINER:

Rob, that's got to be the biggest beard in Hollywood, aside from Nicole Kidman.

JEFFREY ROSS TO JANEANE GAROFALO:

That movie left the theater so fast they held the premiere at Blockbuster. She's made more bad pictures than fotomat.

Books (Like movies, but you have to work)

A classic is something that everybody wants to have read and nobody wants to read.

MARK TWAIN

I went to a bookstore and asked a saleswoman, "Where's the self-help section?"

She answered, "If I tell you, it will defeat the purpose."

THE SHORTEST BOOKS EVER WRITTEN

1000 Years of German Humor

Everything Men Know about Women

The Code of Ethics for Lawyers

Italian War Heroes

Who's Who in Puerto Rico

America's Guide to Etiquette

Royal Family's Guide to Good Marriages

Safe Places to Travel in the USA

Jerry Garcia's Guide to Beating Drug Addiction

Contraception by Pope John Paul II

Career Opportunities for Liberal Arts Majors

Cooking Gourmet Dishes with Tofu

There are three rules for writing a novel. Unfortunately, no one knows what they are.

SOMERSET MAUGHAM

From the moment I picked your book up until I put it down I was convulsed with laughter. Some day I intend on reading it.

GROUCHO MARX

Groucho Marx
"You Bet Your Life"

Julius Henry (Groucho) Marx was born in 1890 and died on August 19, 1977, at Cedars Sinai Medical Center in Los Angeles. What happened in between changed the face of American comedy, and spanned from vaudeville through the golden age of television.

If you have to make a toast, tell a joke, speak at your company retreat, or are just looking for some clever things to say to impress someone you've met at a bar and want to spend the rest of the night with, there is no one better to quote than Groucho Marx. No matter the occasion, Groucho will lend you a quip or a quote.

On screen he played a wisecracking, cigar-toting, middle-aged lech. His prominent nose, bristling, animated eyebrows, impossibly bushy, black mustache, and hunched, gliding gait have spawned decades of impersonations. Just buy a pair of "Groucho glasses" and you're in business. Of course, nothing measures up to the real thing.

"I'm going to Iowa for an award. Then I'm appearing at Carnegie Hall, it's sold out. Then I'm sailing to France to be

honored by the French government. I'd give it all up for one erection."

Wouldn't you?

Groucho Marx made a total of 26 movies, 15 of them with his brothers Chico and Harpo, and Zeppo. Some of your favorites might include *A Day at the Races, Duck Soup*, and *A Night at the Opera*. Of those 15, only 14 were actually released. The first movie was a silent film that Groucho is said to have cut up into guitar picks to prevent its release. Guess he didn't like it.

Groucho and his siblings, The Marx Brothers as they were always known, were one of the world's most famous comedy teams, with their own brand of intelligent slapstick. They mixed anarchic physical comedy with quick-witted one-liners, the cappers often delivered by Groucho himself.

Groucho was best at using humor to defuse potentially awkward situations, as well as to force people to recognize their own ignorance or prejudices.

"I resign. I wouldn't want to belong to any club that would have me as a member."

Groucho was once informed that he would not be allowed to go in the swimming pool at a private club because it did not admit Jews. He responded, "Well, my son is half Jewish. Can he go in up to his waist?"

Today's humor is extremely irreverent, bold, exciting. Well, no one was more irreverent than Groucho. He could thumb his nose at you, make you look like an ass, and still make you feel as if you were in on the joke.

When discovered by his wife kissing the maid, Groucho said "I was just whispering in her mouth."

"The months before my son was born,
I used to yell from night to morn,
Whatever it is, I'm against it!
No matter what it is or who commenced it,
I'm against it!'"

"There is only one way to find out if a man is honest—ask him. If he says 'yes,' you know he is crooked."

So use Groucho as a resource and an inspiration. He'll make your friends wonder how is it possible that you've grown so much wittier, seemingly overnight.

"Those are my principles. If you don't like them, I have others."

"Look, if you don't like my parties, you can leave in a huff. If that's too soon, leave in a minute and a huff. If you can't find that, you can leave in a taxi."

"Last night I shot an elephant in my pajamas. How he got in my pajamas I'll never know."

Groucho is regarded as the most popular and well-known of the Marx Brothers. In his later years, he became indispensable to radio and then television fans for his show, *You Bet Your Life*, for which he won the "Best Comedian of the Year" award in 1949. To the end, he remained irascible, unpredictable, irreverent—irrevocably Groucho.

"I have had a perfectly wonderful evening, but this wasn't it."

I find television very educational. Every time someone switches it on I go into another room and read a good book.

GROUCHO MARX

BOOKS-ON-TAPE WE DON'T WANT TO HEAR:

The Communist Manifesto as read by Ronald Reagan

The Torah as read by Louis Farrakhan

The Koran as read by Salman Rushdie

The Anarchist's Cookbook as read by Theodore Kaczinski

How to Win Friends and Influence People as read by Dennis Rodman

Europe on $10 a Day as read by Steve Forbes

The Godfather as read by John Gotti

Uncle Tom's Cabin as read by George Wallace

I'm Okay, You're Okay as read by Rush Limbaugh

Moby Dick as read by Jonah

Crime and Punishment as read by O. J. Simpson

A Tale of Two Cities as read by Ed Koch and Rudy Giuliani

The Gulag Archipelago as read by Josef Stalin

Feynman's Lectures on Physics as read by Dan Quayle

The Joy of Cooking as read by Hannibal Lecter

The Wealth of Nations as read by Fidel Castro

The Book Signing (I didn't know you could read one, let alone write one)

This is not a novel to be tossed aside lightly. It should be thrown with great force.

DOROTHY PARKER

He leads his readers to the latrine and locks them in.

OSCAR WILDE

Great editors do not discover nor produce great authors; great authors create and produce great publishers.

JOHN FARRAR

Movies (Like TV shows, but you have to pay)

43 THINGS YOU WOULD NEVER KNOW WITHOUT THE MOVIES

1. During all police investigations it will be necessary to visit a strip club at least once.

2. If being chased through town, you can usually take cover in a passing St. Patrick's Day parade—at any time of year.

3. All beds have special L-shaped cover sheets which reach up to the armpit level on a woman but only to waist level on the man lying beside her.

4. All grocery shopping bags contain at least one stick of French bread.

5. It's easy for anyone to land a plane providing there is someone in the control tower to talk you down.

6. Once applied, lipstick will never rub off—even while scuba diving.

7. The ventilation system of any building is the perfect hiding place. No one will ever think of looking for you in there and you can travel to any other part of the building you want without difficulty.

8. If you need to reload your gun, you will always have more ammunition, even if you haven't been carrying any before now.

9. You're very likely to survive any battle in any war unless you make the mistake of showing someone a picture of your sweetheart back home.

10. Should you wish to pass yourself off as a German officer, it will not be necessary to speak the language. A German accent will do.

11. If your town is threatened by an imminent natural disaster or killer beast, the mayor's first concern will be the tourist trade.

12. The Eiffel Tower can be seen from any window in Paris.

13. A man will show no pain while taking the most ferocious beating, but will wince when a woman tries to clean his wounds.

14. If a large pane of glass is visible, someone will be thrown through it before long.

15. When paying for a taxi, don't look at your wallet as you take out a bill—just grab at random and hand it over. It will always be exact fare.

16. Interbreeding is genetically possible with any creature from elsewhere in the universe.

17. Kitchens don't have light switches. When entering a kitchen at night, you should open the fridge door and use that light instead.

18. If staying in a haunted house, women should investigate any strange noises while wearing their most revealing underwear.

19. Mothers routinely cook eggs, bacon, and waffles for their family every morning even though their husband and children will never have time to eat them.

20. Cars that crash will almost always get airborne and burst into flames.

21. The Chief of Police will always suspend his star detective—or give him 48 hours to finish the job.

22. A single match will be sufficient to light up a room the size of RFK Stadium.

23. Medieval peasants had perfect teeth.

24. Although in the 20th century it is possible to fire weapons at any object out of our visual range, people of the 23rd century will have lost this technology.

25. Any person waking from a nightmare will sit bolt upright and pant.

26. It is not necessary to say hello or good-bye when beginning or ending phone conversations.

27. Even when driving down a perfectly straight road you must turn the steering wheel vigorously from left to right every few moments.

28. All bombs are fitted with electronic timing devices with large red readouts so you know exactly when they're going to go off.

29. It is always possible to park directly outside the building you are visiting.

30. A detective can only solve a case once he has been suspended from duty.

31. It does not matter if you are heavily outnumbered in a fight involving martial arts—your enemies will wait patiently to attack you one by one by dancing around in a threatening manner until you have knocked out their predecessors.

32. When a person is knocked unconscious by a blow to the head, they will never suffer a concussion or brain damage.

33. No one involved in a car chase, hijacking, explosion, volcanic eruption, or alien invasion will ever go into shock.

34. Police departments give their officers personality tests to make sure they are deliberately assigned a partner who is their total opposite.

35. When they are alone, all foreigners prefer to speak English to each other.

36. You can always find a chainsaw when you need one.

37. Any lock can be picked by a credit card or a paper clip in seconds, unless it's the door to a burning building with a child trapped inside.

38. An electric fence powerful enough to kill a dinosaur will cause no lasting damage to an eight-year-old child.

39. Television news bulletins usually contain a story that affects you personally at that precise moment.

40. The average hotel pool is deep enough for you to survive a fall from any floor.

41. An Asian crime lord will always have a beautiful daughter named either "Jade" or "Lotus Blossom."

42. Traveling between any two points in New York City

will always take you past the Statue of Liberty, Lincoln Center, Washington Square Park, and the New York Public Library.

43. By the 23rd century, everyone in the human race will be beautiful. Humanity will compensate for this by wearing awful clothes.

Be honest: how many times have you gone to a multi-screen theatre complex and just stood there, looking up at the marquee, trying to decide which movie sucked the least?

DENNIS MILLER

MOVIE SEQUELS NOBODY WANTS TO SEE

Commandments 11-20: Moses Strikes Back

Three Men and a Sheep

Rocky 10: Rocky Fights Irregularity

Police Academy IX: Beating a Dead Horse

Babe III: Side of Bacon

Showgirls 2001: A Silicone Odyssey

Dumbo: First Blood

Waterworld 2: The Red Ink Sea

Eliminating Raoul

Home Alone 4: Under House Arrest

Dead Man Rotting

Driving Miss Daisy's Hearse

Pee-Wee's Felonious Adventure

Lawrence of Bolivia

Kickboxer 3: Right in the Groin!

Weekend At Bernie's 3: Starting to Reek

To Kung Fu, Thanks for Everything, David Carradine

Codependence Day

The Englishman Who Drove Into LA a Hugh and Came Out a John

Il Postino Disgruntilo

I went to the cinema. Adults five dollars, and children, two-fifty. I said, "All right, give me two boys and a girl."

STEVEN WRIGHT

The Big Premiere
(I want to thank all the little people...)

A celebrity is any well-known TV or movie star who looks like he spends more than two hours working on his hair.

STEVE MARTIN

There is only one thing in the world worse than being talked about, and that is not being talked about.

OSCAR WILDE

Any fool can criticize—and many of them do.

Television (A thousand channels and nothing to watch)

DAVID HYDE-PIERCE—ROAST OF KELSEY GRAMMER:

When it comes to Kelsey and women, all his taste is in his mouth. Comedy is easy. Kelsey is hard.

Kelsey's dick looks just like him only it has more hair.

HAZELLE GOODMAN—ROAST OF KELSEY GRAMMER:

When it comes to oral sex, let's just say that he has bad Grammer.

CARTOON CHARACTERS WHO MAY BE GAY

Fred Flintstone

His nickname on the Bedrock bowling team is "Twinkle-toes Flintstone." The show's theme song ends, "…we'll have a gay old time!" He wears an orange dress with little triangles on it. He hangs out with Barney far more than Wilma.

Velma (from *Scooby Doo*)

She always tries to sit next to Daphne in the Mystery Machine, she sports an obvious butch haircut, she has broad shoulders, she is always wearing a thick turtle-neck sweater and knee socks, and she never once attempted to shag Shaggy.

Bugs Bunny

He often stands with hand on hip, plays hairdresser in one episode, frequently dresses in drag. He loves to throw on a top hat and tails and to belt out Broadway show tunes with his buddy Daffy—who, it's worth noting, has a lisp.

Popeye

He eats a lot of salad, and wears a sailor suit even though he hasn't been on a ship in years. He does little sailor-dances, dates a flat-chested transvestite named Olive Oyl, and his best friend is named Wimpy.

Batman and Robin

Robin's nickname: Boy Wonder. Batman's real name: Bruce. Both wear tights, they're in great shape, and they like to show each other their "grappling hooks."

Peppermint Patty (from *Peanuts*)

She has a deep, gravely voice, wears pants, not dresses like the other *Peanuts* gals and wears comfortable shoes. She plays a mean game of football, likes to taunt Charlie Brown, and is always hanging out with the androgynous Marcie. Nickname: Sir.

The Pink Panther

Enough said.

AN ACTOR CHANGES HIS NAME

Back in the early 1960s, a television actor went to one of the major networks to audition for a new situation comedy. When he read his lines for the producers, everyone loved his performance. A few days later, the network executives called him in for a meeting.

"We loved your audition," said one of the executives to the actor. "We think you're very funny, and you have a great talent for physical humor. You're just what we're looking for. We have one problem, though. We don't think that your name will work. The country is just not ready for a television star named Penis Van Lesbian."

"But," protested the actor, "I think Penis Van Lesbian is a great name! It's very catchy!" A long discussion followed, during which the network executives and the actor debated the merits of the name Penis Van Lesbian. Finally, the network promised to name the entire show after him, if the actor would only change his name.

The actor agreed, and the program went on to become a huge success. It was called *The Dick Van Dyke Show*.

CHAPTER EIGHT:
BATTLE OF THE SEXES

The debacle that ensued after Eve tempted Adam with that damn apple was only the beginning of this eternal battle between men and women. And the Friars will lay you ten to one that if you called Eve on it today, she'd still tell you that if Adam had communicated better what this tree of knowledge deal was, then we wouldn't be in this pickle. Adam, on the other hand, would still have his mouth too full of apple to give any coherent opinion on the subject.

Try as they might, the two genders will never be at peace. Oh, they might share an occasional truce perhaps but for the most part the battle lines have been drawn and therein lies the premise for some of the funniest jokes ever told. Let's face it, men will never learn how to correctly answer the age-old question, "How do I look?" And women will never be able to stop asking it, knowing full well that they'll never be satisfied with the answer.

Men will always assume women just plain hate sex before they cop to the fact that a beer gut and hairy ass are not an aphrodisiac. Women on the other hand don't seem to understand that while a sexy outfit is the perfect eye candy, they might as well lick themselves if they wear it on Super Bowl Sunday.

The ultimate evidence of this battle is that the Friars didn't even allow women into the Club until almost eighty years after they began—talk about war! This is the chapter about bachelor parties, dumb blondes, and frat boys. From the "games" to the "tests" to the "differences," it's all here. So read up and the next time you consider giving your other half the silent treatment, think about spewing your newfound wit instead.

Whenever someone tells me not to do something I feel that I have to do it. I hate rules. At a Democratic fundraiser, I did stand-up for the National Organization of Women in Washington. It was a big benefit and there were all these hardened feminists who've struggled their entire lives for women's rights. All I wanted to do was get on the stage and say, "So the other day, I was cleaning the toilet while my husband was fucking me up the ass, and I said, 'Honey what's wrong,' and he said, 'You forgot to pick up my dry cleaning,' and then he hit me and I said 'I'm sorry, I love you and I'm nothing without you.'"

JUDY GOLD

The important thing, ladies and gents, is that we all got together tonight and we learned that lesbianism is a beautiful thing. Is there anything more beautiful than two women together? Except for maybe, two women plus me right there at the end....

DOM IRRERA

JOY BEHAR—DANNY AIELLO ROAST:

The Friars Club is just a gay bar without the good-looking guys.

Men (Lord of the remote control)

I like two kinds of men: domestic and foreign.

MAE WEST

Q: Why did God create men?

A: Because a vibrator can't mow the lawn.

Why are women so much more interesting to men than men are to women?

VIRGINIA WOOLF

THE DIFFERENCE BETWEEN MEN AND WOMEN

On the one hand, we'll never experience childbirth; on the other hand, we can open all our own jars.

BRUCE WILLIS

Women want mediocre men, and men are working hard to become as mediocre as possible.

MARGARET MEAD

Women might be able to fake orgasms, but men can fake whole relationships.

SHARON STONE

The idea behind the tuxedo is the woman's point of view that men are all the same, so we might as well dress them that way. That's why a wedding is like the joining together of a beautiful, glowing bride and some guy. The tuxedo is a wedding safety device, created by women because they know that men are undependable. So in case the groom chickens out, everybody just takes one step over, and she marries the next guy.

JERRY SEINFELD

Women love men in a patronizing way, kind of how you love the village idiot.

SUSIE ESSMAN

Q: What is the difference between men and women?

A: A woman wants one man to satisfy her every need... A man wants every woman to satisfy his one need.

Q: How does a man keep his youth?

A: By giving her money, furs and diamonds.

If a man is talking in the forest and there is no woman there to hear him, is he still wrong?

Honesty is the key to a relationship. If you can fake that, you're in.

COURTENEY COX

When women go wrong, men go right after them.

MAE WEST

Q: Why are men like commercials?

A: You can't believe a word they say.

Q: What do you call a handcuffed man?

A: Trustworthy.

Q: How does a man keep his youth?

A: By giving her money, furs, and diamonds.

Q: What is the thinnest book in the world?

A: *What Men Know About Women.*

Q: What's the fastest way to a man's heart?

A: Through his chest with a sharp knife.

Q: Why do men talk so dirty?

A: So they can wash their mouth out with beer.

Q: Why don't men often show their true feelings?

A: Because they don't have any.

Q: Why are there no female astronauts on the moon?

A: It doesn't need cleaning yet.

Q: Why did God create Adam first?

A: So he'd have a chance to talk before Eve came along.

Q: How can you tell a woman with PMS from a woman without PMS?

A: Beats the hell out of me.

Q: Why is psychoanalysis quicker for men than for women?

A: When it's time to go back to childhood, he's already there.

Q: How many men does it take to open a beer?

A: None. It should be opened by the time she brings it to the couch.

Q: Why is it good that there are women astronauts?

A: So that when the crew gets lost in space, at least the women will ask for directions.

RESTROOMS

Men use restrooms for purely biological reasons.

Women use restrooms as social lounges.

Men in a restroom never speak a word to each other.

Women who've never met will leave a restroom giggling together like old friends.

SEX

Women prefer 30–40 minutes of foreplay.

Men prefer 30–40 seconds of foreplay.

Men consider driving back to her place part of the foreplay.

THE TELEPHONE

Men see the telephone as a communications tool. They use it to send short messages to other people.

A woman can visit her girlfriend for two weeks, and upon returning home, call the same friend and they will talk for three hours.

Here's to the man that kisses his wife
And kisses his wife alone.
For there's many a man kisses another man's wife
When he ought to be kissing his own.
And here's to the man who kisses his child
And kisses his child alone.
For there's many a man kisses another man's child
When he thinks he is kissing his own.

Men are like candles,
They gleam and are bright.
Men are like candles,
They shine best at night.
Men are like candles,
They sputter about,
And when they are needed
The darn things go out.

CHARLIE JONES LAUGHBOOK

Billy Crystal

"Face"

"I can't be funny if my feet don't feel right."

Billy Crystal's production company is called "Face." It takes its name from a nickname given to Billy by of one his favorite babysitters, Billie Holliday. Crystal's father managed the Commodore Record store and eventually started the Commodore Jazz record label. Many of the artists at the label became close friends with the family from Long Beach, New York, and some would babysit for the very young Billy. Crystal would often attend live jazz performances, and would suddenly jump up on stage and tap dance along with the music.

But like many young New Yorkers, Billy dreamed of playing shortstop for the Yankees. So he enrolled in Marshall University, in West Virginia, on a baseball scholarship. Unfortunately, the school dissolved the program after his first year. So Billy came home for a brief stint at Nassau Community College, eventually going on to NYU, where he studied film and television directing under the guidance of Martin Scorsese. After receiving his degree, Billy married his college sweetheart, Janice, and moved back to Long Beach where he worked as a substitute teacher. When he wasn't teaching, Crystal was developing his standup act and eventually started performing at comedy clubs in New York City.

"I'm completely obsessive. I haven't slept since 1948 worrying about whether my shtick is going to be funny or not."

Billy, Janice, and daughter Jennifer (born in 1973) moved to Los Angeles where Billy worked his act at The Comedy Store. One night at the club, legendary TV producer Norman Lear spotted Billy and that was all Crystal needed. Lear placed Billy into guest spots on *All in the Family* and the short-lived *Howard Cosell Show*. But Billy's big break came when Norman Lear handed him the plum role of Jodie Dallas on *Soap*. Billy became television's first openly gay character.

"I had a dream that Connie Chung is doing a newscast about my death and they show a clip from Soap.*"*

Comedienne Joan Rivers was so charmed by his performance as the acerbic Jodie that she tapped him to star in her 1978 directorial-debut film *Rabbit Test*, in which Crystal played a man who discovers that he is pregnant in the wake of a one-night-stand atop a pinball table.

Unfortunately, Crystal's film career didn't immediately skyrocket. He returned to New York in the early '80s and kept his career moving forward by appearing in cable specials, TV movies, and TV series. He kept his stand-up skills in shape by touring nightclubs and college campuses. He was becoming well known for his impersonations of Sammy Davis Jr. and Fernando Lamas ("You look mahhh-hhvelous!"). He was invited to join the cast of *Saturday Night Live* in 1984. During his one season on the show, Crystal emerged as the most popular cast member and earned an Emmy nomination in the Best Individual Performance category.

"Did you ever reach a point in your life, where you say to yourself, 'This is the best I'm ever going to look, the best I'm ever going to feel, the best I'm ever going to do,' and it ain't that great?" (from *City Slickers*)

Since then, Crystal has turned in many memorable performances including his role as Morty the Mime in *This Is Spinal Tap* and Miracle Max in *The Princess Bride*. He starred in the comedy *Throw Momma from the Train* before achieving star status in the romantic comedy *When Harry Met Sally* and the mid-life-crisis comedy *City Slickers*. He returned to Los Angeles, where he capitalized on his screen success by writing, directing, producing, and starring in *Mr. Saturday Night*, a bittersweet and heartfelt film about the six-decade career of a stand-up comic.

"Change is such hard work."

In 1998, Crystal scored a hit in the role of a cynical, two-bit talent agent who at first exploits then ultimately befriends his good-natured, oversized client (played by Washington Wizards star Gheorghe Muresan) in the Crystal-produced comedy *My Giant*. The following year, he starred as a psychiatrist who reluctantly treats a Mafia don (Robert De Niro) in the mega-hit comedy *Analyze This*.

Aside from hosting the Oscars six times, Crystal has united every year since 1986 with fellow comedian-actors Robin Williams and Whoopi Goldberg to co-host the popular "HBO's Comic Relief" benefit. Crystal also produced and directed the movie *61** for HBO, a story very close to his heart. The film recounts the summer of 1961 when two Yankees, Mickey Mantle and Roger Maris, captured the nation's attention by chasing Babe Ruth's single-season home run record.

"When you realize you want to spend the rest of your life with somebody, you want the rest of your life to start as soon as possible." (from *When Harry Met Sally*)

High Holy Days (Poker night, Super Bowl Sunday, and the Final Four)

Q: Why do men pay more than women for car insurance?

A: Because women don't get blowjobs while driving.

Q: What did the left ball say to the right ball?

A: Don't talk to the guy in the middle—he's a dick.

MEN ARE LIKE...

Men are like laxatives: They irritate the shit out of you.

Men are like bananas: The older they get, the less firm they are.

Men are like vacations: They never seem to be long enough.

Men are like bank machines: Once they withdraw they lose interest.

Men are like weather: Nothing can be done to change either one of them.

Men are like blenders: You need one but you're not sure why.

Men are like cement: After getting laid, they take a long time to get hard.

Men are like chocolate bars: Sweet, smooth, and they usually head right for your hips.

Men are like coffee: The best ones are rich, warm, and can keep you up all night long.

Men are like commercials: You can't believe a word they say.

Men are like department stores: Their clothes should always be half off.

Men are like government bonds: They take so long to mature.

Men are like horoscopes: They always tell you what to do and are usually wrong.

Men are like lawn mowers: If you're not pushing one around, then you are riding it.

Men are like mascara: They usually run at the first sign of emotion.

Men are like popcorn: They satisfy you, but only for a little while.

Men are like snowstorms: You never know when one is coming, how long it will last or how many inches you'll get.

A man is driving up a steep mountain road.

A woman is driving down the same road.

As they pass each other, the woman leans out her window and yells, "Pig!"

The man immediately leans out and replies, "Bitch!"

They each continue on their way and, as the man rounds the next corner, he crashes into a pig in the middle of the road and dies.

ADVANTAGES OF BEING MALE

Your ass is never a factor in a job interview.

Your orgasms are real. Always.

Your last name stays put.

Wedding plans take care of themselves.

Chocolate is just another snack.

You can be President.

You can wear a white shirt to a water-theme park.

Foreplay is optional.

You never feel compelled to stop a friend from getting laid.

Car mechanics tell you the truth.

You don't give a rats ass if someone doesn't notice your new haircut.

The world is your urinal.

Same work...more pay.

Wrinkles add character.

You don't retain water.

People never glance at your chest when talking to you.

Hot wax never comes near your pubic area.

You never have to drive to another gas station because this one is "too icky."

THE MANLY WISDOM OF WILL ROGERS

Never slap a man who's chewing tobacco.

Never kick a cow chip on a hot day.

Never miss a good chance to shut up.

Always drink upstream from the herd.

If you find yourself in a hole, stop digging.

There are three kinds of men: The ones who learn by reading. The few who learn by observation. The rest of them have to pee on the electric fence for themselves.

Good judgment comes from experience, and a lot of that comes from bad judgment.

If you're riding ahead of the herd, take a look back every now and then to make sure it's still there.

Letting the cat outta the bag is a whole lot easier then putting it back.

After eating an entire bull, a mountain lion felt so good he started roaring. He kept it up until a hunter came along and shot him...The moral: When you're full of bull, keep your mouth shut!

WHAT MEN WANT FROM WOMEN:

1. We want you to understand that we don't give a shit about clothes, all right? Yours *or* ours.

2. Don't talk to us while the television is on, all right? Very simple: Television is off, we talk. Television is on, we don't talk.

3. Would it kill you to watch *The Godfather* with me for the 57th time?

4. Hey I'm sorry, but some of us see a beautiful sunset and think, "You know, I betcha my accountant is boning me up the ass."

5. Don't ask us to cry. As much as you say you want us to cry, you don't really want us to cry. You hate it when we cry. I've tried crying in front of my wife. She enjoyed it for about thirty seconds and then started thinking, "Why in the fuck did I marry this hamster?"

6. Be patient. Hold us. Love us unconditionally. Help us out of this testosterone-induced fog we dwell in, and lead us into the light.

7. Or if that's asking too much, how's about a big, sloppy blowjob once in awhile?

They say...love thy neighbor as thy self. What am I supposed to do? Jerk him off, too?

RODNEY DANGERFIELD

Q: Who is the most popular man in a nudist colony?

A: The one who can carry two large coffees and a dozen donuts.

Q: Who is the most popular woman in a nudist colony?

A: The one who can eat the last two donuts.

"I can't find it."

Really means, "It didn't fall into my outstretched hands, so I'm completely clueless."

"That's women's work."

Really means, "It's dirty, difficult and thankless."

"Will you marry me?"

Really means, "Both my roommates have moved out, I can't find the washer, and there is no more peanut butter."

"It's a guy thing."

Really means, "There is no rational thought pattern connected with it, and you have no chance at all of making it logical."

"Can I help with dinner?"

Really means, "Why isn't it already on the table?"

"It would take too long to explain."

Really means, "I have no idea how it works."

"I'm getting more exercise lately."

Really means, "The batteries in the remote are dead."

"We're going to be late."

Really means, "Now I have a legitimate excuse to drive like a maniac."

"Take a break, honey, you're working too hard."

Really means, "I can't hear the game over the vacuum cleaner."

"That's interesting, dear."

Really means, "Are you still talking?"

"Honey, we don't need material things to prove our love."

Really means, "I forgot our anniversary again."

"You expect too much of me."

Really means, "You want me to stay awake."

"It's really a good movie."

Really means, "It's got guns, knives, fast cars, and naked women."

"You know how bad my memory is."

Really means, "I remember the words to the theme song of *F Troop*, the address of the first girl I kissed, the Vehicle Identification Number of every car I've ever owned, but I forgot your birthday."

"I was just thinking about you, and got you these roses."

Really means, "The girl selling them on the corner was a real babe, wearing a thong."

"Oh, don't fuss. I just cut myself. It's no big deal."

Really means, "I have actually severed a limb, but will bleed to death before I admit I'm hurt."

"I do help around the house."

Really means, "I once threw a dirty towel near the laundry basket."

"Hey, I've got reasons for what I'm doing."

Really means, "I sure hope I think of some pretty soon."

"What did I do this time?"

Really means, "What did you catch me doing?"

"She's one of those rabid feminists."

Really means, "She refused to make my coffee."

"I heard you."

Really means, "I haven't the foggiest clue what you just said, and am hoping desperately that I can fake it well enough so that you don't spend the next three days yelling at me."

"You really look terrific in that outfit."

Really means, "Please don't try on another outfit. I'm starving."

"I brought you a present."

Really means, "It was free ice-scraper night at the ball/hockey game."

"I missed you."

Really means, "I can't find my sock drawer, the kids are hungry and we are out of toilet paper."

"I'm not lost. I know exactly where we are."

Really means, "No one will ever see us alive again."

"This relationship is getting too serious."

Really means, "I like you as much as I like my truck."

"We share the housework."

Really means, "I make the messes. She cleans them up."

"I don't need to read the instructions."

Really means, "I am perfectly capable of screwing it up without printed help."

A businessman boards a flight and is lucky enough to be seated next to an absolutely gorgeous woman. They exchange brief hellos and he notices she is reading a manual of sexual statistics.

He asks her about it and she replies, "This is a very interesting book. It says that American Indians, on average, have the longest penises and Polish men have the biggest average diameters. By the way, my name is Jill. What's yours?"

He coolly replies, "Tonto Kawalski. Nice to meet you."

Q: What's the useless flesh attached to a penis called?

A: A man.

Q: What's the best way to kill a man?

A: Put a naked woman and a six-pack in front of him. Then tell him to pick only one.

Q: What do men and pantyhose have in common?

A: They either cling, run, or don't fit right in the crotch!

Bachelor Party (Does anyone have change for a $20?)

WHAT MEN WOULD DO IF THEY HAD A VAGINA

Immediately go shopping for zucchini and cucumbers.

Squat over a hand-held mirror for an hour and a half.

See if it's really possible to launch a Ping-Pong ball twenty feet.

Cross their legs without rearranging their crotch.

Get picked up in a bar in less than ten minutes.

Have consecutive multiple orgasms and still be ready for more without sleeping first.

Sit on the edge of the bed and pray for breasts, too.

GENTLEMAN QUIZ

1. In the company of feminists, coitus should be referred to as:

a. Lovemaking.

b. Screwing.

c. The pigskin bus pulling into tuna town.

2. You should make love to a woman for the first time only after you've both shared:

a. Your views about what you expect from a sexual relationship.

b. Your blood test results.

c. Five tequila slammers.

3. You time your orgasm so that:

a. Your partner climaxes first.

b. You both climax simultaneously.

c. You don't miss Sports Center.

4. Passionate, spontaneous sex on the kitchen floor is:

a. Healthy, creative love play.

b. Not the sort of thing your wife/girlfriend would ever agree to.

c. Not the sort of thing your wife/girlfriend need ever find out about.

5. Spending the whole night cuddling a woman you've just had sex with is:

a. The best part of the experience.

b. The second best part of the experience.

c. $100 extra.

6. Your girlfriend says she's gained five pounds in the last month. You tell her that it is:

a. No concern of yours.

b. Not a problem—she can join your gym.

c. A conservative estimate.

7. You think today's sensitive, caring man is:

a. A myth.

b. An oxymoron.

c. A moron.

8. Foreplay is to sex as:

a. Appetizer is to entrée.

b. Priming is to painting.

c. A queue is to an amusement park ride.

9. Which of the following are you most likely to find yourself saying at the end of a relationship?

a. "I hope we can still be friends."

b. "I'm not in right now. Please leave a message after the tone…"

c. "Welcome to Dumpsville. Population: You."

10. A woman who is uncomfortable watching you masturbate:

a. Probably needs a little more time before she can cope with that sort of intimacy.

b. Is uptight and a waste of time.

c. Shouldn't have sat next to you on the bus in the first place.

If you answered "a" more than seven times, check your pants to make sure you really are a man.

If you answered "b" more than seven times, check into therapy, you're still a little confused.

If you answered "c" more than seven times, call me up. Let's go drinking.

A man is never drunk if he can lay on the floor without holding on.

JOE E. LEWIS

The Confirmed Bachelor
(Just say it ... he's gay)

Q: What are the three things homosexuals like most?

A: To eat, drink, and be Mary.

Q: How do you separate men from boys in San Francisco?

A: With a crowbar.

Q: What's a hobosexual?

A: A bum fuck.

Q: How do we know that Adam was gay?

A: Because he had Eve and an apple, and he ate the apple.

Once upon a time there was a frog who lived in a lake all by himself. He had been given special powers by a local witch.

One day he finally ventured out of the lake to get his first glimpse of the world outside. The first thing he saw was a bear chasing a rabbit and so he called out to them and asked them to stop. Then he said to them, "I am a magical frog and since you are the first two animals I have ever seen, I am going to grant you each three wishes. You will take turns using them and you have to use them now."

The bear (being greedy) went first. "I would like for every bear in this forest to be female except for me." A magical sound, and it was done.

Then the rabbit. "I would like a helmet." This confused both the frog and the bear, but, after a magical sound, there was a helmet.

It was the bear's turn again. "I would like for every bear in the neighboring forest to be female." A magical sound, and it was done.

The rabbit went again. "I would like a motorcycle." Both the frog and the bear wondered why the rabbit didn't just ask for a lot of money with which he could buy himself a motorcycle but, after a magical sound, there was a motorcycle.

The bear took his last wish. "I would like for all the bears in the world to be female except for me." A magical sound, and it was done.

The rabbit then put on his helmet, started up the motorcycle, and said "I wish the bear was gay" and took off like a bat out of hell!

Women (Forget the "B" word and don't even <u>think</u> about the "C" word)

A woman without a man is like a fish without a bicycle.

GLORIA STEINEM

Here's to the women that I've loved and all the ones I've kissed.
As for regrets, I just have one; that's all the ones I've missed.
Oh, women's faults are many, us men have only two:
Every single thing we say, and everything we do.

HOW TO ANNOY A MAN

Do not say what you mean, ever.

Be ambiguous. Always.

Cry. Often.

Bring up how good your old boyfriend was in bed.

Stash feminine products in their cars.

Look them in the eye and laugh.

Discuss your period with them.

Have your friends discuss their periods with them.

Discuss how you and your friends all have your periods at the same time—isn't that funny?

Gather female friends and dance to "I Will Survive" while they are present.

Sing all the words. Loud.

Constantly ask them if your butt looks fat.

Criticize the way they dress.

Act upset, and when they ask you what's wrong, get mad at them for not knowing.

Try to get them to dance to "I Will Survive."

Whenever there is silence, ask them, "What are you thinking?"

Tell them you want them to be "more open."

Q: What did the left boob say to the right boob?

A: "Quit hanging so low or people are going to think we're nuts!"

I saw a woman wearing a sweatshirt with Guess on it. I said, "thyroid problem?"

ARNOLD SCHWARZENEGGER

Don't give a woman advice. One should never give a woman anything she can't wear in the evening.

OSCAR WILDE

A woman went into a pet shop and said to the man, "I want a parrot, but sell me one that definitely talks."

The man sold her a parrot, saying "This one definitely talks."

The woman took him home, set the cage up on a table and said to the parrot, "Okay, talk."

The parrot said, "Show me your tits." The woman was outraged. So she put him in the refrigerator. After a while, she took him out and said, "So talk."

Again, the parrot said, "Show me your tits." The woman put him in the fridge for a longer time, but again the same thing happened. She was quite annoyed. This time she put him in the freezer.

There was a turkey in the freezer. The parrot said to the turkey, "How did *you* get here? Did you ask for a blowjob?"

FINALLY A BARBIE I CAN RELATE TO!

At long last, here are some *new* Barbie dolls to celebrate the fact that we aren't as young as we used to be:

Bifocals Barbie

Comes with her own set of blended-lens fashion frames in six wild colors (half-frames too!), neck chain, and large-print editions of *Vogue* and *Martha Stewart Living*.

Hot Flash Barbie

Press Barbie's bellybutton and watch her face turn red while tiny drops of perspiration appear on her forehead. Comes with hand-held fan and tiny tissues.

Facial Hair Barbie

As Barbie's hormone levels shift, see her whiskers grow. Available with teensy tweezers and magnifying mirror.

Flabby Arms Barbie

Hide Barbie's droopy triceps with these new, roomier-sleeved gowns. Good news on the tummy front, too— muumuus with tummy-support panels are included.

Bunion Barbie

Years of disco dancing in stiletto heels have definitely taken their toll on Barbie's dainty arched feet. Soothe her sores with the pumice stone and plasters, then slip on soft terry mules.

No-More-Wrinkles Barbie

Erase those pesky crow's-feet and lip lines with a tube of Skin Sparkle-Spackle, from Barbie's own line of exclusive age-blasting cosmetics.

Soccer Mom Barbie

All that experience as a cheerleader is really paying off as Barbie dusts off her old high school megaphone to root for Babs and Ken, Jr. Comes with minivan in robin-egg blue or white, and cooler filled with doughnut holes and fruit punch.

Midlife Crisis Barbie

It's time to ditch Ken. Barbie needs a change, and Alonzo (her personal trainer) is just what the doctor ordered, along with Prozac. They're hopping in her new red Miata and heading for the Napa Valley to open a B&B. Includes a real tape of "Breaking Up is Hard to Do."

Divorced Barbie

Sells for $199.99. Comes with Ken's house, Ken's car, and Ken's boat.

Recovery Barbie

Too many parties have finally caught up with the ultimate party girl. Now she does Twelve Steps instead of dance steps. Clean and sober, she's going to meetings religiously. Comes with a little copy of *The Big Book* and a six-pack of Diet Coke.

Post-Menopausal Barbie

This Barbie wets her pants when she sneezes, forgets where she puts things, and cries a lot. She is sick and tired of Ken sitting on the couch watching the tube, clicking through the channels. Comes with Depends and Kleenex. As a bonus this year, the book *Getting In Touch with Your Inner Self* is included.

Ever notice how all of women's problems start with MEN?

MENtal illness, MENstrual cramps, MENtal breakdown, MENopause. And when you have real trouble, it's HISterectomy!

A woman who strives to be like a man lacks ambition.

The Women's Movement hasn't change my sex life at all. It wouldn't dare.

ZSA ZSA GABOR

IT IS GOOD TO BE A WOMAN

We got off the *Titanic* first.

We can scare male bosses with mysterious gynecological disorder excuses.

Taxis stop for us.

We don't look like a frog in a blender when dancing.

No fashion faux pas we make could ever rival the Speedo.

We don't have to pass gas to amuse ourselves.

If we forget to shave, no one has to know.

We can congratulate our teammate without ever touching her rear.

We don't have to reach down every so often to make sure our privates are there.

We have the ability to dress ourselves.

We can talk to people of the opposite sex without having to picture them naked.

If we marry someone 20 years younger, we're aware that we look like an idiot.

We know that there are times when chocolate really can solve all our problems.

We'll never regret piercing our ears.

We can fully assess a person just by looking at his/her shoes.

We can make comments about how silly men are in their presence because they aren't listening anyway.

INSECTS

A boy and his father were playing catch in the front yard when the boy saw a honeybee. He ran over and stomped it.

"That was a honey bee," his father said, "one of our friends. For stomping him, you will do without honey for a week."

Later the boy saw a butterfly, so he ran over and stomped it.

"That was a butterfly," his father said, "one of our friends, and for stomping him you will do without butter for a week."

The next morning the family sat down for breakfast. The boy ate his plain toast with no honey or butter.

Suddenly a cockroach ran out from under the stove. His mother stomped it.

The boy looked at his father and said, "Are you going to tell her, Dad, or should I?"

Q: What's the best thing to come out of a dick?

A: The wrinkles.

Seems God was just about done creating the universe, but he had two extra things left in his bag of creations. So, he decided to split them between Adam and Eve. He told the couple that one of the things he had to give away was the ability to stand up while urinating. "It's a very handy thing," God told the couple who he found under an apple tree. "I was wondering if either one of you wanted the ability."

Adam jumped up and blurted, "Oh, give that to me! I'd love to! Please, oh please, oh please, let me have that ability. It'd be so great! When I'm out working in the garden or naming the animals, I could just stand there and let it fly! It'd be so cool, I could write my name in the sand. Oh, please God, let it be me who you give that gift to, let me stand and pee, oh please!"

On and on he went, like an excited little boy who...well... had to pee.

Eve just smiled and told God that if Adam really wanted that so badly, that he should have it. It seemed to be the sort of thing that would make him happy, and she really wouldn't mind if Adam were the one given this ability. And so, Adam was given the ability to control the direction of his micturition while in a vertical position. He was so happy, he celebrated by wetting down the bark on the tree nearest him, laughing with delight all the while. And it was good.

"Fine," God said, looking back into his bag of leftover gifts, "What's left in here?"

"Oh yes," he said, "Multiple orgasms..."

Q: Why do men like smart women?

A: Opposites attract.

Q: How do men define a "50/50" relationship?

A: We cook—they eat; we clean—they dirty; we iron—they wrinkle.

Q: How do you get a man to stop biting his nails?

A: Make him wear shoes.

Q: What did God say after creating man?

A: I can do so much better.

Q: What's the smartest thing a man can say?

A: "My wife says..."

Q: Why are all dumb blonde jokes one-liners?

A: So men can understand them.

Q: Why do female black widow spiders kill the males after mating?

A: To stop the snoring before it starts.

Q: Why do men need instant replay on TV sports?

A: Because after 30 seconds they forget what happened.

Q: Why does it take 100-million sperm to fertilize one egg?

A: Because none of them will stop to ask for directions.

MENOPAUSE

When a woman reaches menopause, she goes through a variety of complicated emotional, psychological, and biological changes. The nature and degree of the changes varies with the individual. Menopause in a man provokes a uniform reaction. He buys aviator glasses, a snazzy French cap and leather driving gloves, and goes shopping for an expensive foreign sports car and a mistress half his age.

Blondes (How many does it take...?)

A young brunette goes to the doctor's office and tells him that her body hurts wherever she touches it. "Impossible," says the doctor. "Show me."

She takes her finger and pushes on her elbow and screams in agony. She then pushes on her knee and screams, pushes on her ankle and screams...and so it goes.

No matter where she touches herself, her agony is apparent. The doctor says, "You're not really a brunette, are you? You're really a BLONDE."

She sheepishly admits that indeed she is a blonde. "I thought so," he says. "Your finger is broken."

A blonde driving a car got lost in a snowstorm. She didn't panic however, because she remembered what her dad had once told her. "If you ever get stuck in a snowstorm, just wait for a snow plow to come by and follow it."

Sure enough, pretty soon a snow plow came by, and she started to follow it. She followed the plow for about forty-five minutes. Finally the driver of the truck got out and asked her what she was doing, and she explained what her dad had told her.

The driver nodded and said, "Well, I'm done with the Wal-Mart parking lot, do you want to follow me over to K-Mart now?

Q: What do you call a blonde driving a car?

A: An air bag.

Q: How are blondes and postage stamps alike?

A: You lick'em, stick'em, and send them away.

Q: Why do blondes like tilt steering wheels?

A: More head room.

Q: What do you call two blondes in the freezer?

A: Frosted flakes.

Q: How do you get a twinkle in a blonde's eye?

A: Shine a flashlight in her ears.

Q: What do you call a blonde with half a brain?

A: Gifted.

Q: How does a blonde hemophiliac cure herself?

A: With acupuncture.

Q: Why don't blondes breast-feed their babies?

A: It hurts too much to boil the nipples.

Q: Why did eighteen blondes go to the R-rated movie?

A: They heard that those under 17 were not admitted.

Q: What's blonde, brunette, blonde, brunette...?

A: A blonde doing cartwheels.

Q: What do you call a blonde on a college campus?

A: A visitor.

Q: What do you call a brunette between two blondes?

A: An interpreter.

Q: Why do blondes write "TGIF" on their sneakers?

A: To remind them that "Toes Go In First."

Q: Why did the blonde have a square chest?

A: She forgot to take the Kleenex out of the box.

Q: How did the blonde break her arm while raking leaves?

A: She fell out of the tree.

Q: What do you call 22 blondes standing ear to ear?

A: A wind tunnel.

Q: What do blondes and beer bottles have in common?

A: Both are empty from the neck up.

Q: What do a UFO and a "smart" blonde have in common?

A: You keep hearing about them, but you never see one.

Q: What do you have when three blondes are in a corner?

A: An air pocket.

Q: What's the first thing a blonde does in the morning?

A: Introduce herself.

Q: Why don't blondes eat pickles?

A: Because they always get their head stuck in the jar.

Q: Why did the blonde put ice in her boyfriend's condom?

A: To keep the swelling down.

Q: What's the quickest way to get into a blonde's pants?

A: Pick them up off the floor and put them on.

Q: Why should you keep a blonde on the job seven days a week?

A: Takes too much to retrain them every Monday.

Q: Why didn't the blonde have any ice cubes at her party?

A: She lost the recipe.

Q: How can you tell when a blonde has used your computer?

A: There's whiteout all over the screen

Q: Why do blondes wash their hair in the kitchen?

A: Because that's where you're supposed to wash vegetables.

Q: How do you kill a blonde?

A: Put a scratch-and-sniff sticker at the bottom of the pool.

Q: What goes "Vroom-screeech, vroom-screech, vroom-screech"?

A: A blonde at a flashing red light.

Q: What did the blonde say when she opened her box of Cheerios?

A: "Oh, look, doughnut seeds."

Q: How can you tell if a blonde has been using your lawn mower?

A: Your green "welcome" mat is ripped to shreds.

Q: What's the difference between blondes and the Bermuda triangle?

A: Blondes swallow more seamen.

Q: What happened when the blonde got locked in the car?

A: Her blond boyfriend had to use a clothes hanger to get her out.

Q: Why did the blonde resolve to have only three children?

A: Because she read that one child out of every four born is Chinese.

Q: Did you hear about the blonde who won the gold medal at the Olympics?

A: She had it bronzed.

Q: Did you hear about the new paint by Benjamin Moore?

A: It's called "blonde." It's not real bright but it spreads real easy.

Q: Why was the blonde so happy when she finished her puzzle in six months?

A: It said on the box 2–4 years!

Q: How do you confuse a blonde?

A: Give her a bag of M&Ms and tell her to put them in alphabetical order.

Q: What do you call a group of blondes standing in a circle, holding hands?

A: A dope ring.

Q: How did the blonde respond when the job interviewer said, "Spell your name?"

A: Y-O-U-R N-A-M-E.

Q: If a blonde and a brunette fell out of an airplane, who would land first?

A: The brunette, the blonde would stop to ask for directions.

Q: Why don't blondes like making Kool-Aid?

A: They can't figure out how to get two quarts of water into the little package.

Q: Why did the blonde couple freeze to death in their car at a drive-in theater?

A: They went to see *Closed for the Winter*.

A blonde went to her mailbox several times before it was even time for the mailman to make his rounds. A neighbor noticed her repeated trips to the curb and asked if she was waiting for a special delivery.

Her reply, "My computer keeps telling me I have mail."

A police officer stops a blonde for speeding and asks her very nicely if he can see her license.

She replies in a huff, "I wish you guys could get your act together. Just yesterday you take away my license and then today you expect me to show it to you."

BLOND GUYS!!!

A blond guy gets home early from work and hears strange noises coming from the bedroom. He rushes upstairs to find his wife naked on the bed, sweating and panting. "What's up?" he says.

"I'm having a heart attack," cries the woman.

He rushes downstairs to grab the phone, but just as he's dialing, his four-year-old son comes up and says, "Daddy! Daddy! Uncle Ted's hiding in your closet and he's got no clothes on!"

The guy slams the phone down and storms upstairs into the bedroom, past his screaming wife, and rips open the wardrobe door. Sure enough, there is his brother, totally naked, cowering on the closet floor. "You rotten bastard," says the blond husband, "my wife's having a heart attack and you're running around naked scaring the kids!"

I had a spiritual revelation yesterday. I was wandering along in Central Park in the afternoon, admiring the scenery, and thinking about what a good wife I have, how good she is to me, and how fortunate I am to have her. I looked up at the sky and asked, "God, why did you make my wife so kind-hearted?"

Suddenly there was a rumble, then a voice said, "So you could love her, my son."

I was startled and could hardly believe what I was hearing. Realizing that this was truly a special moment, I decided to take full advantage of it. I pressed on further by asking, "Why did you make her so good-looking?"

"So you could love her, my son." The voice in the sky responded.

"Why did you make her such a good cook?" I inquired.

"So you could love her, my son," the Lord answered with a bit of irritation in his voice.

I thought about this for a moment, then said, "I don't mean to seem ungrateful or anything, but why did you make her a dumb blonde?"

"So she could love you, my son."

Now who said God doesn't have a sense of humor?

A blonde went into a world-wide message center to send a message to her mother overseas. When the man told her it would cost $300, she exclaimed, "I don't have any money. But I'd do *anything* to get a message to my mother."

The man arched an eyebrow. "Anything?" he asked. "Yes, yes, anything" the blonde promised.

"Well, then, just follow me," said the man as he walked towards the next room.

The blonde did as she was told and followed the man.

"Come in and close the door" the man said. She did. He then said, "Now get down on your knees." She did. "Now take down my zipper." She did. "Now go ahead...take it out..." he said. She reached in and grabbed it with both hands...then paused.

The man closed his eyes and whispered, "Well...go ahead."

The blonde slowly brought her mouth closer to it...and while holding it close to her lips, tentatively said, "Hello ...Mom? Can you hear me?"

Baby Showers (Better you than me)

I'm trying to decide whether to have children or not to have children. My time is running out. I know I want to have children while my parents are still young enough to take care of them.

RITA RUDNER

Bridal Showers (Better me than you)

REASONS WHY GOD CREATED EVE

God worried that Adam would always be lost in the garden because men hate to ask directions.

God knew that Adam would one day need someone to hand him the TV remote. (Men don't want to see what's on television, they want to see what else is on!)

God knew that Adam would never buy a new fig leaf when his wore out and would therefore need Eve to get one for him.

God knew that Adam would never remember which night was garbage night.

God knew that if the world was to be populated, men would never be able to handle childbearing.

As "Keeper of the Garden," Adam would never remember where he put his tools.

When God finished the creation of Adam, he stepped back, scratched his head and said, "I *know* I can do better than that!"

TO THE BRIDE-TO-BE

We've been friends through thick and thin,
Through every type of weather,
So we don't care if you wear white to your wedding,
Even though you've been living together.

Funny, isn't it? You never hear of a man being asked how he combines marriage with a career.

Bachelorette Party (What are we supposed to do at these things again?)

IF YOU EVER HEAR THE FOLLOWING, SHE'S LYING

It happens to all men.

Size doesn't matter.

I'm happy as long as *you* came.

Great, I'd love to hang out with your mother.

I think you're so smart.

Don't be silly, I like taking the bus.

I could never be with another man.

Small jewelry is pretty.

THINGS YOU'LL NEVER HEAR A WOMAN SAY
(REGARDLESS IF SHE IS LYING)

Go ahead, leave the seat up, I love surprises.

I think hairy butts are really sexy.

Please don't throw that t-shirt away, I love the smell, and the holes.

This diamond is way too big.

I won't even put my lips on that thing unless I get to swallow.

Wow! It really is fourteen inches!

Would it distract you if I went down on you while you're driving?

Let's stay at that cheap hotel on the highway instead of the Four Seasons, that way we can spend the money we save on beer.

Does this make my butt look too small?

I'm wrong, you must be right again.

I think belching is really sexy.

Why don't you go out with your friends to a strip club?

It's so romantic when you cum on my face. Do it again.

Your buddies tell the best stories. Let's have them over again tonight.

Just because she slept with the whole team doesn't make her a slut. I think she's nice.

Oh yeah, any hole you want.

Things you'll never hear a woman say: My, what an attractive scrotum!

PATRICIA ARQUETTE

Here's to the men we love.
Here's to the men who love us
And if the men we love don't love us,
Then forget the men. Here's to us.

Chastity is curable, if detected early.

The Confirmed Bachelorette (You can tell by the shoes)

A woman visits her gynecologist and during the course of her examination, the doctor comments on the fact that she has a large *Y* on her chest.

"Oh yes," she replies. "That's because my boyfriend goes to Yale and every time we do it, the *Y* makes an indentation on my chest."

Later that same week, the doctor is examining another woman, this one with a large *H* on her chest. The doctor asks how she got this.

"Oh, my boyfriend goes to Harvard, and every time we do it, he leaves an *H* imprint on my chest."

A little later, a third woman comes in to be examined and when she disrobes, the doctor notices a large *W* on her chest.

"Let me guess," He says. "Your boyfriend goes to Wisconsin and every time you do it, the *W* makes an impression on your chest."

"No," she answers. "My girlfriend goes to Michigan."

Q: Why can't lesbians wear makeup when they're on a diet?

A: Because it's too hard to eat Jenny Craig when you have Mary Kay on your face.

Q: What does a lesbian bring on the second date?

A: A U-Haul.

Q: What do you call a lesbian dinosaur?

A: Lick-a-lotta-pus.

Q: What do you call a lesbian with long fingers?

A: Well-hung.

CHAPTER NINE:
POLITICS AND POLITICAL EVENTS

If death and taxes are the two topics that guarantee an argument—although, it's a no-brainer to figure out that the Friars find them equally hilarious—then politics can literally assassinate an entire friendship. Because people tend to get so passionate about this touchy subject, it's important to diffuse the situation with a little laughter.

Whether we need to learn to laugh at ourselves or try to laugh at the views of others, the one constant is keeping our sense of humor intact, in spite of the intensity of our political convictions. Everyone and everything is up for grabs and the jokes are there for the taking. Pick a topic, any topic—the Presidency, congress, elections, foreign policy, domestic upheaval—there's plenty to choose from and they're all here in this chapter.

If you need a quick joke about decision-making to open up that PTA meeting (before you get on to that condom discussion); or a toast for your son-in-law's inauguration as Town Mayor (it figures, of course, that he'd be a member of that OTHER party); or a little quote for your son to say in his acceptance speech as secretary of the student council (what, exactly, does he do in that capacity, anyway?) you need to look no further than this chapter.

It all fits and it's all here. These quips will even prepare you if you're called to appear on Larry King (yeah, like that will happen) or on *Politically Incorrect* (now that could happen—they'll take anyone). So good luck throwing your hat in the joke-pool portion of the political arena.

Patty Hearst is also here—the second time she's been held against her will.

GREAT MOMENTS IN POLITICS

"I resent your insinuendoes."

"No man is an Ireland."

"If Lincoln were alive today, he'd roll over in his grave."

"Candidly, I cannot answer that. The question is too suppository."

"I deny the allegations, and I defy the allegators."

"If somebody's gonna stab me in the back, I want to be there."

"When you're talking to me, keep your mouth shut."

"I hate to confuse myself with the facts."

"My knowledge is no match for his ignorance."

Q: Why are politicians proof of reincarnation?

A: You just can't get that screwed up in one lifetime.

How can you call the mayor a cheap politician? He's cost the town a fortune!

People who don't know why America is the "land of promise" should be here during an election campaign.

One candidate was so dull, there's a rumor he had a charisma bypass!

I'm wondering if a certain politician is on the take. He's learned how to say "For me?" in twelve languages!

THE DEMOCRATS' EMBLEM

Democrats announced today that they are changing their emblem from a donkey to a condom because it more clearly reflects their party's political stance.

A condom stands up to inflation, halts production, discourages cooperation, protects a bunch of dicks and gives a sense of security while screwing others.

Politics is comprised of two sides and a fence.

Politicians like to stand on their records. That way, nobody can see them.

A politician was speaking to a large gathering. Concluding, he said, "My opponent has been stealing you blind for eight years. Give me a chance!"

Politicians make strange bedfellows because they share the same bunk.

Meet the Pundits (The lunatics have taken over the asylum)

(Sing to the tune of *The Beverly Hillbillies*
Theme Song)

Come listen to my story 'bout a boy named Bush,
His IQ was zero and his head was up his tush.
He drank like a fish while he drove all about,
But that didn't matter 'cause his daddy bailed him out.
DUI, that is. Criminal record. Cover up.

Well first thing you know, little Georgie goes to Yale.
He can't spell his name but they never let him fail.
He spends all his time hanging out with student folk.
And that's when he learns how to snort a line of coke.
Blow, that is. White gold. Nose candy.

The next thing you know there's a war in Vietnam.
Kin folks say, "George, stay at home with Mom."
Let the common people get maimed and scared.
We'll buy you a spot on the Texas Air Guard.
Cushy, that is. Country Clubs. Nose candy.

Twenty years later, George gets a little bored.
He trades in his booze, says that Jesus is his Lord.
He said, "Now the White House is the place I wanna be,"
So he called his Daddy's friends and they called the GOP.
Gun owners, that is. Falwell. Jesse Helms.

Come Nov. 7, the election ran late.
Kin folks said, "Jeb, give the boy your state!"
"Don't let those colored folks get into the polls."
So they put up barricades so they couldn't punch their
    holes.
Chads, that is. Duval County. Miami-Dade.

Before the votes were counted five supremes stepped in.
Told all the voters, "Hey, we want George to win."
"Stop counting votes!" was their solemn invocation.
And that's how George finally got his coronation.
Rigged, that is. Illegitimate. No moral authority.

Y'all come vote now. Ya hear?

While undressing for bed one night, the President notices something like a red rash around his penis.

Alarmed he thinks, "I can't tell the First Lady about this!" and makes a point of getting to his doctor the very next day.

"Doc," he says, "I've got this red ring around my, you know. What is it, and how do I get rid of it?"

The doctor says, "Well, I'm not exactly sure what it is, but take these pills for a week, and see if that takes care of it. If not, come back and we'll try something else."

The President takes the pills for a week, but unfortunately, the red rash is still there after seven days. He goes back to his doctor and tells him the pills didn't help. So the doctor prescribes another medication, capsules this time, and gives him the same instructions. He tells him to take them for another week, and to come back if it's not improved.

He takes the capsules for a week, and the red rash is still there. So he goes back to his doctor and asks, "What's next?"

The doctor gives him a cream in a tube this time. "Rub this on every day for a week and let me know."

He goes back in a week and says, "Great news, Doc! The rash is gone! That stuff in the tube was wonderful! What was it?"

The doctor replies, "Lipstick remover."

The White House is not just getting a new team, but a whole new language. George W. Bush will be bringing with him many friends from Texas, and for anyone not born in the Lone Star State, the Texan accent and the cowboy colloquialisms can seem a bit strange. Here is a guide to a few of the more colorful expressions you might encounter:

1. The engine's runnin' but ain't nobody driving. (Not overly-intelligent.)

2. As welcome as a skunk at a lawn party. (Self-explanatory.)

3. Tighter than bark on a tree. (Not very generous.)

4. Big hat, no cattle. (All talk and no action.)

5. We've howdied but we ain't shook yet. (We've made a brief acquaintance, but not been formally introduced.)

6. He thinks the sun come up just to hear him crow. (He has a pretty high opinion of himself.)

7. She's got tongue enough for 10 rows of teeth. (That woman can talk.)

8. It's so dry the trees are bribin' the dogs. (We really could use a little rain around here.)

9. Just because a chicken has wings doesn't mean it can fly. (Appearances can be deceptive.)

10. This ain't my first rodeo. (I've been around awhile.)

11. He looks like the dog's been keepin' him under the porch. (Not the most handsome of men.)

12. They ate supper before they said grace. (Living in sin.)

13. Time to paint your butt white and run with the antelope. (Stop arguing and do as you're told.)

14. As full of wind as a corn-eating horse. (Rather prone to boasting.)

15. You can put your boots in the oven, but that doesn't make them biscuits. (You can say whatever you want about something, but that doesn't change what it is.)

16. Yankees are kinda like hemorrhoids. They're not too bad when they come down and go back up, but they're a real pain in the butt when they come down and hang out for awhile.

There are a lot of folks who can't understand how we came to have an oil shortage here in the USA. Well, there's a very simple answer. Nobody bothered to check the oil. We just didn't know we were getting low. The reason for this is purely geographical.

All the oil is in Oklahoma, Texas, Louisiana, and Wyoming.

All the dipsticks are in Washington, D.C.

There was a man who, every day, would buy a newspaper on the way to work, glance at the headline, and hand the paper back to the newsboy. Day after day the man would go through this routine. Finally the newsboy could not stand it and he asked the man, "Why do you always buy a paper and only look at the front page before discarding it?"

The man replied, "I am only interested in the obituaries."

"But they are on page 21. You never even unfold the newspaper."

"Young man," he said, "the son of a bitch I'm looking for will be on the front page."

FRANKLIN DELANO ROOSEVELT

More than 5,000 years ago, Moses said to the children of Israel, "Pick up your shovels, mount your asses and camels, and I will lead you to the Promised Land."

Nearly 5,000 years later, Roosevelt said, "Lay down your shovels, sit on your asses, and light up a Camel; this is the Promised Land!"

Now, Bush Jr. wants to steal your shovels, kick your asses, raise the price of your Camels, and mortgage the Promised Land.

THE WIT OF RONALD REAGAN

In the Soviet Union, if you want to buy an automobile, there is a ten-year wait, and you have to put the money down ten years before you get the car. So, there was this young fellow there who had finally made it, and he was going through all the bureaus and agencies and signing all the papers, and finally, he got to the last agency, where they put the stamp on it. And then he gave them his money and the man at the agency said, "Come back in ten years and get your car."

The fellow said, "Morning or afternoon?"

And the agent said, "We're talking abut ten years from now. What difference does it make?"

The car-buyer said, "The plumber is coming in the morning."

It's no secret that I wear a hearing aid. Well, just the other day, all of a sudden it went haywire. We discovered that the KGB had put a listening device in my listening device!

Two Soviets were talking to each other. And one of them asked, "What's the difference between the Soviet Constitution and the United States Constitution?"

And the other one said, "That's easy. The Soviet Constitution guarantees freedom of speech and freedom of gathering. The American Constitution guarantees freedom after speech and freedom after gathering."

It seems that they were having some trouble with speeders in the Soviet Union, even though they don't have automobiles. So, an order was issued that everyone, no matter who it was, caught speeding got a ticket. And one day, General Secretary Gorbachev was coming out of his country home. He's late getting to the Kremlin. So, he told his driver to get in the backseat and he'd drive. And down the road he went, past two motorcycle policemen.

One of them took off after him. In just a few minutes, he was back with his buddy. And the buddy said, "Well, did you give him a ticket?"

And he said, "No." The buddy said, "You didn't? Why not? We're supposed to give everyone a ticket."

He said, "No, he was too important."

"But," his buddy said, "who was it?"

"Well," he said, "I couldn't recognize him. But his driver was Gorbachev."

My favorite cartoon of the last few years came out right after we really began rebuilding our military—of two Russian generals. And one of them was saying to the other, "I liked the arms race better when we were the only ones in it."

Comments at a White House briefing on Foreign Policy: I was wondering... why we don't get together more often. You know, it kind of reminds me of the fellow who asked his friend what the problem really was: ignorance or apathy. And the friend responded, "I don't know and I don't care."

I'd like to run for president. It's inside work, and you don't have to do any heavy lifting.

MILTON BERLE

RUSH LIMBAUGH ON A LIMO RIDE

Rush Limbaugh was riding through plush rural New England sitting in his black, chauffeured limousine. All of a sudden a pig darted out in front of the limo and was instantly killed. Mr. Limbaugh felt really bad and instructed his driver to head to the closest farmhouse, find out if the farmer owned the pig, and offer to pay for damages.

They soon arrived in front of the farmhouse and the chauffeur went to the front door. He was escorted inside by the farmer and remained for over two hours.

When he reappeared his clothes were in disarray, he was carrying a brown paper bag, and had the biggest smile on his face that Rush had ever seen. Rush demanded to know where the chauffeur had been and what had taken him so long.

The chauffeur reported that he had gone to the door, just as instructed, and had told the farmer and his wife what had happened. They invited him in and prepared a fine steak with all the fixin's for him.

Then they took him upstairs to meet their 24-year-old, recently divorced daughter who was a finalist in the Miss America Pageant. They left him with the daughter for them to "get to know one another better" for an hour.

When he came back downstairs the farmer's wife had baked chocolate chip cookies and had given him the brown bag full of fresh, hot cookies, then they sent him on his way.

"Wow!" exclaimed Rush. "What did you tell them?"

"Well…" replied the chauffeur, sheepishly. "I just told them the truth, that I was Rush Limbaugh's chauffeur and I had just killed the pig."

A man takes the day off work and decides to go out golfing. He is on the second hole when he notices a frog sitting next to the green. He thinks nothing of it and is about to shoot when he hears, "Ribbit nine iron." The man looks around and doesn't see anyone. Again, he hears, "Ribbit nine iron." He looks at the frog and decides to prove the frog wrong, puts the club away, and grabs a nine iron. Boom! He hits it 10 inches from the cup. He is shocked. He says to the frog, "Wow that's amazing. You must be a lucky frog, eh?"

The frog replies, "Ribbit lucky frog."

The man decides to take the frog with him to the next hole. "What do you think frog?" the man asks.

"Ribbit three wood."

The guy takes out a three wood and, Boom! Hole in one. The man is befuddled and doesn't know what to say. By the end of the day, the man golfed the best game of his life and asks the frog, "Okay, where to next?"

The frog replies, "Ribbit Las Vegas."

They go to Las Vegas and the guy says, "Okay, frog, now what?"

The frog says, "Ribbit Roulette."

Upon approaching the roulette table, the man asks, "What do you think I should bet?"

The frog replies, "Ribbit three thousand dollars, black six."

Now, this is a million-to-one shot to win, but, after the golf game, the man figures what the heck. Boom! Tons of cash come sliding back across the table. The man takes his winnings and books the best room in the hotel. He sits the frog down and says, "Frog, I don't know how to repay you. You've won me all this money and I am forever grateful."

The frog replies, "Ribbit Kiss Me."

He figures why not, since after all the frog did for him, he deserves it. With a kiss, the frog turns into a gorgeous 15-year-old girl.

"And that, your honor, is how the girl ended up in my room. So help me God or my name is not William Jefferson Clinton."

A tourist parked his car in downtown Washington, D.C. He said to a man standing near the curb, "Listen, I'm going to be only a couple of minutes. Would you watch my car while I run into this store?"

"What?" the man huffed. "Do you realize that I am a member of the United States Congress?"

"Well no," the tourist said, "I didn't realize that. But it's all right. I'll trust you anyway."

Did you hear the news about Hitler? Well, there's good news and there's bad news.

First, the good news: They found Hitler. He's alive, living in Buenos Aires, and they're bringing him to trial.

The bad news: They're holding the trial in LA.

Working for the People
(Elevating lying to a fine art)

Clinton lied. A man might forget where he parks or where he lives, but no one ever forgets oral sex, no matter how bad it is.

BARBARA BUSH

Conservatives aren't necessarily stupid, but most stupid people are conservatives.

JOHN STUART MILL

Power corrupts. Absolute power is kind of neat.

JOHN LEHMAN

George Bush and Dick Cheney go to a diner for lunch. They look at the menu, and Cheney says to the waitress, "I'll have the health salad, hold the dressing."

Bush looks at the waitress and says, "I'll have a quickie."

The waitress gets mad. "You know, we've just had eight years of that kind of talk. I'm so sick of it."

The waitress leaves and Cheney looks at Bush. "George, it's 'Quiche.'"

Rita Rudner:
High Anxiety

"Men are very confident people. My husband is so confident that when he watches sports on television, he thinks that if he concentrates he can help his team. If the team is in trouble, he coaches the players from our living room, and if they're really in trouble, I have to get off the phone in case they call him."

Rita Rudner and her husband, former BBC comedy writer Martin Bergman, co-wrote Kenneth Branagh's film, *Peter's Friends*. Their second collaboration, the Bergman-directed *A Weekend in the Country*, stars Jack Lemmon, Christine Lahti, Dudley Moore, and Richard Lewis, along with Rudner. She and her husband have their partnership as writers down to a science.

"We make each other feel really guilty, and the person who makes the other feel the guiltiest doesn't write. The guilty person sits down and writes until the other person feels really guilty, and then they take over."

Rita started in show business as a Broadway dancer, but really thinks that her brains are better than her legs.

"That's why I had to become funny. I wasn't going to get attention the way beautiful women do. And that's why I had

to learn how to dance really well—I stood next to girls that would get jobs just because they had the best legs anyone had ever seen."

Her anxiety about the way she looks inspires a lot of her comedy.

"Now they can suck the fat out of one part of your body and put it into other parts. Boy, that's a bad idea! I want them to suck the fat out of my body and put it into Cindy Crawford!"

Rita was born and raised in Florida, but she left for New York at age fifteen to become a professional dancer. She appeared in many Broadway shows, including *Promises, Promises*, and *Annie*. She eventually switched to stand-up comedy because it seemed less competitive than dance and it allowed her to stay in New York.

"There were so many talented dancers and so few Broadway shows that the odds were phenomenally against you. I wanted to get into television, except I didn't want to move to LA, since I was afraid to drive. So I became a comedienne."

Rudner and Bergman live in Beverly Hills. She has actually learned to drive. Rita often mines the ripe field of her own marriage for some of her best material.

"Men hate to lose. I once beat my husband at tennis. I asked him, 'Are we going to have sex again?' He said, 'Yes, but not with each other.'"

"All men are afraid of eyelash curlers. I sleep with one under my pillow, instead of a gun."

Rita and her husband have a pet dog but have never had any children, nor do they want any.

"Kids are cute, but we'd rather have a movie."

The Democrats are the party that says government will make you smarter, taller, richer, and remove the crabgrass on your lawn. The Republicans are the party that says government doesn't work and then they get elected to prove it.

P.J. O'ROURKE

The Republicans have a new health-care proposal: Just say no to illness!

MARK RUSSELL

I don't know exactly what democracy is, but we need more of it.

When I was a boy I was told that anybody could become President; I'm beginning to believe it.

CLARENCE DARROW

Republican boys date Democratic girls. They plan to marry Republican girls, but feel they're entitled to a little fun first.

A government is the only known vessel that leaks from the top.

JAMES RESTON

People never lie so much as after a hunt, during a war, or before an election.

OTTO VON BISMARCK

It is better to be feared than loved, if you cannot be both.

NICCOLÒ MACHIAVELLI, *THE PRINCE*

A little boy goes to his dad and asks, "What is politics?"

Dad says, "Well, son, let me try to explain it this way: I'm the breadwinner of the family, so let's call me 'Capitalism.' Your mom, she's the administrator of the money, so we'll call her 'the Government.' We are here to take care of your needs, so we'll call you 'the People.' We consider the nanny as 'the Working Class.' And your baby brother, we'll call him 'the Future.' Now, think about that and think if it makes sense."

So the little boy goes to bed thinking about what Dad has said.

Later that night, he hears his baby brother crying, so he gets up to check on him. He finds that the baby has severely soiled his diaper. So the little boy goes to his parents' room and finds his mother sound asleep.

Not wanting to wake her, he goes to the nanny's room. Finding the door locked, he peeks in the keyhole and finds his father in bed with the nanny. He gives up and goes back to bed.

The next morning the little boy says to his father, "Dad, I think I understand the concept of politics now."

"Good, Son," the father says, "Tell me in your own words what you think politics is about."

The little boy replies, "Well, while Capitalism is screwing the Working Class, the Government is sound asleep, the People are being ignored, and the Future is in deep shit."

If God had wanted us to vote, He would have given us candidates.

BUMPER STICKER

Move election day to April 15. Pay your taxes and hold elections on the same day. See if any of these duplicitous sons of bitches would try to get away with their crap, if we paid their salaries on the same day we voted for them.

DENNIS MILLER

It was election time and a politician decided to go out to the local reservation and try to get the Native American vote. They were all assembled in the council hall to hear the speech. The politician had worked up to his finale, and the crowd was getting more and more excited. "I promise better educational opportunities for Native Americans!" he said.

The crowd went wild, shouting "Hoya! Hoya!"

The politician was a bit puzzled by the native word, but was encouraged by their enthusiasm. "I promise gambling reforms to allow a casino on the reservation!"

"Hoya! Hoya!" cried the crowd, stomping their feet.

"I promise more social reforms and job opportunities for Native Americans!" The crowd reached a frenzied pitch, shouting, "Hoya! Hoya! Hoya!"

After the speech, the politician was touring the reservation and he saw a tremendous herd of cattle. Since he had been raised on a ranch and knew a bit about cattle, he asked the chief if he could get closer to take a look at the cattle.

"Sure," the chief said, "but be careful not to step in the hoya."

YOU MIGHT BE A REPUBLICAN IF...

You think Huey Newton is a cookie.

You think you might remember laughing once as a kid.

You think "proletariat" is a cheese.

You've named your kids "Deduction One" and "Deduction Two."

You've tried to argue that poverty could be abolished if people were just allowed to keep more of their minimum wage.

You've ever referred to someone as "my [insert racial or ethnic minority here] friend."

You're a pro-lifer but support the death penalty.

You confuse Lennon with Lenin.

You once broke loose at a party and removed your necktie.

You've ever referred to the moral fiber of something.

Vietnam made sense to you.

You've ever uttered the phrase, "Let's just bomb those suckers!"

You've ever urged someone to pull themselves up by their bootstraps when they didn't have any shoes.

You own a bumper sticker that says, "Ollie North, American Hero."

You answer to "The Man."

You fax the FBI a list of "commies on my block."

You accuse Bert and Ernie on *Sesame Street* of sexual deviance.

You've ever told a child that Oscar the Grouch lives in a garbage can because he is lazy and doesn't want to contribute to society.

You think Birkenstock was that radical rock concert in 1969.

On election day I stay home. Because if you vote, you have no right to complain. You elect dishonest, incompetent people, they get into office and screw everything up—you caused the problem. I am in no way responsible, and have every right to complain as loud as I want to about the mess you people created.

GEORGE CARLIN

In this world of sin and sorrow there is always something to be thankful for; as for me, I rejoice that I am not Republican.

H.L. MENCKEN

Any man who is under 30 and is not a liberal has not a heart; and any man who is over 30 and is not a conservative, has no brains.

WINSTON CHURCHILL

Politics is not the art of the possible. It consists of choosing between the disastrous and the unpalatable.

JOHN KENNETH GALBRAITH

The inherent vice of capitalism is the unequal sharing of blessings; the inherent virtue of socialism is the equal sharing of miseries.

WINSTON CHURCHILL

We need a President who's fluent in at least one language.

BUCK HENRY

It was Ronald Reagan, the former President of the United States, who said to his wife, "Nancy, darling, as long as I have a face, you have a place to sit." She's been sitting on his face for thirty years now. We don't know where her ass ends and his face begins.

PROFESSOR IRWIN COREY

Military intelligence. Isn't that a contradiction in terms?

GROUCHO MARX

How do you tell the difference between a Liberal and a Conservative?

Easy. Watch a man drowning fifty feet offshore.

The Conservative will throw out twenty-five feet of rope and shout "Swim for it!"

The Liberal will toss out fifty feet of rope, drop his own end, and go off to do another good deed.

Dear Abby,

I am a sailor in the U.S. Coast Guard. My parents live in a suburb of Philadelphia and one of my sisters, who lives in Bensenville, is married to a transvestite.

My father and mother have recently been arrested for growing and selling marijuana and are currently dependent on my other two sisters, who are prostitutes in Jersey City. I have two brothers; one is currently serving a non-parole life sentence in Attica for the rape and murder of a teenage boy. The other brother is currently being held in the Wellington Remand Center on charges of incest with his three children.

I have recently become engaged to marry a former Thai prostitute who lives in the Bronx and indeed is still a part-time "working girl." However, we hope to open a brothel soon, where she'll be the manager. I am hoping my two sisters will be interested in joining our team. Although I would prefer them not to prostitute themselves, at least it would get them off the street... and hopefully, the heroin.

Abby, my problem is this: I love my fiancée and look forward to bringing her into the family, and of course I want to be totally honest with her....

Should I tell her about my cousin who voted for Bush?

THE PRESIDENT'S PRIVATE BATHROOM

George W. Bush was invited to the White House for a foreign policy orientation session. After drinking several glasses of iced tea, he asked Bill Clinton if he could use his personal bathroom. He was astonished to see that the President had a solid gold urinal. That afternoon, W. told his wife Laura about the urinal. "Just think," he said, "when I am President, I'll get to have a gold urinal!"

The next day Laura Bush had lunch with a group of female senators. She told Hillary Clinton how impressed W. had been with his discovery that the President had a gold urinal in his private bathroom. That evening, Bill and Hillary were getting ready for bed. Hillary turned to Bill and said, "Well, I found out who peed in your saxophone."

George W. Bush was thrilled at being able to spend his first night in the White House, but something very strange happened. On the first night he was awakened by George Washington's ghost.

"President Washington, what is the best thing I could do to help the country?" Bush asked.

"Set an honest and honorable example, just as I did," advised Washington.

With all the excitement of the White House, Bush still couldn't sleep well and, the next night, the ghost of Thomas Jefferson moved through the dark bedroom.

"Tom, what is the best thing I cold do to help the country?" Bush asked.

"Cut taxes and reduce the size of the government," Jefferson said.

Bush still couldn't sleep well and, on the third night, he saw another ghostly figure moving in the shadows. It was Abraham Lincoln's ghost.

"Abe, what is the best thing I could do to help the country?" Bush asked.

"Go see a play," Lincoln replied.

My father was not a failure. After all, he was the father of a President of the United States.

HARRY S TRUMAN

When Bill and Hillary first got married, Bill said, "I am putting a box under our bed. You must promise never to look in it." In all their 30 years of marriage, Hillary never looked. However, on the afternoon of their 30th anniversary, curiosity got the better of her and she lifted the lid and peeked inside.

In the box there were 3 empty beer cans and $1,874.25 in cash.

After dinner, Hillary could no longer contain her guilt and she confessed, saying, "I am so sorry. For all these years I kept my promise and never looked in the box under our bed. However, today the temptation was too much and I gave in. But now I need to know, why do you keep the empty cans in the box?"

Bill thought for a while and said, "I guess that after all these years you deserve to know the truth. Whenever I was unfaithful to you, I put an empty beer can in the box under the bed to remind myself not to do it again."

Hillary was shocked, but said, "I am very disappointed and saddened, but I guess after all those years on the road, three cans in the box is not that bad considering the number of years we've been together." They hugged and made their peace.

A little while later, Hillary asked Bill, "So why do you have all that money in the box?"

Bill answered, "Well, whenever the box filled up with empty cans, I took them to the recycling center and redeemed them for cash."

While visiting England, George W. Bush is invited to tea with the Queen. He asks her what her leadership philosophy is.

She says that it is to surround herself with intelligent people.

He asks how she knows if they're intelligent.

"I do so by asking them the right questions," says the Queen. Allow me to demonstrate." She phones Tony Blair and says, "Mr. Prime Minister. Please answer this question: Your mother has a child, and your father has a child, and this child is not your brother or sister. Who is it?" Tony Blair responds, "It is I, ma'am."

"Correct. Thank you and good-bye, sir," says the Queen. She hangs up and says, "Did you get that, Mr. Bush?"

"Yes, ma'am. Thanks a lot. I'll definitely be using that!"

Upon returning to Washington, he decides he'd better put the Chairman of the Senate Foreign Relations Committee to the test. He summons Jesse Helms to the White House and says, "Senator Helms, I wonder if you can answer a question for me."

"Why, of course, sir. What's on your mind?"

"Uhh, your mother has a child, and your father has a child, and this child is not your brother or your sister. Who is it?"

Helms hems and haws and finally asks, "Can I think about it and get back to you?"

Bush agrees, and Helms leaves. He immediately calls a meeting of other senior Republican senators, and they puzzle over the question for several hours, but nobody can come up with an answer. Finally, in desperation,

Helms calls Colin Powell at the State Department and explains his problem.

"Now look here, son, your mother has a child, and your father has a child, and this child is not your brother or your sister? Who is it?"

Powell answers immediately, "It is I, of course, you dumb cracker."

Much relieved, Helms rushes back to the White House and exclaims, "I know the answer, sir! I know who it is! It's Colin Powell!"

Bush replies in disgust, "Wrong, you dumb bastard, it's Tony Blair!"

CHAPTER TEN:
IT'S JUST A GAME—ISN'T IT?

It is not just a game. It's the most important thing in the world. It is the most significant event to ever take place on earth. It is what makes boys out of men and girls out of women. It is The Game. And it is sacred. Doesn't much matter which game, or what they are playing, as long as we are watching and eating at the same time. It's really not the same without the eating. Or the drinking. That is key, too. But the best is when we are playing. Then, we are the athletes, the chosen ones, the invincible. (Ouch, there goes my trick knee again.) We are the players and we take ourselves way too seriously.

Every sport has its distinct characteristics, as do the people who play the sport, watch the sport, or read about it. And they are all spoken for in this chapter. You can poke fun at basketball, hockey, skydiving, and almost any other sport that comes to mind. For something that should be all fun and games, sports encourages a lot of really bad behavior in people who should just calm down, have a good time, and take it all less seriously. After all, it's only a game—isn't it?

CyberSport: The Thrill of Access... The Agony of Disconnecting.

Sports are the only entertainment where, no matter how many times you go back, you'll never know the ending.

Baseball (A stick and a couple of balls)

BASEBALL IN HEAVEN

Two buddies, Bob and Earl, were two of the biggest baseball fans in America.

Their entire adult lives, Bob and Earl discussed baseball history in the winter, and they pored over every box score during the season. They went to 60 games a year. They even agreed that whoever died first would try to come back and tell the other if there was baseball in heaven.

One summer night, Bob passed away in his sleep, after watching a Yankee victory. He died happy.

A few nights later, his buddy Earl awoke to the sound of Bob's voice from beyond.

"Hey Earl!"

"Bob, is that you?" Earl asked.

"Of course it's me," Bob replied.

"This is unbelievable! So tell me, is there baseball in heaven?"

"Well, I have some good news and some bad news. Which do you want to hear first?"

"Tell me the good news first."

"Well, the good news is that, yes, there is baseball in heaven, Earl."

"Oh, that is wonderful! So what could possibly be the bad news?"

"You're pitching tomorrow night."

FIRST TIME AT A BASEBALL GAME

A Scottish man was at a baseball game.

It was the first time he had ever seen the sport, so he sat quietly. The first batter approached the plate, took a few swings, and then hit a double. Everyone was on their feet screaming, "Run, Run!"

This happened two more times, with a single and a triple. The Scottish man was now excited and ready to get into the game.

The next batter came up and four balls went by. The umpire called "Walk," and the batter started on a slow trot to first. The Scotsman, extremely excited now, stood up and screamed, "R-R-Run ye basstarrd, rrrun!"

Everyone around him started laughing. So the Scotsman, extremely embarrassed, sat back down. A friendly fan, seeing the Scotsman's embarrassment, leaned over and said, "He can't run—he got four balls."

The Scotsman then stood up and screamed, "Walk with pride, man...walk with pride!"

Q: What do baseball players eat on?

A: Home plates!

Football is for men. Baseball is for intelligent men.

I like baseball as a sport, because in baseball when you hit a ball into the stands, you just let it go. In golf, you have to go looking for it.

Baseball is a beautiful thing. In baseball, you hit the ball and someone else chases it.

Some of our hitters are so bad that they can strike out on two pitches.

MILTON BERLE

Baseball players make a lot of money nowadays. Even guys who don't make the team are getting seven figures.

Baseball players are getting too rich. They hit the ball now, and have their chauffeurs run to first for them.

A player was just signed for over $10 million a season. If I made that much money, I wouldn't steal second. I'd buy it.

Basketball (More ball jokes)

Q: What do you get when you cross Michael Jordan and a groundhog?

A: Six more weeks of basketball.

Bowling (Please, no more ball jokes)

TOP 23 THINGS TO DO AT A BOWLING ALLEY

1. Every time you throw, exclaim "TAKE THAT, YOU!!!" Continue this behavior until forcefully thrown out.

2. Whenever a strike "**X**" appears on the screen, start yelling about how this is a Black Panther conspiracy.

3. Explain to the owner how your game has been ruined due to plate tectonics, then demand compensation.

4. Wear golf shoes.

5. Pray to the pins. Leave a sacrifice.

6. Make lewd and graphic references to your "ball." (Works well on Seniors Ladies night.)

7. Play bocce with extra lane balls.

8. Try to juggle the balls. When you drop them, start screaming about plate tectonics again.

9. Completely cover your ball in duct tape (sticky side out) then loudly bitch about how your hook is off.

10. Hide behind the pins. Stick your head up, laughing hysterically.

11. Throw refuse down the ball return, then tell the owner the trash compactor is busted.

12. Root for the other team. Bring banners.

13. Bring a foghorn to use at crucial moments.

14. Even if you miss totally—at the top of your lungs scream STEEEEEEEEEEEEEERIKE.

15. Bring a small gold idol, and demand the other team pray to it.

16. Rent all the lanes, but don't bowl.

17. Blatantly underscore yourself, then accuse the other team of cheating.

18. When an opponent is on his backswing, race up and take his ball, then run home.

19. If your team is in the finals, throw nothing but gutterballs, blame plate tectonics.

20. Wear a baseball uniform, and bowl sidearm.

21. Walk around asking people why they are here. Do this the whole night.

22. Name your ball something like "Killer." Openly boast to everyone how great you are. Bowl terribly. Do this all night.

23. Run around sprinkling "magic fairy dust" on everyone's balls. Tar works nicely.

Boxing (This is a sport?)

Q: What has four legs and only one ear?

A: Mike Tyson's dog.

I went to the boxing matches the other night, and a hockey game broke out.

RODNEY DANGERFIELD

It's crazy when you figure boxers get all that money for fighting and hockey players do it every night for free.

I have a problem with boxing. I don't understand any sport where a guy who makes $11 million is called "the loser."

Fishing (THIS is a sport?)

Give a man a fish and he will eat for a day. Teach him how to fish and he will sit in a boat and drink beer all day.

Enjoy the stream, O harmless fish,
And when an angler for his dish,
Through gluttony's vile sin,
Attempts, the wretch, to pull the out,
God give thee strength, O gentle trout,
To pull the rascal in.

Here's to the fish that I may catch;
So large that even I,
When talking of it afterward,
Will never need to lie.

Here's to our fisherman bold;
Here's to the fish he caught;
Here's to the one that got away,
And here's to the ones he bought.

If you don't do anything the entire day, you're called a bum. If you do it in a boat, you're called a fisherman.

I once knew a one-armed fisherman. He had a terrible time telling you how big the one that got away was.

I used to enjoy fishing tremendously until, one day, I happened to look at it from the worm's point of view.

Fishing is a jerk on one end of the line waiting for another jerk at the other.

Good fishing is just a matter of timing. You have to get there yesterday.

Last week I caught a fish so big, I nearly dislocated my shoulders just describing it.

The great thing about fishing is that it gives you something to do while you're not doing anything.

There are two types of fishermen: those who fish for sport and those who catch something.

Fishing season hasn't opened and a fisherman who doesn't have a license is casting for trout as a stranger approaches and asks, "Any luck?"

"Any luck? This is a wonderful spot. I took 10 out of this stream yesterday," he boasts.

"Is that so?　By the way, do you know who I am?" asks the stranger.

"Nope."

"Well, meet the new game warden."

"Oh," gulped the fisherman. "Well, do you know who I am?"

"Nope."

"Meet the biggest liar in the state."

Football (What fun, I can't feel my toes...)

FOOTBALL AND THE TV REPAIRMAN

A woman called in a repairman to fix her television. Just as he finished, the woman heard her husband's key in the lock. "Hurry," she said to the repairman, "you'll have to hide. My husband is insanely jealous."

There was no time to run out the back door, so the repairman hid inside the TV console. The husband came in and plopped down in his favorite chair to watch some football. Inside the TV, the repairman was all squished up and getting hotter and hotter. Finally, he couldn't stand it anymore. He climbed out, marched across the room and out the front door.

The husband looked at the TV set, looked at his wife, looked back at the set again and said, "I didn't see the referee send that guy off the field, did you?"

Mary was watching the local news and turned to her husband, who was involved in a crossword puzzle.

"Darling," she said, "did you hear that? A man in New York swapped his wife for a season pass to the Islanders' games. Would you do a thing like that?"

"Hell no," he replied. "The season's half over."

Football is a game in which a handful of men run around for two hours watched by millions of people who could really use the exercise.

Q: What is a cheerleader's favorite soft drink?

A: Root beer!

Football players are measured by the yard.

I think football is a sport the way ducks think hunting is a sport.

It's all fun and games, till someone loses an eye! Then it's a sport.

It's not sport if you can talk afterwards.

My favorite football team is whoever plays the Cowboys.

Pro football is like nuclear warfare. No winners, just survivors.

Tackle, block, illegal use of hands.
That's not on the field,
That's just in the stands.

I'm a football fan, but I think there are too many games on over the holidays. At our Thanksgiving dinner, Dolores passed me the turkey and I spiked it.

BOB HOPE

Football players say the fans are so noisy that they can't even hear themselves think. At most, that would affect maybe one or two players on the team.

Golf (Who came up with the outfits?)

Hockey is a sport for white men. Basketball is a sport for black men. Golf is a sport for white men dressed like black pimps.

TIGER WOODS

Give me my golf clubs, fresh air, and a beautiful partner, and you can keep my golf clubs and the fresh air.

JACK BENNY

A married man was having an affair with his secretary. One day, their passions overcame them and they took off for her house, where they made passionate love all afternoon.

Exhausted from the wild sex they fell asleep, and didn't wake up until 8:00 P.M. As the man threw on his clothes, he told the woman to take his shoes outside and rub them through the grass and dirt. Mystified, she nonetheless complied. He put on his shoes and drove home.

"Where have you been?!" demanded his wife when he entered the house.

"Darling, I can't lie to you. I've been having an affair with my secretary and we've been having sex all afternoon. I fell asleep and didn't wake up until eight."

The wife glanced down at his shoes and said, "You lying bastard! You've been playing golf!"

At a golf club, a bunch of women are having tea. Then one woman discovers that the men's locker room below their balcony has its door ajar. A man is taking a shower. They can see his naked body but not his face. The woman chuckles and says, "I am glad that that is not my husband—how embarrassing!"

A second woman acknowledges, "I am glad that he is not my boyfriend...hmmmm!"

A third woman says, "I don't know whether he is my husband or not, but I sure know that he is not any of the men here at this golf club."

The other day I broke 70. That's a lot of clubs.

HENNY YOUNGMAN

I was playing golf. I swung, missed the ball, and got a big chunk of dirt. I swung again, missed the ball, and got another big chunk of dirt. Just then, two ants climbed on the ball, saying, "Let's get up here before we get killed!"

HENNY YOUNGMAN

The reason most people play golf is to wear clothes they would not be caught dead in otherwise.

ROGER SIMON

It was a sunny Saturday morning, and Joe was on the links, addressing the golf ball, visualizing his shot, when a voice came over the clubhouse loudspeaker: "Would the gentleman on the lady's tee please back up to the men's tee?"

Joe was still deep in his routine, seemingly impervious to the interruption. Again the announcement: "Would the man on the women's tee kindly back up to the men's tee!"

Finally Joe had had enough. He shouted, "WOULD THE STARTER IN THE CLUBHOUSE KINDLY SHUT UP AND LET ME PLAY MY SECOND SHOT!!!"

Q: What's the hardest thing about playing golf with your wife?

A: Having to say, "Great shot, Honey!" 142 times.

Two men are talking at work Monday morning.

"What did you do this weekend?"

"Dropped hooks into water."

"Fishing, eh?"

"No, golfing."

A golf match is a test of your skill against your opponent's luck.

Avid golfers have a fairway look in their eyes.

Bankers' Hours: That part of the day when it is too hot to play golf.

Golfer: A person who hits and lies.

Dunebogey: Golf course sand trap.

Golfer: Yells "Fore!" takes Five, writes down Three.

Golf Tip #17: To get more distance, smack the ball and run backwards.

Golf is a good walk spoiled.

Golf scores are directly proportionate to the number of witnesses.

Golf separates the men from the poise.

Golf: Baseball for those that don't have eight friends.

Q: How do golfers celebrate?

A: Par tee.

I own the erasers for all the miniature golf pencils.

I'm too young to take up golf and too old to rush up to the net.

If there were no golf balls, how would we measure hail?

It takes a lot of balls to golf the way I do.

More lies are told on the golf course than to the IRS.

My golf is improving. Yesterday I hit the ball in one.

Old: When you are a 17 neck, 44 waist, and shoot 106 in golf.

PROFILE
Drew Carey
"Regular Guy"

*"He brings a lot of joy when-
ever he leaves the room."*

Drew Carey, the character
on the TV show that bears
his name, is just a regular
guy trying to make the best
of his average life and average job. In reality, Drew
Carey the celebrity has a
superlative career that many
people envy. He has accom-
plished a lot in his eight
years as a stand-up comedian.

*"I see fulfilling my five-year
contract and disappearing."*

Mirroring his TV alter ego, Drew was born the youngest
child of working-class parents in Cleveland, Ohio. His
father, a draftsman for General Motors, died of a brain
tumor when Carey was eight years old. Drew was often left
at home alone, where he spent his time watching cartoons
and listening to comedy records.

"Weirdo. Weirdo. Underachiever. Weirdo. Weirdo."
DREW CAREY, SUMMING UP HIS CHILDHOOD

In 1980, while visiting his brother Neal in San Diego,
Drew impulsively enlisted in the Marine Corps Reserve,
hoping that the experience would teach him self-disci-
pline. He served for the next six years, working odd jobs

during the week and sweating it out with the Corps on the weekends. By 1986, Drew was back living in Cleveland, and back waiting tables to pay the bills. A friend of his who was a local radio personality told Drew that if he came up with some funny material for the radio show, he would get paid. Carey found a book at the local library on how to write jokes. In January 1986, he made good on his New Year's resolution and made his stand-up debut at a local comedy club.

"I was mobbed in the adult section of a video store in Las Vegas, and I thought, 'I've got to get out of this madness.' I want to grow a beard, have money and retire. Meanwhile I'm gonna have fun."

The turning point in Drew's career came with his first appearance on *The Tonight Show with Johnny Carson* in 1991. Johnny asked Drew to come over and sit on the couch after his set, and part of that now-famous performance is included in the *Best of Carson* home video.

"It's hard to believe that he beat out 1,000,000 other sperm."

In 1997, *People* magazine included him in its list of the year's 25 Most Intriguing People.

"If he were any more stupid, he'd have to be watered twice a week."

Fame hasn't changed Drew very much, who is still just a regular guy. Though he now calls Los Angeles home, Carey remains accessible to his homies: during a 1996 visit to Cleveland for an interview with *TV Guide*, Drew patiently chatted with fans and signed hundreds of autographs.

"He sets low personal standards and then consistently fails to achieve them."

THOUGHTS ON GOLF

In primitive societies, when native tribes beat the ground with clubs and yelled, it was called witchcraft; today, in civilized society, it is called golf.

The man who takes up golf to get his mind off his work soon takes up work to get his mind off golf.

The secret of good golf is to hit the ball hard, straight and not too often.

There are three ways to improve your golf game: take lessons, practice constantly, or start cheating.

Many a golfer prefers a golf cart to a caddy because it cannot count, criticize, or laugh.

Golf is a game in which the slowest people in the world are those in front of you, and the fastest are those behind.

Golf: A five-mile walk punctuated with disappointments.

There's no game like golf: You go out with three friends, play eighteen holes, and return with three enemies.

GOLF LAWS

Law 1: No matter how bad your last shot was, the worst is yet to come.

This law does not expire on the 18th hole, since it has the supernatural tendency to extend over the course of a tournament, a summer and, eventually, a lifetime.

Law 2: Your best round of golf will be followed almost immediately by your worst round ever.

The probability of the latter increases with the number of people you tell about the former.

Law 3: Brand-new golf balls are water-magnetic.

Though this cannot be proven in the lab, it is a known fact that the more expensive the golf ball, the greater its attraction to water.

Law 4: Golf balls never bounce off of trees back into play.

If one does, the tree is breaking a law of the universe and should be cut down.

Law 5: No matter what causes a golfer to muff a shot, all his playing partners must solemnly chant "You looked up," or invoke the wrath of the universe.

Law 6: The higher a golfer's handicap, the more qualified he deems himself as an instructor.

Law 7: Every par-three hole in the world has a secret desire to humiliate golfers. The shorter the hole, the greater its desire.

Law 8: Topping a three-iron is the most painful torture known to man.

Law 9: Palm trees eat golf balls.

Law 10: Sand is alive. If it isn't, how do you explain the way it works against you?

Law 11: Golf carts always run out of juice at the farthest point from the clubhouse.

Law 12: A golfer hitting into your group will always be bigger than anyone in your group.

Likewise, a group you accidentally hit into will consist of a football player, a professional wrestler, a convicted murderer, and an IRS agent—or some similar combination.

Law 13: All three-woods are demon-possessed.

Law 14: Golf balls from the same "sleeve" tend to follow one another, particularly out of bounds or into the water (See Law 3).

Law 15: A severe slice is a thing of awesome power and beauty.

Law 16: "Nice lag" can usually be translated to "lousy putt." Similarly, "tough break" can usually be translated "way to miss an easy one, sucker."

Law 17: The person you would most hate to lose to will always be the one who beats you.

Law 18: Golf should be given up at least twice per month.

Law 19: All vows taken on a golf course shall be valid only until the sunset.

Here's to your woods, here's to your irons,
Here's to your putter, too.
May every shot you hit with them,
Fall in the hole for you.

Truth is something you leave in the locker room with your street shoes when you play golf.

Skiing (I'm in complete controlIIIIIIIIIIIIIIIII)

HOW TO PREPARE FOR THE SKI SEASON

1. Visit your local butcher and pay thirty dollars to sit in the walk-in freezer for two hours. Afterward, burn two hundred dollar bills warming up.

2. Fasten a small, wide rubber band around the top half of your head before you go to sleep each night.

3. Soak your gloves and store them in the freezer after every use.

4. If you wear glasses, rub glue all over them.

5. Go to an ice skating rink, walk across the ice twenty times in your ski boots, while holding your skis over one shoulder and your bag and poles over the other. Sporadically drop things.

6. Buy a new pair of gloves and throw one away.

7. Clip a lift ticket to the zipper of your jacket and ride a motorcycle fast enough to make the ticket lacerate your face.

8. Put on as many layers of clothing as possible and then go to the bathroom and take them all off. Twice.

9. Fill a blender with ice, hit the start button and let the spray blast your face. Leave the ice on your face until it melts.

10. Place a small but angular pebble in each of your shoes, line them with crushed ice, and then tighten a C-clamp around your toes.

Skydiving (When "oops" matters)

You do not need a parachute to skydive. You only need a parachute to skydive twice.

Q: Why don't blind people like to skydive?

A: Because it scares the hell out of the dog.

Skydiving...Only one direction—No decisions!

If at first you don't succeed, then skydiving isn't for you.

A man went skydiving for the first time. After listening to the instructor for what seemed like days, he was ready to go. Excited, he jumped out of the airplane. About five seconds later, he pulled the ripcord. Nothing happened. He tried again. Still nothing. He started to panic, but remembered his back-up chute. He pulled that cord. Nothing happened. He frantically began yanking both cords to no avail.

Suddenly he looked down, and he couldn't believe his eyes. Another man was in the air with him, but this guy was going up! Just as the other guy passed by, the skydiver yelled, "Hey, do you know anything about skydiving?"

The other guy yelled back, "No! Do you know anything about gas stoves?"

Biplane: The last words a pilot says before baling out.

Tennis (More balls)

Taking up a new sport, I have always subscribed to the rule, Whatever you lack in skill, make up for in silly accessories.

"How's your tennis game?"

"Not great. But I have a hat with a tiny solar-powered fan that keeps me cool, and a racket the size of an outdoor grill."

PAUL REISER

Q: What can be served but never eaten?

A: A tennis ball.

The trouble with being a good sport is you have to lose to prove it.

Gambling (Don't bet the ranch)

There are these two friends, a white guy and a black guy. One evening, they're in a bar arguing over which of them can have sex the most times in one night. They decide to settle the issue by going to the local whorehouse and gathering empirical evidence, as it were.

So they get to the whorehouse, pair off with a couple of the ladies, and go to their respective rooms.

The white guy energetically balls his whore and, reaching up with a pencil, makes a "*I*" mark on the wall. Then he falls asleep. He wakes up in a couple of hours and screws the whore again, albeit a little less enthusiastically this time. Again, he reaches back and marks a "*I*" on the wall. Again, he falls asleep. He wakes up again in a couple of hours and lethargically humps the hooker again. He drowsily marks another "*I*" on the wall and falls asleep for the rest of the night.

The next morning, the black guy barges into the white guy's room to see how he did. He takes one look at the wall and exclaims, "A hundred and eleven?! You beat me by three!"

THE BET

Jolson said he liked the kid in the white trunks. Burns said he liked the kid in the dark trunks.

Jolson said, "I'll bet you a hundred the kid in the white trunks wins."

"It's a bet," said Burns.

The kid in the dark trunks wiped out his white-clad opponent in two rounds.

The fighters came into the ring for the second match. Jolson said, "Double or nothing, I get the white trunks."

"It's a bet," said Burns.

The kid in the dark trunks knocked out his opponent in the first round.

The third fight was about to begin. Jolson said, "Double or nothing, okay?"

"Okay." said Burns.

Jolson lost again. He lost the first four fights and was eight hundred dollars behind.

Burns said, "Look Al, forget about the last fights. Let's make believe you lost only a hundred. Forget the rest."

Jolson said, "Deal!"

"Good. Give me my hundred," said Burns.

"Tell you what," Jolson said, "On the next fight, double or nothing."

HOW TO END AN ARGUMENT

Two women were at a bar. One looked at the other and said, "You know, eighty percent of all men think the best way to end an argument is to make love."

"Well," said the other woman, "that will certainly revolutionize the game of hockey!"

CHAPTER ELEVEN:
ALL THE WORLD IS A JOKE

Well, if you made it this far then you certainly have come a long way in the fun department. Some might say it with a song, others might kill 'em with kindness, but for the Friars, if you really want to get your point across, a joke, a poke, or a Roast is the only way to go. And don't worry about insulting anyone because, well, frankly that is the point.

Of course, you do need to choose your victims—er, subjects—wisely. You don't want to give Aunt Emma a coronary by dipping into the penis portion of your joke stash. Nor do you want to be quoting jokes from a Friars Roast to the new postulates at Immaculate Conception convent. Not that they won't find them funny but it will only remind them of all the sex acts they are no longer allowed to perform.

So throw away your prejudices and embrace jokes about all races, colors, and creeds. Don't care what people will think of you while quoting the crème de la crème of comedy—just make sure you don't have spinach between your teeth. For the Friars, religion, nationality, and culture can all be reduced to four-letter words that add up to one hilarious punch line.

Don't take life too seriously—better yet, don't let those stuffy, stuck-up people around you take it seriously. Read the chapter and bone up on a brand new repertoire guaranteed to make you the life of the party!

I love The Friar's Club. It reminds me of the old days, seeing so many straight Jews in show business.

I'm not saying James Caan is connected, but I hear he knows where Abe Vigoda is buried.

Ethnic/Regional
(No, nothing is sacred)

On a group of beautiful, deserted islands in the middle of nowhere, the following people are stranded:

Two Italian men and one Italian woman...

Two French men and one French woman...

Two German men and one German woman...

Two Greek men and one Greek woman...

Two English men and one English woman...

Two Bulgarian men and one Bulgarian woman...

Two Japanese men and one Japanese woman...

Two Chinese men and one Chinese woman...

Two American men and one American woman...

Two Irish men and one Irish woman.

One month later on these stunningly beautiful islands, the following things have occurred:

One Italian man killed the other Italian man for the Italian woman.

The two French men and the French woman are living happily in a ménage-à-trois.

The two German men have a strict weekly schedule of alternating visits with the German woman.

The two Greek men are sleeping with each other and the Greek woman is cleaning and cooking for them.

The two English men are waiting for someone to introduce them to the English woman.

The two Bulgarian men took one long look at the endless ocean, one long look at the Bulgarian woman, and started swimming.

The two Japanese men have faxed Tokyo and are awaiting instructions.

The two Chinese men have set up a laundry-liquor store-restaurant and have gotten the Chinese woman pregnant in order to provide staff for the business.

The two American men are contemplating suicide because the American woman keeps complaining about her body and talks endlessly about the true nature of feminism, how she can do everything they can do, the necessity of fulfillment, the equal division of household chores, how sand and palm trees make her look fat, how her last boyfriend respected her opinion and treated her nicer than they do, how her relationship with her mother is improving, and how at least the taxes here are low and it isn't raining.

The two Irishmen divided the island into north and south and set up a distillery. They don't remember if sex is in the picture 'cause it gets sort of hazy after a few litres of coconut whiskey—but they are satisfied because at least the English aren't having any fun!

A Jewish man and a Chinese man were talking. The Jewish man commented on what wise people the Chinese are. "Yes," replied the Chinese man, "Our culture is over four thousand years old. But you Jews are very wise people, too."

The Jewish man replied, "Yes, our culture is over five thousand years old."

The Chinese man was incredulous. "That's impossible," he replied. "Where did your people eat for a thousand years?"

A young man was wandering, lost, in a forest when he came upon a small house. Knocking on the door, he was greeted by an ancient Chinese man with a long gray beard.

"I'm lost," said the young man. "Can you put me up for the night?"

"Certainly," the Chinese man said, "but on one condition. If you so much as lay a finger on my daughter, I will inflict upon you the three worst Chinese tortures known to man."

"OK," said the young man, thinking that the daughter must be pretty old as well, and he entered the house.

Before dinner the daughter came down the stairs. She was young, beautiful and had a fantastic figure. She was obviously attracted to the young man as she couldn't keep her eyes off him during the meal. Remembering the old man's warning, he ignored her and went up to bed alone.

During the night, the young man could bear it no longer and sneaked into her room. He was careful to keep his lovemaking quiet so the old man wouldn't hear and, near dawn, he crept back to his room, exhausted, but happy.

He awoke to a heavy feeling. Opening his eyes he saw a large rock on his chest with a note on it that read: "Chinese Torture 1: Large rock on chest."

"Well, that's pretty crappy," he thought. "If that's the best the old man can do, then I don't have much to worry about." He picked the boulder up, walked over to the window and threw the boulder out.

As he did so, he noticed another note on it that read: "Chinese Torture 2: Rock tied to left testicle."

In a panic he glanced down and saw the rope that was already getting close to taut. Figuring that a few broken bones was better than castration, he jumped out of the window after the boulder.

As he plummeted towards the ground he saw a large sign on the ground that read: "Chinese Torture 3: Right testicle tied to bed post."

An Italian, a Scotsman, and a Chinese fellow are hired at a construction site.

The foreman points out a huge pile of sand and says to the Italian guy, "You're in charge of sweeping."

To the Scotsman, he says, "You're in charge of shoveling."

And to the Chinese guy, "You're in charge of supplies."

He then says, "Now, I have to leave for a little while. I expect you guys to make a big dent in that there pile."

So the foreman goes away for a couple hours and, when he returns, the pile of sand is untouched. He asks the Italian, "Why didn't you sweep any of it?"

The Italian replies, "I no hav-a no broom. You said-a to the Chinese a-fella that he a-was-a ina charge of-a supplies, but he has-a disappeared and I no could-a find-a him nowhere."

Then the foreman turns to the Scotsman and says, "And you; I thought I told you to shovel this pile."

The Scotsman replies, "Aye, ye did, lad; boot ah couldnay get meself a shoovel! Ye left th' Chinese gadgie in chairge of supplies, boot ahcouldnay fin' him either."

The foreman is really angry now and storms off toward the pile of sand to look for the Chinese guy.

Just then, the Chinese guy leaps out from behind the pile of sand and yells, "SUPPLIES!!"

In the good ol' U.S. of A., buses have a sign saying, "Don't speak to the driver."

In Germany, the sign reads, "It is strictly forbidden for passengers to speak to the driver."

In England, "You are graciously requested to refrain from speaking to the driver."

In Scotland, "What have you got to gain by speaking to the driver?"

And in Italy, "Don't answer the driver."

In America, everyone knows that it is terribly dangerous to be in Israel now, and it is not recommended to travel there.

In Israel, everyone knows that it is dangerous only in the territories and in a little bit of Jerusalem.

In Jerusalem, everyone knows there is shooting going on, but only in the neighborhood of Giloh.

In Giloh, everyone knows that it is dangerous, but only on Ha'anafa Street.

On Ha'anafa Street, everyone knows that it is dangerous, but not all along the street, just in the houses that face Beit Jalla.

In the houses facing Beit Jalla, everyone knows it is dangerous, but mostly in a few apartments on specific floors that get shot at occasionally.

In the apartments that get shot at, they know it is dangerous, but not in all the rooms, just in the kitchen. In the bedrooms and bathrooms, for instance, it is totally safe.

In the kitchen that gets shot into, they know it is really dangerous, but not in the entire kitchen, just near the refrigerator and toaster.

Those near the refrigerator know that where it is really dangerous is in the freezer, which is directly in the sights of the sharpshooter from Beit Jalla. You can take milk and cheese out of the fridge part without getting hit, usually. Word of honor.

And in the freezer over the fridge part of the refrigerator on one part of Ha'anafa Street at the edge of Giloh in Jerusalem in Israel? Oh boy, it is dangerous there. If you stand there and get some frozen blintzes out of the freezer—you're taking your life in your hands. So for a few months, just until things calm down, we're not going to use the freezer. Now, this you call dangerous?

Texans
(Guns, oil, and a pick-up)

A woman from Texas and a woman from New York meet at a party. The woman from Texas says to the woman from New York, "Hi! Where y'all from?"

The woman from New York replies, "Where I come from we don't end our sentences with prepositions…"

So the woman from Texas says, "Fine! Where y'all from, BITCH?!"

A few minutes later, the woman from New York meets the woman from Texas's husband. She's steamed at the Texas broad, so she asks (in a very suggestive voice) "Is there anything I can do for you, handsome??"

"Welllllll," replies the Texan, "I sure could use a piece of ass."

The woman from New York nods, takes the Texan into the bedroom, takes off all of her clothes, takes off all of his clothes, and engages in a hot session of mad, passionate lovemaking with him. After they are done, she again says suggestively, "Now, handsome, is there anything else I can do for you?"

"Well, ma'am, " he replies, "I could still use that piece of ass. Mah drink is gettin' mighty warm."

TEXAS THREE-KICK RULE

A big-city California lawyer went duck-hunting in rural Texas. He shot and dropped a bird, but it fell into a farmer's field on the other side of a fence.

As the lawyer climbed over the fence, an elderly farmer drove up on his tractor and asked him what he was doing. The litigator responded, "I shot a duck and it fell in this field, and now I'm going into retrieve it."

The old farmer replied. "This is my property, and you are not coming over here."

The indignant lawyer said, "I am one of the best trial attorneys in the U.S. and, if you don't let me get that duck, I'll sue you and take everything you own."

The old farmer smiled and said, "Apparently, you don't know how we do things in Texas. We settle small disagreements like this with the Texas Three-Kick Rule."

The lawyer asked, "What is the Texas Three-Kick Rule?"

The farmer replied, "Well, first I kick you three times and then you kick me three times, and so on, back and forth, until someone gives up."

The attorney quickly thought about the proposed contest and decided that he could easily take the old codger. He agreed to abide by the local custom.

The old farmer slowly climbed down from the tractor and walked up to the city feller. His first kick planted the toe of his heavy work boot into the lawyer's groin and dropped him to his knees. His second kick nearly ripped the man's nose off his face. The barrister was flat on his belly when the farmer's third kick to a kidney nearly caused him to give up.

The lawyer summoned every bit of his will and managed to get to his feet and said, "Okay, you old coot, now it's my turn."

The old farmer smiled and said, "Naw, I give up. You can have the duck."

A Texan was taking a taxi tour of London, and was in a hurry.

As they went by the Tower of London the cabbie explained what it was and that construction started in 1346 and it was completed in 1412. The Texan replied, "Shoot, a little ol' tower like that? In Houston we'd have that thing up in two weeks!"

House of Parliament next: Started construction in 1544, completed 1618. "Hell boy, we put up a bigger one than that in Dallas and it only took a year!"

As they passed Westminster Abbey, the cabby was silent. "Whoah! What's that over there?"

"Damned if I know, wasn't there yesterday..."

TEXAN EMERGENCY FIRST AID

Two men from Texas were sitting at a bar when a young lady nearby began to choke on a hamburger. As she gasped and gagged, one Texan turned to the other and said, "That gal is havin' a bad time. I'm gonna go over there and help."

The Texan ran over to the young lady, held both sides of her head in his big, Texan hands, and asked, "Kin ya swaller?"

Gasping, she acknowledged that she couldn't swallow. Then, the Texan asked, "Kin ya breathe?" Still gasping, she motioned that she couldn't breathe. With that, the Texan yanked up her skirt, pulled down her panties, and licked her butt. The young woman was so shocked and humiliated that she coughed up the piece of hamburger and began breathing on her own.

The Texan sat back down with his friend and said, "Ya know, it's sure amazin' how that hind-lick maneuver always works!"

Americans (You bet!)

Q: How can you tell it's midnight at an American airport?

A: When you see the 8:00 P.M. flights taking off.

Q: What do Americans call a TV set that goes five years without need of repair?

A: An import.

Q: How can an American be certain that the car he's just bought is actually new?

A: When it's recalled by the factory.

Three guys are in a bar: a Texan, a Californian, and a Seattleite. They drink, they get crazy.

The Texan grabs a bottle of tequila, unscrews the top, takes a good swig, and throws the bottle into the air. He then pulls out a forty-five-caliber pistol and shoots the bottle, spraying tequila all over everything.

The other patrons at the bar shout, "Hey why'd you waste that?"

The Texan says, "Hell, it's just tequila. Where I come from, we got lotsa tequila."

The Californian, not to be outdone, whips out a corkscrew and opens a bottle of Chardonnay, pours a bit into a glass, swirls it around, sips it, then throws the bottle in the air and shoots it with a little silver pistol.

The patrons again express their displeasure and astonishment at the waste of a bottle of good wine.

The Californian says, "Napa Valley, we got lots of great wine up there."

The Seattleite borrows the corkscrew, pops the top off a bottle of Red Hook and downs the whole bottle. He throws the empty bottle into the air, shoots the Californian, and simultaneously catches the falling bottle.

Now the people are screaming, "Why'd you do that?"

The Seattleite replies, "I'm from Seattle. We've got lots of Californians, but I got to recycle this bottle."

America is the only country in the world where the poor have a parking problem.

San Francisco is like muesli: take away the fruits and the nuts and all you have left is the flakes.

New Yorkers (You talkin' to me?)

Living in California adds ten years to a man's life. And those extra ten years, I'd like to spend in New York.

A New Yorker was forced to take a day off from work to appear for a minor traffic summons. He grew increasingly restless as he waited hour after endless hour for his case to be heard.

When his name was called late in the afternoon, he stood before the judge, only to hear that court would be adjourned for the rest of the afternoon and he would have to return the next day.

"What for?!?!?" he snapped at the judge.

His honor, equally irked by a tedious day and sharp query, roared out loud, "Twenty dollars contempt of court! That's why!"

Then, noticing the man checking his wallet, the judge relented, "That's all right. You don't have to pay now."

The young man replied, "I know. But I'm just seeing if I have enough for two more words."

Canadian (Sorry, my mind wandered...)

Q: Why do Canadians like to do it doggie-style?

A: So they can both watch the hockey game.

Q: How do you get a bunch of Canadians out of the pool?

A: Tell them to get out of the pool.

A Newfie was going to Toronto on an airplane and started talking to a Mainlander.

NEWFIE: Lord Tundrin' Geeses Bye, what do you do for a livin'?

MAINLANDER: Well, I'm a psychoanalyst.

NEWFIE: Psychoanalyst, what the heck is that?

MAINLANDER: It's hard to explain, so I'll give you an example. Do you own a fishtank?

NEWFIE: Yes, I got a tank.

MAINLANDER: Well, I bet you like fish, then?

NEWFIE: Yeah, I like fish.

MAINLANDER: Well, if you like fish, then you probably like the water.

NEWFIE: Yeah, I love the water.

MAINLANDER: Well, if you like the water, then you probably like to go to the beach.

NEWFIE: I love to go to the beach.

MAINLANDER: I bet you like to look at girls in bikinis while you're at the beach.

NEWFIE: You betcha.

MAINLANDER: And as you're looking at girls on the beach I bet you thinkin' about taking them home and having your way with them.

NEWFIE: Gosh, how did you know that?

MAINLANDER: Well, that's what a psychoanalyst is.

NEWFIE: Oh.

The Newfie was going back to St. John's and started to talk to another Mainlander on the plane.

NEWFIE: Hi, How ya doin'?

MAINLANDER: Oh, fine, I guess.

NEWFIE: I'm a psychoanalyst.

MAINLANDER: You're a psychoanalyst?

NEWFIE: Yeah, let me explain it to ya. Do you own a fish-tank?

MAINLANDER: No.

NEWFIE: What are ya!? Some kind of a faggot?

Irish (Enough said)

Something irascible, quite inexplicable, Irish.
Strange blend of shyness, pride and conceit
And stubborn refusal to bow in defeat.
He's spoiling and ready to argue and fight,
Yet the smile of a child fills his soul with delight.
His eyes are the quickest to well up in tears,
Yet his strength is the strongest to banish your fears.
His faith is as fierce as his devotion is grand
And there's no middle ground on which he will stand.
He's wild and he's gentle, he's good and he's bad,
He's proud and he's humble, he's happy and sad.
He's in love with the ocean, the earth and the skies,
He's enamored with beauty wherever it lies.
He's victor and victim, a star and a clod,
But mostly he's Irish and in love with his God.

God then made man.

The Italians for their beauty.

The French for fine food.

The Swedes for intelligence.

The Jews for faith.

And on and on, until he looked at what he had created and said, "This is all very fine but no one is having fun. I guess I'll have to make me an Irishman."

Wherever you go and whatever you do,
May the luck of the Irish be there with you.

Q: What's the Irish version of a queer?

A: Someone who prefers women to liquor.

A man stumbles up to the only other patron in the bar and asks if he can buy him a drink.

"Why, of course," comes the reply.

The first man then asks, "Where are you from?"

"I'm from Ireland," replies the second man.

The first man responds, "You don't say. I'm from Ireland, too! Let's have another round to Ireland!"

"Of course," replies the second man, knocking back another one.

Curious, the first man asks, "Where in Ireland are you from?"

"Dublin," comes the reply.

"I can't believe it," says the first man, "I'm from Dublin too! Let's have another drink to Dublin!"

Both men continue drinking.

Curiosity strikes again and the first man asks, "What school did you go to?"

"St. Mary's," replies the second man. "I graduated in '82."

"This is unbelievable," the first man says. "I went to St. Mary's and I graduated in '82, also!"

About this time, one of the regulars comes into the bar and takes a seat.

"What's been going on?" he asks the bartender.

"Nothin' much," answers the bartender. "The O'Malley twins are drunk again."

Q: What's the difference between an Irish wedding and an Irish funeral?

A: One drunk Irishman.

This Irish guy shows up in a pub one day and orders three pints of Guinness. He takes sips from each glass until they are empty and calls the bartender for three more. The bartender says, "Hey, pal, I don't mind bringing one at a time, then they'll be fresh and cold."

"Nah...ahm preferrin' that ya bring 'em three at a time. You see, me and me two brothers would meet at a pub and drink and have good times. Now one is in Australia, the other in Canada, and I'm here. We agreed before we split up that we'd drink this way to each other's honor."

"Well," says the bartender, "that's a damn good sentimental thing to do. I'll bring the pints as you ask."

Well, time goes on and the Irishman's peculiar habit is known and accepted by all the pub regulars. One day, the Irishman comes in and orders only two pints. A hush falls over the pub. Naturally, everyone figures something happened to one of the brothers. A bunch of the regulars corner the bartender and finally persuade him to find out what happened.

With a heavy heart, the bartender brings the two pints and says, "Here's your pints...and let me offer my sincerest condolences. What happened?"

The Irishman looks extremely puzzled for a moment. When the light comes on in his head, he starts laughing. "No, no! 'Tis nothing like that. You see, I've given up drinking for Lent."

May there always be work for your hands to do.
May your purse always hold a coin or two.
May the sun always shine on your windowpane.
May a rainbow be certain to follow each rain.
May the hand of a friend always be near you.
May God fill your heart with gladness to cheer you.

May you have the hindsight to know where you've been, the foresight to know where you're going, and the insight to know when you're going too far.

Italian (Points for the food)

Why does the New Italian Navy have glass-bottom boats?

To see the Old Italian Navy!

HENNY YOUNGMAN

An American tourist was driving outside of Rome when he decided to stop for a hitchhiker. To his surprise, the hitchhiker pulled a gun and, with a thick Italian accent, demanded that the tourist get out of the car.

"Don't kill me, please. Just take my money, take the car."

"I no-a kill you," the Italian replied, "as long as you do-a what I say. Now take-a out your dick and masturbate."

The shocked tourist did what he was told.

"Okay," said the Italian, "now do it again." The tourist wanted to protest, but the Italian had the gun pointed at him, so he did it one more time.

"Now one more-a time, or I-a kill you." With extreme effort the tourist brought himself to a third orgasm.

Then the Italian gave a signal and a bellisima young woman stepped out from behind a big tree. "Now," said the Italian, "you can-a give my sister a ride to town."

Polish (No points for the food)

SOME POLISH JOKES BY HENNY YOUNGMAN:

In a blackout, a Polish man was stuck on an escalator for two hours. I asked him, "Why didn't you walk down?" He said, "Because I was going up!"

Have you seen the new Polish jigsaw puzzle? One piece.

A Polish terrorist was sent to blow up a car. He burned his mouth on the exhaust pipe!

Are you Polish? Okay, I'll talk slower.

Russians (...are coming)

The farmers of a Russian commune are gathered together by some officials for an announcement. The government spokesman steps up and declares that production is up, tractors are being manufactured in record quantities, and the economy is wonderful. He then asks if there are any questions. A farmer named Perchek raises his hand. "Yes, Comrade, a question. If everything is so wonderful, why are we hungry, ill-housed and ill-clothed?"

"An excellent question," comes the reply. "I will ask it to my superiors and return to you with an answer."

Three months later, the farmers are once again gathered and the same type of news is announced. The spokesman again asks if there are questions.

"Yes," says one farmer. "Where is Perchek?"

Two Russian border guards, Ivan and Vladimir, are on duty on a cold winter morning. Looking across the border, Ivan is smiling to himself, then he notices that Vladimir is also smiling.

IVAN (suspiciously): "What were you thinking about?"

VLADIMIR: "Same thing you were thinking about, comrade."

IVAN: "Then it is my duty to arrest you."

WASPs (Cocktail time)

Q: What's a WASP's version of mass transit?

A: The ferry to Martha's Vineyard.

Over lunch one day, Steinberg and DeLorenzo were discussing whether or not WASPs could be said to have a sense of humor.

Steinberg staunchly maintained they did not. "After all," he pointed out, "why does a WASP need a sense of humor?"

"Not so," protested DeLorenzo. "My WASP acquaintances always laugh at my jokes. In fact, I get three laughs out of them...once when they hear the joke, once when I explain it, and the third when they understand it."

Religion (Hallelujah!)

THREE RELIGIOUS TRUTHS

1. Jews do not recognize Jesus as the Messiah.

2. Protestants do not recognize the Pope as the leader of the Christian faith.

3. Baptists do not recognize each other in the liquor store or at Hooters.

WHY GOD NEVER RECEIVED A PH.D.

1. He had only one major publication.

2. It was in Hebrew.

3. It had no references.

4. It wasn't published in a refereed journal.

5. Some even doubt he wrote it by himself.

6. It may be true that he created the world, but what has he done since then?

7. His cooperative efforts have been quite limited.

8. The scientific community has had a hard time replicating his results.

9. He never applied to the ethics board for permission to use human subjects.

10. When one experiment went awry, he tried to cover it by drowning his subjects.

11. When subjects didn't behave as predicted, he deleted them from the sample.

12. He rarely came to class, just told students to read the book.

13. Some say he had his son teach the class.

14. He expelled his first two students for learning.

15. Although there were only ten requirements, most of his students failed his tests.

16. His office hours were infrequent and usually held on a mountain top.

17. No record of working well with colleagues.

Amish (Is nothing sacred?)

I love making fun of the Amish, you know why? 'Cause they are never going to find out.

DAVE ATTELL

An Amish lady is trotting down the road in her horse and buggy when she is pulled over by a cop.

"Ma'am," he says, "I'm not going to ticket you, but you have a broken reflector on your buggy."

"Oh, I'll tell my husband, Jacob, as soon as I get home."

"That's fine," he replied. "Another thing, I don't like the way that one rein loops across the horse's back and around one of his balls. I consider that animal abuse. Have your husband take care of that right away!"

Later that day, the lady is home telling her husband about the encounter with the cop. "Well, dear, what exactly, did he say?"

"He said the reflector was broken."

"I can fix that in two minutes. What else?"

"I'm not sure, Jacob. Something about the emergency brake."

Catholics (Bless me, Father...)

A priest decides to take a walk to the pier. He looks around and stops to watch a fisherman load his boat.

The fisherman asks if the priest has ever fished before, to which the priest answers, no. The fisherman asks him if he'd like to join him for a couple of hours. The priest agrees. The fisherman baits his hook for him and says, "Give it a shot, Father."

After a few minutes, the priest hooks a big fish and struggles to get it in the boat.

The fisherman says, "Whoa, look at that big sonofabitch!"

PRIEST: Pardon me, I am a man of God. Would you please mind your language?

FISHERMAN (thinking quickly): I'm sorry father, but that is what the fish is called—a sonofabitch.

PRIEST: I didn't know. Sorry.

After the trip, the priest brings the fish to the church and stops to see the bishop. "Would you look at the size of this sonofabitch!" the priest exclaims.

BISHOP: Father, I am shocked, you are a priest and this is a house of the Lord.

PRIEST: No, you don't understand, that is what the fish is called, a sonofabitch, and I caught it.

BISHOP: Hmm, you know, I could clean this sonofabitch and we could have him for dinner.

So the bishop cleans the fish and takes it to the mother superior.

BISHOP: Mother, could you cook this sonofabitch for dinner?

MOTHER SUPERIOR: Your Grace! What language!

BISHOP: No, Mother, that's what this fish is called, a sonofabitch! Father caught it, I cleaned it and we want you to cook it!

MOTHER SUPERIOR: Well, I'd love to cook up that sonofabitch!

As luck would have it, the Pope is in town and stops by the diocese, where he is invited to dinner. He thinks the fish is great and asks where they got it.

PRIEST: I caught the sonofabitch.

BISHOP: And I cleaned the sonofabitch.

MOTHER SUPERIOR: And I cooked the sonofabitch.

The Pope stares at them for a minute with a steely gaze and then takes off his hat, leans back in his chair, and puts his feet up on the table, lights a cigarette and says, "You know, you fuckers are all right!"

I remember I was so depressed I was going to jump out a window...so they sent a priest up to talk to me.

He said, "On your mark..."

RODNEY DANGERFIELD

Four young novice nuns were about to take their vows, dressed in their white gowns. They came into the chapel where the mother superior was waiting for them for the ceremony to marry them to God.

In front of them on the table were the four wedding rings.

Just as the ceremony was about to begin, four Hasidic men with their yarmulkes, payes, and long beards came in and sat silently in the front row.

Somewhat taken aback, the mother superior said to them. "I am honored that you would want to share this experience with us, but do you mind if I ask you why you came?"

"We're from the groom's side."

A Sunday School teacher asked her class why Joseph and Mary took Jesus with them to Jerusalem. A small child replied: "They couldn't get a baby-sitter."

Heaven was getting a bit crowded, so Peter began giving quizzes to see who should get in. A man ascended to heaven, and came to the gates. "Who was the first man?" asked Peter.

"Adam."

"That's correct. Enter."

Soon another man came along. "Where did Adam and Eve live?"

"Eden."

"That's correct. Enter."

Then Mother Theresa came along. "Ooh, I'll have to give you a hard one. What did Eve say when she met Adam for the first time?"

"Mmm, that IS a hard one."

"Enter."

One day a cat dies of natural causes and goes to Heaven and meets the Lord Himself. The Lord says to the cat, "You lived a good life and if there is any way I can make your stay in Heaven more comfortable, please let me know." The cat thinks for a moment and says, "Lord, all my life I have lived with a poor family and had to sleep on a hard wooden floor." The Lord stops the cat and says, "Say no more," and a wonderful fluffy pillow appears.

A few days later 6 mice are killed in a tragic farming accident and go to Heaven. Again, the Lord is there to greet them with the same offer. The mice answer, "All of our lives we have been chased. We have had to run from cats, dogs, and even women with brooms. We are tired of running. Do you think we could have roller skates so we don't have to run any more?" The Lord says, "Say no more," and fits each mouse with a beautiful pair of roller skates.

About a week later the Lord stops by to see the cat and finds him snoozing on the pillow. The Lord gently wakes the cat and asks him, "How are things since you have been here?" The cat stretches and yawns and replies, "It is wonderful here. Better than I could have ever expected. And those Meals on Wheels you have been sending by are the best!!"

SISTER MARY AND THE BET

Sister Mary burst into the office of the principal of Our Lady of Perpetual Motion parochial school in an advanced state of agitation.

"Father!" she cried, "just WAIT until you hear this!"

The priest led the sister to a chair, and said, "Now just calm down and tell me what has you so excited."

"Well, Father," the nun began, "I was just walking down the hall to the chapel and I heard some of the older boys wagering money!"

"A serious infraction, indeed!" said the priest.

"But that's not what has me so excited, father" replied the nun. "It was WHAT they were wagering on! They had wagered on a contest to see who could urinate the highest on the wall!!"

"What an incredible wager!" exclaimed the priest, "What did you do?"

Sister Mary said, "Well, I hit the CEILING, father."

He asked, "How much did you win?"

As man is driving and sees a sign which reads:

SISTERS OF MERCY HOUSE OF PROSTITUTION—10 MILES.

He thinks it was a figment of his imagination and drives on. Soon, he sees another sign which says...SISTERS OF MERCY HOUSE OF PROSTITUTION—5 MILES.

Realizing these signs are for real, he drives on and sure enough, there is a third...SISTERS OF MERCY HOUSE OF PROSTITUTION—NEXT RIGHT.

His curiosity gets the best of him and he pulls into the driveway. On the far side of the parking lot is a somber stone building with a sign on the door that reads... SISTERS OF MERCY HOUSE OF PROSTITUTION.

He climbs the steps, rings the bell and the door is answered by a nun in a long black habit, who asks, "What may we do for you my son?"

"I saw your signs along the highway and was interested in possibly doing some business," he answers.

"Very well, my son. Please follow me," says the nun.

He is led through many winding passages, and soon he is very disoriented. The nun stops at a closed door and tells the man, "Please, knock on this door" and leaves.

The man does as he is told and this door is opened by another nun in a long black habit, holding a tin cup. This nun instructs: "Please place $50.00 in the cup, then go through the large wooden door at the end of this hallway."

He places the money in this nun's tin cup. He trots eagerly down the hallway and slips through the door, pulling it shut. As the door locks behind him, he finds himself back in the parking lot, facing another small sign:

"Go in Peace. You have just been screwed by the Sisters of Mercy."

Two nuns, Sister Marilyn and Sister Helen, are traveling through Europe in their car. They get to Transylvania and are stopped at a traffic light.

Suddenly, out of nowhere, a tiny little vampire jumps onto the hood of the car and hisses through the windshield.

"Quick, quick!" shouts Sister Marilyn. "What shall we do?" "Turn the windshield wipers on. That will get rid of the abomination," says Sister Helen. Sister Marilyn switches them on, knocking the vampire about, but he clings on and continues hissing at the nuns.

"What shall I do now?" she shouts. "Switch on the windshield washer. I filled it up with Holy Water at the Vatican," says Sister Helen.

Sister Marilyn turns on the windshield washer. The vampire screams as the water burns his skin, but he clings on and continues hissing at the nuns.

"Now what?" shouts Sister Marilyn?

"Show him your cross," says Sister Helen. "Now you're talking," says Sister Marilyn. She opens the window and shouts, "Get the hell off our car!"

A nun got into a cab, and the driver was staring at her. She asked him why he was staring at her, and he said, "I want to ask you a question, but I don't want to offend you."

She said, "You can't offend me, not as old as I am and as long as I have been a nun. I've heard just about everything."

The cabdriver said, "Well, I've always had a fantasy to have a nun give me a blow job."

She said, "Well let's see what we can work out. I have two conditions: One—you have to be single. Two—you have to be Catholic."

The cabdriver said, "Oh I'm single and I am Catholic."

She said, "Okay, pull in to the alley," and he did. So she performed the act. Then they were on the street again.

Suddenly the cabdriver started laughing, and the nun said, "My child, what's so funny?"

He said, "Ha ha, I pulled a fast one on you, sister. The truth is I'm married, and I'm Jewish!"

She said, "That's okay. My name is Steve, and I'm on my way to a costume party."

A priest and a rabbi were talking when the rabbi asked the priest about confession. "I have an idea," said the priest. "Why don't you sit with me on my side of the confession booth and hear it for yourself? No one will ever know."

A woman came into the booth and said, "Bless me, Father, for I have sinned."

The priest asked, "What did you do?"

"I cheated on my husband."

"How many times?"

"Three times."

"Well," said the priest, "say five Hail Marys and put five dollars in the offering box."

Another woman came and said, "Bless me, Father, for I have sinned."

The priest asked, "What did you do?"

"I cheated on my husband."

"How many times?"

"Three times."

Again the priest said, "Say five Hail Marys and put five dollars in the offering box."

Then the priest said to the rabbi, "Would you like to do the next confession?"

The rabbi started to object, but the priest said, "Go ahead. It's easy."

So another woman came in and said, "Bless me, Father, for I have sinned."

This time the rabbi asked, "What did you do?"

"I cheated on my husband."

"How many times?"

The woman said, "Twice."

Then the rabbi said, "Well, go do it again. They're three for five dollars today."

A priest and a nun went golfing one day. The priest seemed to have an extremely foul mouth for a priest. He was first to putt.

"Goddamnit, I missed!" exclaimed the priest.

This upset the nun. She replied, "If you say that two more times, God will send a bolt of lightning down from the sky at you!"

The priest then takes his second putt. "Goddamnit, I missed again!" he screamed even louder.

The nun was very unhappy with the priest this time. "If you say that again, I know you will get struck by lightning. God doesn't like his name used in vain."

This priest wasn't a very good golfer, and he missed again. Ignoring the nun's threats, he yelled, "Goddamnit, I missed!"

All of a sudden, down came a huge bolt of lightning from the sky. It hit the nun. The priest blinked in disbelief. Then the clouds moved and God peeked out. He yelled, "Goddamnit, I missed!"

Christians (Fire and brimstone)

Why is it that when we talk to God we are praying, but when God talks to us, we're schizophrenic?

LILY TOMLIN

"Lord, I have a problem!"

"What's the problem, Eve?"

"Lord, I know you've created me and have provided this beautiful garden and all of these wonderful animals and that hilarious comedy snake, but I'm just not happy."

"Why is that, Eve?" came the reply from above.

"Lord, I am lonely. And I'm sick to death of apples."

"Well, Eve, in that case, I have a solution. I shall create a man for you."

"What's a 'man,' Lord?"

"This man will be a flawed creature, with aggressive tendencies, an enormous ego, and an inability to empathize or listen to you properly. He'll basically give you a hard time. He'll be bigger, faster, and more muscular than you. He'll be really good at fighting and kicking a ball about and hunting fleet-footed ruminants. And, he'll be pretty good in the sack."

"I can put up with that," says Eve, with an ironically raised eyebrow.

"Yeah well, he's better than a poke in the eye with a burnt stick. But, there is one condition."

"What's that, Lord?"

"You'll have to let him believe that I made him first."

During his sermon one Sunday, the local preacher told his congregation that the entire range of human experience could be found in the Bible. He confidently stated, "If anything can happen to humans, it is described somewhere in the Bible."

After the service, a woman came up to the preacher and said, "Reverend, I don't think the Bible mentions anything about PMS."

The preacher told the woman he was certain he could find a reference to PMS somewhere in Scripture.

During the following week, he searched diligently, book by book, chapter by chapter, and verse by verse.

On the following Sunday, the woman came up to him and asked, "Did you find any references to PMS in the Bible?"

The preacher smiled, opened his Bible, and began to read, "…and Mary rode Joseph's ass all the way to Bethlehem."

One day, after a near-eternity in the Garden of Eden, Adam calls out to God, "Lord, I have a problem."

"What's the problem, Adam?" God asks.

"Lord, you created me and provided for me and surrounded me with this beautiful garden and all of these wonderful animals, but I'm just not happy."

"Why is that, Adam?" comes the reply from the Heavens.

"Lord, I know you created this place for me, with all this lovely food and all of the beautiful animals, but I am lonely."

"Well Adam, in that case I have the perfect solution. I shall create a woman for you."

"What's a woman, Lord?"

"This woman will be the most intelligent, sensitive, caring, and beautiful creature I have ever created. She will be so intelligent that she can figure out what you want before you want it. She will be so sensitive and caring that she will know your every mood and how to make you happy. Her beauty will rival that of the heavens and earth. She will unquestioningly care for your every need and desire. She will be the perfect companion for you," replies the heavenly voice. "She will love you before herself."

"Sounds great!"

"She will be, but this is going to cost you, Adam."

"How much will this woman cost me, Lord?" Adam replies.

"She'll cost you your right arm, your right leg, an eye, an ear, and your left testicle."

Adam ponders this for some time, with a look of deep thought and concern. Finally Adam says to God, "What can I get for a rib?"

Guy goes to hell. The Devil is in a good mood, so on the first day, he shows the guy around so he can choose which damnation will fall on him.

They go into the first room and see people flogged by demons, with hundreds of flies feasting on their wounds.

Horrified, the guy shuts the door and says, "I think I'll see a few more punishments, please."

He goes into a second room and sees people boiled alive in cauldrons, demons piercing their bodies with spears.

Despairing, he opens the third door. He sees Claudia Schiffer fucking some old guy while ten demons watch. Happy, he tells the devil, "Okay, I want this punishment."

"All right," says the devil, and he calls the demons: "Guys, give this man the same punishment we gave Claudia Schiffer."

Jews (See, also, the rest of this book)

FIFTEEN JEWISH COUNTRY SONGS

1. "I was One of the Chosen People, 'Til She Chose Someone New"

2. "Honky Tonk Nights on the Golan Heights"

3. "I've Got My Foot on the Glass, Where Are You?"

4. "My Rowdy Friend Elijah Is Comin' Over Tonight"

5. "New Bottle of Whiskey, Same Ol' Testament"

6. "Stand by Your Mensch"

7. "Eighteen Wheels and a Dozen Latkes"

8. "I Balanced Your Books but You Are Breaking My Heart"

9. "My Darlin's a Schmendrick and I'm All Verklempt"

10. "That Shiksa Done Made off with My Heart Like a Goniff"

11. "The Second Time She Said Shalom, I Knew She Meant Goodbye"

12. "You're the Lox My Bagel's Been Missing"

13. "You've Been Talking Hebrew in Your Sleep Since That Rabbi Came to Town"

14. "Why Don't We Get Drunk? We're Jews!"

15. "Mamas, Don't Let Your Ungrateful Sons Grow Up to Be Cowboys (When They Could Have Just As Easily Gone into the Family Business)"

Q: What did the waiter ask the group of dining Jewish women?

A: Is anything all right?

Jewish Version of Natural Childbirth:

No makeup.

Q: What's a Jewish "Ten"?

A: A "Seven" with three million dollars in the bank.

Several centuries ago, the Pope decreed that all the Jews had to leave Italy. There was, of course, a huge outcry from the Jewish community, so the Pope offered a deal. He would have a religious debate with a leader of the Jewish community. If the Jewish leader won the debate, the Jews would be permitted to stay in Italy. If the Pope won, the Jews would have to leave.

The Jewish community met and picked an aged Rabbi, Moishe, to represent them in the debate. Rabbi Moishe, however, could not speak Latin and the Pope could not speak Yiddish. So it was decided that this would be a "silent" debate.

On the day of the great debate, the Pope and Rabbi Moishe sat opposite each other for a full minute before the Pope raised his hand and showed three fingers. Rabbi Moishe looked back and raised one finger.

Next, the Pope waved his finger around his head. Rabbi Moishe pointed to the ground where he sat. The Pope then brought out a communion wafer and chalice of wine. Rabbi Moishe pulled out an apple. With that, the Pope stood up and said, "I concede the debate. This man has bested me. The Jews can stay."

Later, the Cardinals gathered around the Pope, asking him what had happened. The Pope said, "First I held up three fingers to represent the Trinity. He responded by holding up one finger to remind me that there was still one God common to both our religions. Then I waved my finger around me to show him that God was all around us. He responded by pointing to the ground to show that God was also right here with us. I pulled out the wine and the wafer to show that God absolves us of our sins. He pulled out an apple to remind me of original sin. He had an answer for everything. What could I do?"

Meanwhile, the Jewish community crowded around Rabbi Moishe, asking what happened. "Well," said Moishe, "first he said to me, 'You Jews have three days to get out of here.' So I said to him, 'Up yours.' Then he tells me the whole city would be cleared of Jews. So I said to him, 'Listen here Mr. Pope, the Jews...we stay right here!'" "And then?" asked a woman. "Who knows?" said Rabbi Moishe. "He took out his lunch, and I took out mine."

What did the Jewish Mother bank teller say to her customer?

You never write, you never call, you only visit when you need money.

What did the Jewish Mother ask her daughter when she told her she had an affair?

Who catered it?

What kind of cigarettes do Jewish Mothers smoke?

Gefiltered.

Why do Jewish Mothers make great parole officers?

They never let anyone finish a sentence.

Why are Jewish Mothers always excused from jury duty?

They all insist that they're the guilty ones.

What is a genius?

An average student with a Jewish Mother.

Anytime a person goes into a delicatessen and orders a pastrami on white bread, somewhere a Jew dies.

MILTON BERLE

Two Jewish matrons were conversing on the porch swing of a large white pillared mansion in Miami Beach.

The first woman says, "Ven mine first child vas born, mine husband built for me dus beautiful menshun."

The second woman says, "Fentestic!"

The first woman continues, "Ven mine second child vas born, mine husband bought for me dot fine Kedillek in de driveway."

Again, the second woman says, "Fentestic!"

The first woman boasts, "Den, ven mine third child vas born, mine husband bought for me this exqvisite diamond bracelet."

Yet again, the second woman comments, "Fentestic!"

The first woman then asks her companion, "Nu, so vat did your husband buy for you ven you had your first child?"

The second woman replies, "Mine husband sent me to charm school."

"Charm school??" the first woman cries, "Vay iss mir! Vot for?"

The first woman responds, "So dot instead of saying, 'Who gives a shit,' I learned to say, 'Fentestic!'"

(This joke is best told and not read. It helps if you can do dialects.)

Time: Late 1940s

Place: New York

There were these two elderly Jewish gentlemen visiting the Big Apple when they decided it was getting late and they needed to find a room for the night. As they passed a hotel, one man said to the other, "Why don't we try this one?"

The other said, "Are you crazy?" It says on the sign that this is a restricted hotel. You know what that means? It means they don't let Jews in!"

To which the first man replied, "Restricted, reschmicted. Let's go in and have a little fun. Just let me do all the talking."

So the two men entered and approached the desk clerk.

MAN (in thick Yiddish accent): We want a room!

CLERK (flustered, with a "Connecticut clench"): I'm sorry, but this is a restricted hotel. We do not allow Jewish people to stay here.

MAN: What makes you think I'm Jewish? I'm just as Christian as you are! Come on, ask me a Christian question!

The clerk decides to humor him.

CLERK: Okay, okay. Where was Jesus born?

MAN: Such a question! Everybody knows that Jesus was born in a stable. Come on, ask me another Christian question!

CLERK (impatient): Look. I know you are Jewish and you are not staying here!

MAN: Come on, ask me a question. Ask me, "What for was Jesus born in a stable!"

CLERK (visibly angry): All right! Why was Jesus born in a stable!?

MAN: Because a schmuck like you wouldn't give *his* mother a room either!

During the war, an Italian girl saved my life. She hid me in her basement in Cleveland.

HENNY YOUNGMAN

A Jewish man pulls up to the curb and asks the policeman, "Can I park here?"

"No" says the cop.

"What about all these other cars?"

"They didn't ask!"

HENNY YOUNGMAN

Q: Why don't Jews drink?

A: It interferes with their suffering.

MORE JEWISH GEMS FROM HENNY YOUNGMAN

Two Jewish women in New York, one says, "Do you see what's going on in Poland?"

The other says, "I live in the back, I don't see anything."

A little Jewish grandma is at the Florida coast with her little Jewish grandson. The grandson is playing on the beach when a big wave comes and washes the kid out to sea. The lifeguards swim out, bring him back to shore, the paramedics work on him for a long time, pumping the water out, reviving him. They turn to the Jewish Grandma, and say, "We saved your grandson."

The little Jewish Grandma says, "He had a hat!"

A Jewish businessman was in a great deal of trouble. His business was failing, he had put everything he had into the business, he owed everybody. It was so bad he was even contemplating suicide. As a last resort he went to a Rabbi and poured out his story of woe.

When he had finished, the Rabbi said, "Here's what I want you to do: Put a beach chair and your Bible in your car and drive down to the beach. Take the beach chair and the Bible to the water's edge, sit down in the beach chair, and put the Bible in your lap. Open the Bible; the wind will rifle the pages, but finally the open Bible will come to rest on a page. Look down at the page and read the first thing you see. That will be your answer, that will tell you what to do."

A year later the businessman went back to the Rabbi and brought his wife and children with him. The man was in a new custom-tailored suit, his wife in a mink coat, the children were all in brand-new clothes. The businessman pulled an envelope stuffed with money out of his pocket, and gave it to the Rabbi as a donation in thanks for his advice.

The Rabbi recognized the benefactor, and was curious. "You did as I suggested?" he asked.

"Absolutely," replied the businessman.

"You went to the beach?"

"Absolutely."

"You sat in a beach chair with the Bible in your lap?"

"Absolutely."

"You let the pages rifle until they stopped?"

"Absolutely."

"And what were the first words you saw?"

"Chapter 11."

AN AMERICAN JEW IN LONDON

An American Jew was on Regent Street in London and entered a posh gourmet food shop. A salesperson in a morning coat with tails approached him and politely asked, "May I be of service to you, sir?"

"Yes," replied the customer, "I would like to buy a pound of lox."

"No, no," replied the dignified salesperson, "You mean 'smoked salmon.'"

"Okay, a pound of smoked salmon."

"Anything else?"

"Yes, a dozen blintzes."

"No, no—you mean 'crepes.'"

"Okay, a dozen crepes."

"Anything else?"

"Yes. A pound of chopped liver."

"No, no. You mean 'paté.'"

"Okay," said the Jewish patron, "A pound of paté, and I'd like you to deliver this Saturday."

"Sir," said the indignant salesperson, "we don't schlep chazzerai on Shabbos!"

A QUESTION FOR THE RABBI

An elderly Italian Jewish man wanted to unburden his guilty conscience by talking to his Rabbi.

"Rabbi, during World War II, when the Germans entered Italy, I pretended to be a goy and changed my name from Levy to Spumoni, and I am alive today because of it."

"Self-preservation is important and the fact that you never forgot that you were a Jew is admirable," said the Rabbi.

"Rabbi, a beautiful Jewish woman knocked on my door and asked me to hide her from the Germans. I hid her in my attic and they never found her."

"That was a wonderful thing you did and you have no need to feel guilty."

"It's worse, Rabbi. I was weak and told her she must repay me with her sexual favors."

"You were both in great danger and would have suffered terribly if the Germans had found her. There is a favorable balance between good and evil and you will be judged kindly. Give up your feelings of guilt."

"Thank you, Rabbi. That's a great load off my mind. But I have one more question."

"And what is that?"

"Should I tell her the war is over?"

JEWISH SURVIVOR

Flush with the success of its latest creation, CBS is launching a new version, called *Jewish Survivor*. Sixteen Jews are put in a two-bedroom co-op on the Upper West Side of New York. Each week they vote out one member until there is a final survivor who gets $1 million (but placed into a trust that does not vest until age 59).

The Rules:

1. No maid service.

2. No use of ATMs or credit cards.

3. No food from any take-out or delivery service (this includes Chinese food).

4. All purchases must be retail.

5. No calls to mother for women, to office for men.

6. Outside trips must be by foot, bus, or subway—no limos or cabs.

7. All workouts/exercise must be done in regular sweats—no designer labels.

8. Zabar's is off limits.

9. No Jewish geography.

10. No *New York Times.* Only *New York Post* or *New York Daily News.*

11. No Pottery Barn, J. Crew, Lands' End or Williams-Sonoma catalogs.

12. Only one phone line for all sixteen Tribe members. No call can last more than three minutes. No cell phones.

13. Maintenance problems must be resolved by the Tribe, without help from any gentiles.

14. All therapy sessions suspended.

15. No consulting with attorneys.

There have been no applicants as yet.

The Jewish businessman is being audited by the IRS. The tax man says, "You're deducting three thousand dollars for the birth of your baby. You can't do that, because she was born in January."

"True," says the Jewish guy, "but the work was done last year."

Q: What's the difference between a Jewish-American Princess and a pit bull?

A: A nose job and a mink coat.

Q: Why was Moses's mother so happy?

A: She not only had fun in bed, she made a prophet.

Mormons (Take my wives...)

A woman visiting Salt Lake City in the latter half of the 18th century sees someone that she thinks may be Brigham Young, the leader of the Mormon church.

WOMAN: Are you Brigham Young?

BRIGHAM YOUNG: I am.

WOMAN: Are you the Brigham Young who is the head of the Mormon church?

BRIGHAM YOUNG: I am.

WOMAN: Are you the Brigham Young who led the Mormons to Utah?

BRIGHAM YOUNG: I am.

WOMAN: Are you the Brigham Young who denounces all religion as false except Mormonism?

BRIGHAM YOUNG: I am.

About this time, the woman is beginning to lose her temper.

WOMAN: Are you the Brigham Young who preaches polygamy?

BRIGHAM YOUNG: I am.

Now she's really getting mad.

WOMAN: Are you the Brigham Young who has 26 wives?

BRIGHAM YOUNG: I am.

Then furiously, she says, "You ought to be hung!"

BRIGHAM YOUNG: I am.

PROFILE
Jerry Seinfeld:
"Did you ever notice...?"

"Now why does moisture ruin leather? Aren't cows outside a lot of the time? When it's raining, do cows go up to the farmhouse and say, "Let us in! We're all wearing leather!"

Jerry Seinfeld's unique "observational humor" has made him one of the most popular comedians in America. Born in Brooklyn, raised in Massapequa, Long Island ("It's an old Indian name that means 'by the mall'"), Seinfeld began working in the comedy clubs of New York City on the same night that he graduated from Queens College. Sometimes he would perform his stand-up routine for free in order to perfect his act.

"The Chalk Outline guy's got a good job. Not too dangerous, the criminals are long gone. I guess these are people who wanted to be sketch artists but they couldn't draw very well. 'Uh, listen, John, forget the sketches, do you think if we left the dead body "fixed" right there on the sidewalk you could manage to trace around it?' How does that help them solve the crime? They look at the thing on the ground, 'Oh, his arm was like that when he hit the pavement.... the killer must have been... Jim.'"

He paid his bills with a variety of jobs that ranged from working for a scam operation selling light bulbs over the phone (a job he has publicly apologized for) and selling fake jewelry on the street.

"I was in front of an ambulance the other day, and I noticed that the word 'ambulance' was spelled in reverse print on the hood of the ambulance. And I thought, 'Well, isn't that clever. I look in the rear-view mirror, I can read the word 'ambulance' behind me. Of course while you're reading, you don't see where you're going, you crash, you need an ambulance. I think they're trying to drum up some business on the way back from lunch."

Jerry's hard work paid off when he became a regular guest on *Late Night with David Letterman* and *The Tonight Show*. In 1990, Jerry and his partner, Larry David (who was the model for the neurotic George Costanza) were given the green light by NBC for their own primetime sitcom. Seinfeld and David created a show about "nothing," devoting entire shows to everything from how to order from the "soup nazi" to waiting for a table in a Chinese restaurant.

"Why is commitment such a big problem for a man? I think that for some reason when a man is driving down that freeway of love, the woman he's with is like an exit, but he doesn't want to get off there. He wants to keep driving. And the woman is like, 'Look, gas, food, lodging, that's our exit, that's everything we need to be happy...Get off here, now!' But the man is focusing on the sign underneath that says, 'Next exit 27 miles,' and he thinks, 'I can make it.' Sometimes he can, sometimes he can't. Sometimes, the car ends up on the side of the road, hood up and smoke pouring out of the engine. He's sitting on the curb all alone, 'I guess I didn't realize how many miles I was racking up.'"

By 1993, the TV series *Seinfeld* had become a huge hit, both with the critics and with viewers, and that year won the Emmy for best comedy series. The extraordinarily successful series remained at the top of the ratings all the way through its ninth and final season.

Miscellany (Wit, wisdom ... whatever)

The Lone Ranger and Tonto are camping in the desert. They set up their tent and go to sleep.

Some hours later, the Lone Ranger wakes his faithful friend.

"Tonto, look up at the sky and tell me what you see."

Tonto replies, "Me see millions of stars."

"What does that tell you?" asks the Lone Ranger.

Tonto ponders for a minute. "Astronomically speaking, it tells me that there are millions of galaxies and potentially billions of planets. Astrologically, it tells me that Saturn is in Leo. Time-wise, it appears to be approximately a quarter past three. Theologically, it's evident the Lord is all-powerful and we are small and insignificant. Meteorologically, it seems we will have a beautiful day tomorrow. What it tell you, Kemo Sabe?"

The Lone Ranger is silent for a moment, then speaks, "Tonto, you dumb-ass, someone has stolen our tent."

TOP TEN SLOGANS BEING CONSIDERED BY VIAGRA

1. Viagra, It's "Whaazzzzz Up!"

2. Viagra, The quicker pecker upper.

3. Viagra, Like a rock!

4. Viagra, When it absolutely, positively has to be there tonight.

5. Viagra, Be all that you can be.

6. Viagra, Reach out and touch someone.

7. Viagra, Strong enough for a man, but made for a woman!

8. Viagra, Tastes great!—More filling!

9. Viagra, We bring good things to life!

10. This is your penis... This is your penis on drugs. Any questions?

In a small Southern town there was a "Nativity Scene." Great skill and talent had gone into creating it.

One small feature bothered me. The Three Wise Men were wearing fireman's helmets.

Totally unable to come up with a reason or explanation, I left. At a "quick stop" on the edge of town, I asked the lady behind the counter about the helmets.

She exploded into a rage. "You Yankees never do read the Bible!"

I assured her that I did, but simply couldn't recall anything about firemen in the Bible.

She jerked her Bible from behind the counter and riffled through the pages, finally jabbing her finger at a passage.

"See, it says right here, 'The Three Wise Men came from afar.'"

Bernard, who is noted for his gracious manners, was awakened one morning at 4:30 A.M. by his ringing telephone.

"Your dog's barking, and it's keeping me awake," said an angry voice.

Bernard thanked the caller, and checked the caller ID to determine which neighbor had called.

The next morning at precisely 4:30 A.M. Bernard called his neighbor back. "Good morning, Mr. Williams. Just called to say that I do not have a dog."

A millionaire threw a magnificent party for his many friends. Much to everyone's dismay, his very large pool was filled with alligators. Towards the end of the evening he stood before a podium and announced to his guests, "The first person who swims across this here pool will get a million dollars!" He then stepped back and waited for a response.

No one responded, so he made another offer: "I'll give the first person a million dollars and my mansion." Once again he stepped back and waited.

Finally he said, "I'll give you a million dollars, my mansion, and a choice between my Corvette or Lamborghini."

Suddenly he heard a splash, turned to see a man swimming across the pool hitting one alligator up side the head, wrestling one after another. With lots of luck the man reached the other end of the pool and climbed out at the millionaire's feet.

The millionaire congratulated the man and invited him up to his office to receive his awards. When they got to his office the millionaire asked, "What do you want, the Corvette or Lamborghini?"

The man replied, "I want the jerk that pushed me into the pool!!"

Tiger Woods drove his BMW Z3 into a service station for a fill-up.

"What can I do for you?" asked the attendant who obviously didn't recognize Tiger.

"Fill er up," replied Tiger. The attendant asked, "What kind of car is this?"

Tiger replied, "BMW Z3, like James Bond's."

The attendant asked, "What it got in it?"

Tiger replied, "It has everything, power steering, power seats, power sun roof, power mirrors, AM/FM radio with a 10-disc CD player in the trunk with 100 watts per channel, 8-speaker stereo, disc brakes all around, leather interior, and best of all, an 8.8 liter V12 engine."

The attendant said, "Wow! That's really something."

Tiger asked, "How much do I owe you?"

The attendant said, "That'll be $30.17."

Tiger pulled out his money clip and a handful of change. Mixed up with the change were a few golf tees.

"What are those little wooden things for?" asked the attendant.

"Those are what I put my balls on when I'm driving," said Tiger.

"Wow," says the attendant, "those BMW people think of everything!"

A little guy gets on a plane and sits next to the window.

A few minutes later, a big, heavy, strong, mean-looking, hulking guy plops down in the seat next to him and immediately falls asleep.

The little guy starts to feel airsick, but he's afraid to wake the big guy up to ask if he can go to the bathroom. He knows he can't climb over him.

Suddenly, the plane hits an air pocket and an uncontrollable wave of nausea passes through the little guy. He can't hold it in any longer and he pukes all over the big guy's chest.

About five minutes later the big guy wakes up, looks down, and sees the vomit all over him.

"So," says the little guy, "are you feeling better now?"

This lady was in a pet shop, when she spotted a parrot and fell instantly in love with it. She went to the shop owner and told him that she'd like to buy the bird. He said he would sell it to her, but he warned her that the bird had been brought up from a chick in a brothel, and had picked up some of the lingo. The woman said that she'd still like to have the parrot, that her kids were old enough to tolerate any bad language.

So she purchased the bird and took it home. When she took the cloth off the cage, the parrot gave a squawk, then said "Wow, how about this, a new brothel and a new madam!"

"I'm not your madam, and this is not a brothel!" the woman exclaimed, but laughed.

A little after that her two daughters arrived home, at which the bird squawked again. "Wow, how about this, a new brothel, a new madam, and two new whores!" The girls were shocked, but they all had a laugh. After all, they could all see the funny side of things.

Later, the woman's husband come home. At that, the bird said "Ah, how about this, a new brothel, a new madam, two new whores, but the same old customers. How are ya, Tony?"

A duck walked into a pet store and asked the owner, "Do you have any duck food?" The owner said, "No."

The next day the duck walked in and asked the owner, "Do you have any duck food?" The owner said, "No, we do not sell duck food."

The next day the duck came back again and asked, "Do you have any duck food?" The owner said "No, and if you come in here again I will nail your beak to the wall!"

The next day the duck walked into the store and asked the owner, "Do you have any nails?" The owner replied with confusion, "No, we don't have any nails!" So the duck asked, "Do you have any duck food?"

WORDS OF WISDOM

Accept that some days you're the pigeon, and some days you're the statue.

Always keep your words soft and sweet, just in case you have to eat them.

Always read a book that will make you look good if you die in the middle of it.

Be wary of strong drink. It can make you shoot at tax collectors, and miss.

Cooking lesson #1: Don't fry bacon in the nude.

Drive carefully. It's not only cars that can be recalled by their maker.

Eat a live toad in the morning and nothing worse will happen to you for the rest of the day.

If life gives you lemons, squeeze the juice into a water-gun and shoot other people in the eyes.

If you're not part of the solution, be part of the problem!

If you can't be kind, at least have the decency to be vague.

If you can't beat your computer at chess, try kickboxing.

If you lend someone $20 and never see that person again, it was probably worth it.

If you think nobody cares if you're alive, try missing a couple of car payments.

If you try and don't succeed, cheat. Repeat until caught. Then lie.

It may be that your sole purpose in life is simply to serve as a warning to others.

Never buy a car you can't push.

Never eat yellow snow.

Never pet a burning dog.

Never put both feet in your mouth at the same time, because then you don't have a leg to stand on.

Never try to teach a pig to sing. It wastes your time and annoys the pig.

Nobody cares if you can't dance well. Just get up and dance.

The early worm gets eaten by the bird, so sleep late.

There are very few personal problems that cannot be solved through a suitable application of high explosives.

When everything's coming your way, you're in the wrong lane.

You are what you eat, so stay away from the jerk chicken.

Be nice to the nerds and geeks in high school—you'll be working for them in the future.

Save the whales. (Collect the whole set.)

A day without sunshine is like night.

On the other hand, you have different fingers.

I feel like I'm diagonally parked in a parallel universe.

I wonder how much deeper the ocean would be without sponges?

Honk if you love peace and quiet.

Despite the cost of living, have you noticed how popular it remains?

Depression is merely anger without enthusiasm.

Eagles may soar, but weasels don't get sucked into jet engines.

The early bird may get the worm, but the second mouse gets the cheese.

Borrow money from a pessimist—they don't expect it back.

If Barbie is so popular, why do you have to buy her friends?

Most people's minds are like steel traps—rusty, and illegal in 37 states.

When everything's coming your way, you're in the wrong lane going the wrong direction.

Bills travel through the mail at twice the speed of checks.

The hardness of butter is directly proportional to the softness of the bread.

The severity of the itch is inversely proportional to the ability to reach it.

A clear conscience is usually the sign of a bad memory.

Change is inevitable—except from vending machines.

Plan to be spontaneous.

Be modest and proud of it!

How many of you believe in telekinesis? Raise my hand....

A cop saw a woman driving and knitting at the same time. As he pulled up beside her car he said, "Pull over!" She replied, "Nope. A pair of socks."

I don't fly Virgin, because they don't go all the way.

MICKEY FREEMAN

The fireman had rushed into a burning building and rescued a beautiful young lady who was clad only in the top half of her baby-doll nightgown. He had carried her in his arms down three flights of stairs.

As they arrived safely outside the building, she looked at him with great admiration and said, "Oh, you are wonderful. It must have taken great strength and courage to rescue me the way you did."

"Yes it did," the fireman admitted. "I had to fight off three other firemen who were trying to get to you."

What happened when Napoleon went to Mount Olive?

Popeye got pissed.

Why do they lock gas station bathrooms?

Are they afraid someone will clean them?

The best way to make a slow horse fast is not to feed him.

I used to know who the men on the side of Mount Rushmore are, but now I just take them for granite.

Did you hear of the latest NASA experiment? They have launched a number of cows into orbit to study the effects of weightlessness on bovines. It was called "The Herd Shot Round the World."

Stupid people should have to wear signs that just say, "I'm Stupid." That way you wouldn't rely on them, would you? You wouldn't ask them anything. It would be like, "Excuse me…oops, never mind. I didn't see your sign."

It's like before my wife and I moved. Our house was full of boxes and there was a U-Haul truck in our driveway. My friend comes over and says "Hey, you moving?" "Nope. We just pack our stuff up once or twice a week to see how many boxes it takes. Here's your sign."

A couple of months ago I went fishing with a buddy of mine, we pulled his boat into the dock, I lifted up this big 'ol stringer of bass and this idiot on the dock goes, "Hey, y'all catch all them fish?" "Nope—Talked 'em into giving up. Here's your sign."

I was watching one of those animal shows on the Discovery Channel. There was a guy inventing a shark bite suit. And there's only one way to test it. "Alright Jimmy, you got that shark suit on, it looks good…They want you to jump into this pool of sharks, and you tell us if it hurts when they bite you." "Well, all right, but hold my sign. I don't wanna lose it."

Last time I had a flat tire, I pulled my truck into one of those side-of-the-road gas stations. The attendant walks out, looks at my truck, looks at me, and I SWEAR he said, "Tire go flat?" I couldn't resist, and said, "Nope. I was driving around and those other three just swelled right up on me. Here's your sign."

We were trying to sell our car about a year ago. A guy came over to the house and drove the car around for about 45 minutes. We get back to the house, he gets out of the car, reaches down and grabs the exhaust pipe, then says, "Darn that's hot!" See? If he'd been wearing his sign, I could have stopped him."

I learned to drive an 18 wheeler in my days of adventure. Wouldn't ya know I misjudged the height of a bridge. The truck got stuck and I couldn't get it out no matter how I tried. I radioed in for help and eventually a local cop shows up to take the report. He went through his basic questioning...ok...no problem. I thought sure he was clear of needing a sign...until he asked, "So...is your truck stuck?" I couldn't help myself! I looked at him, looked back at the rig and then back to him and said, "No, I'm delivering a bridge...here's your sign."

On July 20, 1969, as commander of the Apollo 11 Lunar Module, Neil Armstrong was the first person to set foot on the moon. His first words after stepping on the moon, "That's one small step for man, one giant leap for mankind," were televised to Earth and heard by millions. But just before he reentered the lander, he made the enigmatic remark: "Good luck, Mr. Gorsky."

Many people at NASA thought it was a casual remark concerning some rival Soviet Cosmonaut. However, upon checking, there was no Gorsky in either the Russian or American space programs. Over the years many people questioned Armstrong as to what the "Good luck, Mr.Gorsky" statement meant, but Armstrong always just smiled.

On July 5, 1995, in Tampa Bay, Florida, while answering questions following a speech, a reporter brought up the 26-year-old question to Armstrong. This time he finally responded. Mr. Gorsky had died and so Neil Armstrong felt he could answer the question. In 1938, when he was a kid in a small Midwest town, he was playing baseball with a friend in the backyard. His friend hit a fly ball, which landed in his neighbor's yard by the bedroom windows. His neighbors were Mr. and Mrs. Gorsky. As he leaned down to pick up the ball, young Armstrong heard Mrs. Gorsky shouting at Mr. Gorsky: "Sex! You want sex?! You'll get sex when the kid next door walks on the moon!"

A guy goes into a bar wearing a shirt open at the collar, and is met by a bouncer who tells him he must wear a necktie to gain admission. So the guy goes out to his car and he looks around for a necktie and discovers that he just doesn't have one. He sees a set of jumper cables in his trunk. In desperation he ties these around his neck, and manages to fashion a fairly acceptable looking knot and lets the ends dangle free. He goes back to the restaurant and the bouncer carefully looks him over, and then says, "Well, OK, I guess you can come in—just don't start anything."

The Lone Ranger and Tonto walked into a bar and sat down for a beer. After a few minutes, a big, tall cowboy walked in and said, "Who owns the big, white horse outside?"

The Lone Ranger stood up, hitched his gun belt, and said, "I do... Why?"

The cowboy looked at the Lone Ranger and said, "I just thought you'd like to know that your horse is about dead outside!"

The Lone Ranger and Tonto rushed outside and sure enough Silver was ready to die from heat exhaustion.

The Lone Ranger got the horse water and soon Silver was starting to feel little better. The Lone Ranger turned to Tonto and said, "Tonto, I want you to run around Silver and see if you can create enough of a breeze to make him start to feel better."

Tonto said, "Sure, Kemosabe" and took off running circles around Silver. Not able to do anything else but wait, the Lone Ranger returned to the bar to finish his drink.

A few minutes later, another cowboy strutted into the bar and asked, "Who owns that big, white horse outside?"

The Lone Ranger stood again, and claimed, "I do, what's wrong with him this time?"

The cowboy looked him in the eye and said, "Nothing, but you left your Injun runnin'."

A lonely wife brought a man she had just met at a bar home to her bedroom one evening when she thought her husband was out of town. They immediately tore each other's clothes off and started going at it.

She sat up quickly in bed as she heard the key in the lock.

"Quick!" she said to the man, "It's my husband! You've got to get out of here quick!"

"Where's the back door?" the man asked as he grabbed his clothes.

"There isn't one," she replied.

"O.K. then, where would you like one?" he asked.

Snowmen fall from Heaven unassembled.

There are very few problems that cannot be solved by orders ending with "or die."

ALISTAIR J.R. YOUNG

I discovered I scream the same way whether I'm about to be devoured by a Great White or a piece of seaweed touches my foot.

AXL ROSE

If Mama Cass had shared her ham sandwich with Karen Carpenter, they might both be alive today.

MORE BY HENNY YOUNGMAN

Getting on a plane, I told the ticket lady, "Send one of my bags to New York, send one to Los Angeles, and send one to Miami."

She said, "We can't do that!"

I told her, "You did it last week!"

Was that suit made to order? Where were you at the time?

If you had your life to live over again, do it overseas.

Is that your hat or are you wearing a cabana?

A man went to get his driver's license renewed. The line inched along for almost an hour until the man finally got his license. He inspected his photo for a moment and commented to the clerk, "I was standing in line so long, I ended up looking pretty grouchy in this picture."

The clerk looked at his picture closely. "It's okay," he reassured the man. "That's how you're going to look when the cops pull you over anyway."

THINGS YOU'LL NEVER HEAR

Pamela Lee: My, I have pretty feet! So, I like, get to wear clothes in this movie?

Pauly Shore: I can't do that role. It's degrading to my acting talent.

The Spice Girls: So, what key is this song in?

Michael Jackson: Wow! That woman's hot!

Louis Farrakhan: Well, maybe some things are my fault.

The Democratic National Committee: So, where did this money come from?

MUSINGS BY STEVEN WRIGHT:

Twenty-four hours in a day...24 beers in a case...coincidence?

Why do psychics have to ask you for your name?

When I get real, real bored I like to go downtown and get a good parking spot, then sit in my car and count how many people ask me if I'm leaving.

I went to a place to eat that said "Breakfast Anytime." So I ordered French toast during the Renaissance.

You can't have everything. Where would you put it?

Chickens are the only animals you eat before they are born and after they are dead.

An egotist is someone who is usually me-deep in conversation.

A gossip is a person who will never tell a lie if the truth will do more damage.

A secret is something you tell to one person at a time.

Have you ever noticed? Anybody going slower than you is an idiot, and anyone going faster than you is a moron.

GEORGE CARLIN

Talk to a man about himself and he will listen for hours.

BENJAMIN DISRAELI

She's afraid that if she leaves, she'll become the life of the party.

GROUCHO MARX

The most wasted of all days is one without laughter.

E.E. CUMMINGS

He who laughs last didn't get it.

He who laughs last thinks slowest.

Nothing shows a man's character more than what he laughs at.

JOHANN WOLFGANG VON GOETHE

Index of Contributors

Adams, Joey, 232, 233
Aldrich, Thomas B., 122
Alexander, Jason, 163, 187
Alexis, Kim, 246
Allen, Hervey, 117
Allen, Woody, 95, 196
Alt, Carol, 248
Amiel, Henri Frédéric, 120
Arden, Eve, 92
Arnold, Thomas, 121
Arquette, Patricia, 346
Astaire, Fred, 117
Astor, Nancy, Lady, 123
Attell, Dave, 422

Backus, Jim, 204
Banks, Tyra, 246, 249
Baruch, Bernard M., 123
Becker, May L., 115
Behar, Joy, 275, 286, 304
Belzer, Richard, 108
Benny, Jack, 125, 385
Bergman, Ingmar, 115
Berle, Milton, 59, 64, 96–97, 358, 439
Billings, Josh, 120
Bishop, Joey, 201
Bismarck, Otto Von, 364
Borge, Victor, 283
Brecht, Bertolt, 263
Brinkley, Christie, 245, 247, 248
Brookner, Anita, 120
Brown, Les, 125
Browning, Robert, 138
Bruce, Lenny, 64
Bryant, William Jennings, 262
Burke, Billie, 123
Burns, George, 45, 95, 125, 132, 243
Bush, Barbara, 361
Butler, Brett, 188, 288, 402

Campbell, Naomi, 248
Capri, Dick, 29, 287
Carey, Drew, 390–391
Carey, Joyce, 125
Carlin, George, 368, 466
Carson, Johnny, 64
Carter, Jack, 206
Cavett, Dick, 92
Chesterton, G.K., 64
Cho, Margaret, 32
Christie, Agatha, 54
Churchill, Winston, 368
Coleridge, Samuel Taylor, 126
Colman, Nina, 22–28
Cooper, George, 270
Corey, Professor Irwin, 369
Cosby, Bill, 263
Cox, Courtney, 306
Crawford, Cindy, 245, 246, 248, 249
Crisp, Quentin, 91
Crystal, Billy, 29, 206, 267, 310–312, 350
Cummings, E.E., 467

Dana, Bill, 126
Dangerfield, Rodney, 59, 63, 91, 93, 99, 123, 260–261, 317, 380, 425
Darrow, Clarence, 87, 364
Darwin, Charles, 207
Davis, Bette, 62
Degeneres, Ellen, 105
Devries, Peter, 52
Dickens, Charles, 200
Diller, Phyllis, 55, 137, 272–273
Disraeli, Benjamin, 467
Dougherty, Barry, 19–21
Durant, Will, 150

Einstein, Albert, 209
Emerson, Ralph Waldo, 65

Essman, Susie, 28, 306
Evangelista, Linda, 248, 249

Fabio, 247
Farrar, John, 294
Ferrara, Adam, 29, 147
Fields, W.C., 95, 204
Fitzgerald, F.Scott, 142
Franklin, Benjamin, 63, 65, 116
Freeman, Mickey, 458
Friedman, Bruce, 60
Fromm, Erich, 65
Frost, David, 73

Gabor, Zsa Zsa, 74, 202, 331
Gabriel, Peter, 120
Galbraith, John Kenneth, 368
Gibran, Kahlil, 65
Goethe, Johann Wolfgang Von, 65, 73, 467
Gold, Judy, 304
Goldsmith, Oliver, 184
Goldwyn, Samuel, 66
Goodman, Hazelle, 300
Graves, Robert, 66
Greene, Shecky, 161
Grizzard, Lewis, 66
Guitry, Sacha, 66

Hackett, Buddy, 15–16
Hall, Jerry, 246
Harrigan, John, 66
Hawn, Goldie, 120
Heimel, Cynthia, 66
Henry, Buck, 369
Hepburn, Katharine, 67
Herrick, Robert, 71
Holmes, Oliver Wendell, 132
Hope, Bob, 385
Houseman, A.E., 244
Hyde-Pierce, David, 300

Ireland, Kathy, 245
Irrera, Dom, 304

James, Kevin, 28
Jessel, Georgie, 187
Jobs, Steve, 37
Johnson, Beverly, 245, 247
Johnson, Larry E., 197
Jones, Charlie, 309

Kafka, Franz, 207
Kennedy, John F., 263
King, Alan, 287
Kipling, Rudyard, 200

Lehman, John, 361
Leno, Jay, 270
Letterman, David, 222
Leunig, Michael, 43
Levenson, Sam, 95
Lewis, Anna, 71
Lewis, Joe E., 324
Liebowitz, Fran, 91
Limbaugh, Rush, 358–359
Lovitz, Jon, 108

McCallister, Philip, 239
Machiavelli, Niccolo, 365
McKeon, Michael, 28, 288
McMahon, Ed, 28
Mallory, Carole, 245
Martin, Steve, 299
Marx, Groucho, 54, 63, 128, 197, 228, 289, 290–293, 369, 467
Mason, Jackie, 59
Maugham, Somerset, 289
Mead, Margaret, 305
Mencken, H.L., 61, 368
Messenger, Mary Alice, 88
Midler, Bette, 49
Mill, John Stuart, 361
Miller, Dennis, 298, 366
Miller, Max, 76
Mitford, Nancy, 92
Moss, Kate, 249

Nash, Ogden, 54, 137
Nicholson, Jack, 99

Orban, Robert, 89
O'Rourke, P.J., 364

Paige, Satchel, 258
Parker, Dorothy, 140, 196, 294
Patitz, Tatjana, 245, 247
Pollak, Kevin, 29, 108
Pope, Alexander, 265
Porizkova, Paulina, 246, 248

Reece, Gabrielle, 246
Regan, Ronald, 356–358
Reiser, Paul, 92, 397
Reston, James, 364
Richards, Sal, 286
Roland, Helen, 58
Roman, Freddie, 286
Roosevelt, Franklin Delano, 355
Rose, Axl, 464
Rosen, Marc, 73
Ross, Jeffrey, 17–18, 28, 32, 107, 147, 287, 288
Rouchefoucald, François de la, 65
Rudner, Rita, 55, 343, 362–363
Russell, Bertrand, 213
Russell, Mark, 364

Sales, Soupy, 132, 287
Schiffer, Claudia, 247
Schwarzenegger, Arnold, 328
Scott, Steven, 286
Seinfeld, Jerry, 306, 448–449
Shaffer, Paul, 267
Shakespeare, William, 72, 114, 141
Simon, Roger, 387
Sinatra, Frank, 287

Smith, Bob, 94
Smythers, Ruth, 54
Stander, Lionel, 210
Steinem, Gloria, 59, 326
Stewart, Jon, 281
Stone, Sharon, 305
Stone, Stewey, 147

Tasha, 249
Tennyson, Alfred, Lord, 269
Thackeray, William Makepeace, 200, 283
Tiegs, Cheryl, 247
Tomlin, Lily, 432
Trillin, Calvin, 243
Truman, Harry S., 259, 371
Turlington, Christy, 247, 248, 249
Twain, Mark, 94, 150, 191, 207, 288

Vidal, Gore, 244, 258
Vidor, King, 54
Viorst, Judith, 45

Webb, Veronica, 249
West, Mae, 32, 55, 124, 198–199, 305, 307
Wilde, Oscar, 54, 61, 95, 294, 299, 328
Willis, Bruce, 305
Winters, Shelley, 204
Woods, Tiger, 385
Woolf, Virginia, 305
Wright, Steven, 78, 178–179, 227, 243, 263, 299

Young, Alaistair J.R., 464
Youngman, Henny, 52–53, 59, 67, 78, 92, 106, 130–131, 188, 202, 209, 228, 283, 387, 418, 419, 441

Acknowledgments

The author would like to thank the following individuals for their contributions to this book: first, Carl Ogawa; also, Sandy Barnes, Iris Bass, Nancy Bernstein, Reeve Chace, Barb Coffman, Howard Cohl, Gladys Deitch, Jennifer Dennis, Michael Driscoll, Peter Elkoff, Steve Friedberg, Ed Harrison, Pamela Horn, Morty Lazarus, JP Leventhal, Martin Lubin, Chris Martellino, Michael Matuza, Laurel Meade, Barbara Parker, Brett Parker, Laura Ross, Aldo Savatteri, David Savatteri, Sharon Topel, Brad Walrod, and Charles Weldon.

Photo Credits